MODERN ARCHITECTURE
1851-1919

2

D

Published in the United States of America in 1983 by
RIZZOLI INTERNATIONAL PUBLICATIONS, INC.
712 Fifth Avenue, New York, NY 10019

Copyright © 1981 A.D.A. EDITA Tokyo Co., Ltd.
3-12-14 Sendagaya, Shibuya-ku, Tokyo, Japan

ISBN 0-8478-0507-7
LC   83-61411

Printed and bound in Japan

MODERN ARCHITECTURE
1851-1919
KENNETH FRAMPTON/YUKIO FUTAGAWA

RIZZOLI
NEW YORK

CONTENTS PART 1 1851-1919

Cover: Hill House by Charles R. Mackintosh
Title pages: Eiffel Tower by Gustave Eiffel
Photographs by Yukio Futagawa

MODERN ARCHITECTURE
1851-1919

1 Glass, Iron, Steel, and Concrete 1775-1915

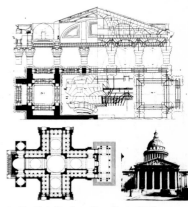

1 *Soufflot, Ste-Geneviève, Paris, 1755.*
Stonework detail.

Perforation is a precious attribute in a substance, for it expands it without destroying it; in a word, it makes one see empty space and makes the void manifest without, for all that, reducing it to its primitive state; one always sees the sky through the tower; through it the 'aerial', interchanges its own substance with the bars of its prison, the iron, flowing in arabesques, becoming itself the air. Without doubt this 'aerial' character of the tower has a practical origin; it must open up the material to its maximum so that it should offer the least possible resistance to the sole dangerous enemy which Eiffel encountered in his venture; the wind; but even in this, one perceives the subtle nature of the aerial to the extent that it is dominated, sublimated and rendered essential by the wind, the wind is always the constant symbol of uncontrollable power and hence of massivity: ... to conquer the wind (like the tower) is to go to the limits of the light and the subtle, it is to reunite the great mythologies of the dreamy spirit and deliverer.

Roland Barthes
'La Tour Eiffel', *Mythologies,* 1957

Steam locomotion and the iron skeleton came into being at around the same time through the interdependent efforts of three men: James Watt, Abraham Darby, and John Wilkinson. The evolution of paleotechnology was symbiotic. Thus Wilkinson's invention of the cylinder boring machine in 1775 was essential to the perfection of Watt's steam engine of 1789. Wilkinson's experience in working iron was to prove equally indispensable to the first structural use of iron, since he assisted Darby and his architect, T.F. Pritchard, in designing and erecting the first cast-iron bridge; a 100-foot-span structure built over the Severn at Coalbrookdale in 1779. The Coalbrookdale achievement aroused considerable interest and in 1786 the Anglo-American revolutionary, Tom Paine, designed a monument to the American Revolution in the form of a cast-iron bridge spanning, the Schuylkill River. In 1796 a 236-foot cast-iron bridge was built across the Wear at Sunderland to the designs of Thomas Wilson, who adopted Paine's voussoir method of assembly. About the same time Thomas Telford built his 130-foot Buildwas Bridge erected over the Severn, a design which employed only 173 tons of iron, as opposed to the 378 tons used at Coalbrookdale.

From 1793 to 1805 Telford was at work building the Ellesmere Canal connecting Ellesmere Port on the Mersey to Chester and then extending the navigability of the River Dee into North Wales via the cast-iron Pontcysyllte aqueduct carried on stone piers, 127 feet above the valley of the Dee. Over the next twenty five years, Telford went on to prove his unparalleled stature as a civil engineer and as the last great canal builder of the waning waterway era. His pioneer career was brought to a close with his brick-encased, iron-framed warehouses at St. Katharine Dock in London, designed with the architect Philip Hardwick and erected in 1829. These docks employed the system of fireproof multi-storey mill construction developed in the Midlands during the last decade of the 18th century. The main structural antecedents for St. Katharine's were William Strutt's calico mill, built at Derby in 1792, and Charles Bage's flax-spinning mill erected at Shrewsbury in 1796. While both of these mills employed cast-iron columns, the pressing need to perfect a fireproof system for mill buildings led, in the space of four years, to the replacement of timber beams by T-section iron beams. These iron beams

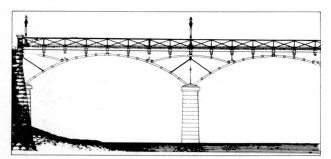

2 *De Cessart and Dillon, Pont des Arts, Paris, 1801-03.*

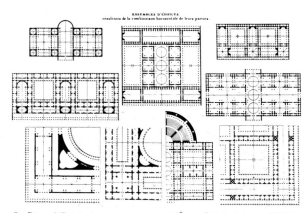

3 *Durand,* Précis des leçons données à l'École Polytechnique, *1802-09.*

invariably supported shallow brick vaults, the whole assembly being stiffened by the outer shell and by wrought-iron tie rods restraining the structure in a lateral direction. This system of vaulting seems to have derived directly from the 18th-century development of the Roussillon or Catalonian vault in France, which was first adopted there as a means of achieving a fireproof structure in Château Bizy, built at Vernon by Constant d'Ivry in 1741.

Aside from its use in 13th-century cathedrals wrought-iron masonry reinforecement in France had its origins in Paris, in Perrault's east facade of the Louvre (1667) and Soufflot's portico of Ste-Geneviève (1772). Both works anticipate the development of reinforced concrete. In 1776 Soufflot proposed a wrought-iron trussed roof for part of the Louvre that prepared the way for the pioneering work of Victor Louis, that is, for Louis's wrought-iron roof for the Théâtre Français of 1786 and his theatre in the Palais-Royal of 1790. This last combined an iron roof with a hollow-pot, fireproof floor structure, a system that once again was derived from the Roussillon vault. That fire was a growing urban hazard can be seen from the Halle au Blés, Paris, whose burnt-out roof was replaced in 1808 by an iron-ribbed cupola, designed by the architect Bélanger and the engineer Brunet. This was one of the first instances of a clear division of labour between architect and constructor.

With the foundation of the École Polytechnique in 1795, the French strove towards establishing a technocracy necessary for the consolidation of the Napoleonic Empire. This imperial emphasis on applied technique served to reinforce the growing specialization of architecture and engineering, a division already institutionalized through the foundation of Perronet's École des Ponts et Chaussées in 1747. The earliest French application of iron to bridge construction came with the elegant Pont des Arts over the Seine, erected to the designs of de Cessart and Dillon in 1803. In his *Traité de l'art de bâtir* of 1802 J.B. Rondelet, who had supervised the completion of Ste-Geneviève after Soufflot's death, began to record the pioneering work of Soufflot, Louis, Brunet, de Cessart, and others. And while Rondelet documented the "means," J.N.L. Durand, lecturer in architecture at the École Polytechnique, catalogued the "ends" in his *Précis des leçons données à l'École Polytechnique* (1802-09). Durand's book propagated a system whereby Classical forms, conceived as modular elements, laid into a grid, could be arranged at will for the accommodation of the market halls, libraries, barracks, museums, law courts, customs houses, etc. First Rondelet and then Durand codified a technique and a design method whereby a rationalized Classicism could be brought to accommodate not only new techniques but also new social demands. This comprehensive programme influenced the Prussian Neo-Classical architect Karl Friedrich Schinkel, who, at the beginning of his architectural career in 1816, began to incorporate elaborate iron elements into his Neoclassical embellishments for the city of Berlin.

From the time of Boulton and Watt's 13-inch cast-iron beam, used in their Salford Mill, Manchester, of 1801, a continual effort was made to improve the spanning capacity of both cast- and wrought-iron beams and rails. The typical iron railroad section was evolved during the first decade of the century and from this section the standard structural I-beam spontaneously emerged. Jessop's cast-iron rail of 1789 gave way to Birkenshaw's wrought-iron T-rail of

4 Saulnier, Menier Chocolate Factory,
Noisiel-sur-Marne, France, 1871-72.

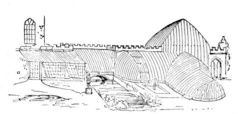

5 Loudon, a prototypical hot house, 1817.

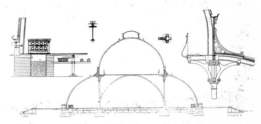

6 Turner and Burton, Palm House, Kew Gardens, London,
1844-48. Cross section and perimeter details of the shed.

1820, and this led to the first American rail, rolled in Wales in 1831, in the form of an I-section broader at the base than at the top. While this form was immediately adopted for railway construction, its general structural use did not begin until after 1854, when heavier versions of the same section were successfully rolled.

Since the rolling of deeper sections proved to be impossible before major improvements in the production of iron, engineers tried various ways to increase the spanning capacity of the material by building up deep members from the standard wrought-iron angles and plates that were then being used in ship building. William Fairbairn reputedly fabricated and tested such composite I-beams as early as 1839. These ingenious attempts to produce wide-span elements through reinforcing or assembling iron components were more or less eclipsed at mid-century by the successful rolling of a wrought-iron beam 7 inches deep. Fairbairn's book *On the Application of Cast and Wrought Iron to Building Purposes* (1854) presented an improved system of mill construction, consisting of rolled iron beams 16 inches deep that supported shallow vaults made of sheet iron, the whole topped out with concrete. Wrought-iron tie rods were still used to stabilized the structure and since these were cast into the concrete floor, this proposal brought Fairbairn fortuitously close to the principles of reinforced concrete. A comparable anticipation of modern steel frame construction came with a remarkable four-storey cast- and wrought-iron framed building erected in the Naval Dockyard at Sheerness. This boat store, clad in corrugated iron, was designed by Col. Greene and erected in 1860, some twelve years before the pioneer-ing iron-framed Menier Chocolate Factory was built by Jules Saulnier at Noisiel-sur-Marne.

The sudden expansion in urban growth and trade on the eastern American seaboard in the 1840s encouraged men like James Bogardus and Daniel Badger to open casting shops in New York for the manufacture of multi-storey architectural fronts in iron. Up to the late 1850s, however, these modular structures relied on the use of large timber beams to span the internal space, iron being reserved for the internal columns and the facades. One of the finest works of Bogardus's extensive career is his Haughwout Building, New York, of 1859, built to the designs of the architect John P. Gaynor. This was the first building to be served by a passenger elevator, just five years after Elisha Graves Otis had demonstrated the device in 1854.

The all glass structure, whose horticultural possibilities were elaborated on by J.C. Loudon in his *Remarks on Hot Houses* (1817), had little chance of being generally applied, at least in England, until the repeal of the excise duty on glass in 1845. Richard Turner and Decimus Burton's Palm House at Kew Gardens (1845-48) was one of the first structures to take advantage of the sudden availability of sheet glass. The first large permanent enclo-sures to be significantly glazed thereafter were the railway termini that were built during the second half of the 19th century; a development that began with Richard Turner and Joseph Locke's Lime Street Station, Liverpool, of 1850.

The railway terminus presented a peculiar challenge to the received canons of architecture, since there was no type available to express and adequately

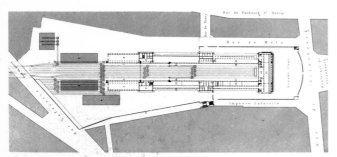

7 Duquesney, Gare de l'Est, Paris, 1852.

8 Scott, St. Pancras Station, London, 1874.

9 Paxton and Fox, Crystal Palace, London, 1851.

articulate the junction between the head building and the shed. This problem, which saw its earliest architectural resolution in François Duquesney's Gare de l'Est, Paris, of 1852, was of some concern since these termini were effectively the new gateways into the capital city. The engineer Léonce Reynaud, designer of the first Gare du Nord in Paris (1847), was aware of this issue of representation when he wrote in his *Traité d'Architecture* of 1850:

Art does not have the rapid progress and sudden developments of industry, with the result that the majority of buildings today for the service of railroads leave more or less to be desired, be it in relation to form or the arrangement. Some stations appear to be appropriately arranged but having the character of industrial or provisional construction rather than that of a building for public use.

Nothing could be more exemplary of this predicament than St. Pancras Station in London, where the 243-foot-span shed, built in 1863-65 to the designs of W.H. Barlow and R.M. Ordish, was totally divorced from the Gothic Revival head building completed in 1874 to the designs of George Gilbert Scott. And what was true for St. Pancras also applied to Brunel's designs for Paddington in London (1852) where once again, despite the embellishments to the shed carried out by Matthew Digby Wyatt, Philip Hardwick's hotel and head building remained inadequately related to the fundamental structure.

In contrast to the terminus, the free-standing exhibition building presented no such problems, for where there was no cultural precedent the engineer reigned supreme. This was never more so than in the case of the Crystal Palace in London, built for the Great Exhibition of 1851, where the gardener Joseph Paxton was given a free hand to design in accordance with Loudon's hothouse principles. When commissioned at the eleventh hour to design the Crystal Palace, Paxton outlined, in eight days, an enormous orthogonal three-tiered glasshouse, whose components were virtually identical to those of the *Victoria regia* lily house that he had designed and built at Chatsworth in the previous year. Except for three entrance porches, symmetrically disposed, the glazed perimeter of the Crystal Palace was uninterrupted. However, during its development, a revised scheme had to be prepared in order to retain a group of mature trees. Since the remaining public opposition to the Great Exhibition of 1851 turned on this question of tree preservation, Paxton was quick to realize that these troublesome items could easily be accommodated by a central transept with a high vaulted roof and thus the double symmetry of the final form emerged.

The Crystal Palace was not so much a particular form as it was a building process made manifest as a total system, from its initial conception, fabrication and trans-shipment, to its final erection and dismantling. Like the railway buildings, to which it was related, it was a highly flexible kit of parts. Its overall form was structured around a basic 8-foot cladding module assembled into a hierarchy of structural spans varying from 24 to 72 feet. Its realization, which took barely four months, was simply a matter of mass production and systematic assembly. As Konrad Wachsman has remarked in his book *The Turning Point of Building,* "Its production requirements included studies

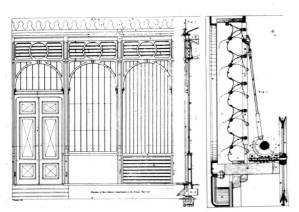

10 Crystal Palace. Typical details of the modular components.

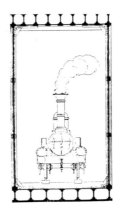

11 Stephenson and Fairbairn, Britannia Tubular Bridge, Menai Straits, 1852. Cross section.

12 Britannia Tubular Bridge. Rendering.

which indicated that for easy handling no part should weigh more than one ton and that the greatest economies could be obtained by using glass panels of the largest possible size."

With the virtual completion of the British railway infrastructure by 1860, British structural engineering entered a fallow period that lasted for the rest of the century. Aside from the great London railway termini, only two works of outstanding brilliance and ingenuity remained to be built after the middle of the century: the Stephenson and Fairbairn Britannia Tubular Bridge over the Menai Straits of 1852 and Brunel's Saltash Viaduct of 1859. Both made use of plated wrought iron, that is to say, riveted rolled sheet, a technique which had been greatly advanced by the studies of Eton Hodgkinson and the experimental work of William Fairbairn. Robert Stephenson had already utilized the findings of Hodgkinson and Fairbairn in his development of the plate girder in 1846, a system that was to be fully demonstrated in the Britannia Bridge. This structure comprised two independent, single-track, iron-plated box tunnels which bridged the straits with two spans of 230 feet and one main span of 460 feet. Stephenson's stone towers had been intended for the anchorage of supplementary suspension members, but the plated "tubes" acting alone proved more than adequate for the span. Comparable spans were achieved in the Saltash Viaduct, where a single track is carried over the Tamar River on two bowstring trusses each spanning 455 feet. Rolled, riveted plates were again used to form the hollow elliptical chords, measuring 16 by 21 feet across their respective axes. These chords interacted with underslung iron chain catenaries to carry vertical standards from which the roadbed was final-ly suspended. In its imaginative stature Brunel's last work equalled the great viaducts which Gustave Eiffel was to build in the Massif Central over the next thirty years, and its use of hollow plated sections anticipated the gigantic tubular steel framing to be employed by John Fowler and Benjamin Baker in the 700-foot, cantilevers of their Forth Bridge, completed in 1890.

The British abandonment of the international exhibition field, after their triumph of 1851, was at once exploited by the French, who mounted five major international exhibitions between 1855 and 1900. The degree to which these displays were regarded as national platforms from which to challenge the British command over industrial production and trade may be judged from the emphasis placed each time on the structure and content of the Galerie des Machines. The young Gustave Eiffel worked with the engineer J.B. Krantz on the most significant exhibition building to be erected after the Crystal Palace, namely the Paris World Exhibition of 1867. This collaboration revealed not only Eiffel's expressive sensibility but also his capacity as an engineer, since in detailing the Galerie des Machines, with its 114-foot span, he was able to verify the validity of Thomas Young's modulus of elasticity of 1807; a hitherto solely theoretical formula for determining the elastic behaviour of material under stress. The whole oval complex, of which the Galerie des Machines was merely the outer ring, was itself a testament to the conceptual genius of Le Play, who had suggested that the building be arranged as seven concentric galleries exhibiting machinery, clothing, furniture, liberal arts, fine arts, and the history of labour.

After 1867 the sheer size and diversity of the objects produced, and the

13 *Krantz and Eiffel, Paris World Exhibition, 1867.*

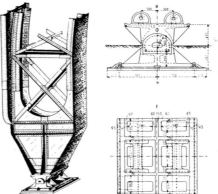

14 *Contamin and Dutert, Galerie des Machines, Paris, 1887-89. Detail of the hinged supports.*

independence favoured by commercial competition, seem to have demanded multiple exhibition structures. By the time of the International Exhibition of 1889 no further effort was made to house the exhibits in one self-contained building. This penultimate exhibition of the century was dominated by two of the most remarkable structures that French engineering was ever to achieve — Contamin's Galerie des Machines, 350 feet in span, designed with architect C.L.F. Dutert, and Eiffel's tower, 984 feet high, designed in collaboration with the engineers Nouguier and Koechlin and the architect Sauvestre. Contamin's structure, based on statical method perfected by Eiffel in his hinged viaducts of the 1880s, was one of the first to use the three-hinged arch form in the achievement of a large span. Contamin's shed not only exhibited machines but it was itself an exhibiting machine, in which mobile viewing platforms, running on elevated tracks, passed over the exhibition space, thereby affording the visitor a fast and comprehensive view over the exhibits laid out beneath his feet.

As to the sublime impact of such a work a contemporary commentary conveys it all too dramatically: "One's gaze can travel over half a kilometre of bright and empty space, revealing from one end to the others the facades of multicoloured glass and the graceful curve of the supports whose two identical arches, joining at the center, resemble two enormous trees . . ."

In the second half of the 19th century the Massif Central had been found to be sufficiently rich in minerals to justify the considerable expense of equipping it with a railway network. The viaducts that Eiffel designed there between 1869 and 1884 exemplify a method and an aesthetic that found their

ultimate celebration in the design of the Eiffel Tower. The typical parabolic profile of the tubular iron pylon that Eiffel evolved for these viaducts is formally indicative of his constant attempt to resolve the dynamic interaction of wind and water.

The need to span wider rivers led Eiffel and his associates to devise an ingenious system of viaduct support. The spur to such a solution came in 1875, with the commission to construct a railway viaduct over the river, Douro in Portugal. The availability of cheap steel after 1870 afforded a material in which a wide-span solution might be readily achieved. A decision was therefore made to cross the ravine in five spans, two short spans supported on pylons on either side and a central longer span of 524 feet carried on a two-pinned arch. The procedure of erection, to be repeated a few years later at Garabit, was to construct the flanking spans with their supporting pylons and then to erect the central section from these continuous structures on either side. Truss extensions were cantilevered out at track level and the hinged arch was constructed, in two halves; prefabricated steel sections being hauled into position from the water below. The hinged abutments were floated and jacked into position and then maintained at a correct incline, during assembly, by cables suspended from the caps of the adjacent pylons. The outstanding success of the Douro Viaduct, completed in 1878, immediately brought Eiffel a commission to build the Garabit Viaduct over the River Truyère in the Massif Central.

Just as the Douro Viaduct provided the necessary experience to build Garabit, so the achievement of Garabit was essential to the design and concep-

15 *Galerie des Machines. Mobile "viewing" machines.*

tion of the Eiffel Tower. Like the Crystal Palace, the Tower was designed and erected under considerable pressure. First exhibited in the spring of 1885, it was in the ground by the summer of 1887 and well over 650 feet high by the winter of 1888. As in Contamin's Galerie des Machines, the structure had to be provided with an access system for the rapid movement of visitors. The elevator was essential, since there was no way of gaining access to the Tower except via elevators that either ran on inclined tracks within its legs or rose vertically from first platform to pinnacle. The guide rails for these elevators were exploited during erection as tracks for climbing cranes, an economy in working method reminiscent of the mounting technique used by Eiffel in the case of the hinged viaducts. As much a by-product of the railway as the Crystal Palace, the Tower was, in effect, a 300-metre-high viaduct pylon, whose type-form had been originally evolved out of the interaction of wind, gravity, water and material resistance. It was a hitherto unimaginable structure that could not be experienced except by traversing the aerial matrix of the space itself. Given the futuristic affinity of the Tower to aviation – celebrated by the aviator Santos Dumont when he circled the structure with his dirigible in 1901 – it is hardly surprising that thirty years after its erection it should have been reinterpreted as the prime symbol of a new social order, in Vladimir Tatlin's Monument to the Third International, projected in 1920.

As iron technology developed through the exploitation of the earth's mineral wealth, so concrete technology, or at least the development of hydraulic cement, seems to have arisen out of traffic on sea. In 1774, John Smeaton established the base of his Eddystone Lighthouse using a "concrete" compound of quicklime, clay, sand, and crushed iron slag, and similar concrete mixes were used in England in bridge, canal, and harbour works throughout the last quarter of the 18th century. Despite Joseph Aspdin's pioneering development of Portland cement for use as imitation stone in 1824 and various other English proposals for metal-reinforced concrete construction, such as that made by the ever inventive J.C. Loudon in 1792, the initial English lead in the pioneering of concrete gradually passed to France.

In France the economic restrictions that followed the Revolution of 1789, the synthesis of hydraulic cement by L.J. Vicat around 1800 and the tradition of building in *pisé* (rammed earth), combined to create the optimum circumstances for the invention of reinforced concrete. The first consequential use of the new material was made by François Coignet, who was already familiar with the *pisé* building method of the Lyons district. In 1861 he developed a technique for strengthening concrete with metal mesh and on the basis of this established the first limited company to specialize in ferro-concrete construction. Coignet worked in Paris under Haussmann's direction, building 3½ inches thick, shell concrete sewers and other public structures in ferro-concrete, including, in 1867, a remarkable series of six-storey apartment blocks. Despite these commissions, Coignet failed to uphold his patent and by the end of the Second Empire his company was dissolved.

Another French pioneer of concrete was the gardener Joseph Monier, who, following his successful production of concrete flower pots in 1850, turned to the exploitation of the material for building. Between 1867 and 1878 Monier

16 Hennebique, patent reinforced concrete frame construction, 1892.

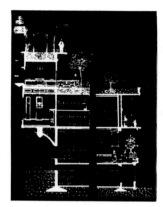

17 Hennebique, concrete house,
Bourg-la-Reine, 1904. Section.

took out a series of patents for metal-reinforced applications, the partial rights of which he ill-advisedly sold in 1880 to the engineers Schuster and Wayss. Further rights were obtained from Monier in 1884 by the firm of Freytag, and soon afterwards the large German civil engineering concern of Wayss and Freytag came into being. Their monopoly over the Monier system was consolidated by G.A. Wayss who commissioned Matthias Koenen to write the standard work on the Monier method, *Das System Monier,* published in 1887. The publication of important theoretical studies on differential stress in reinforced concrete by the German theorists Neuman and Koevern consolidated the German lead in this type of construction.

The period of most intense development in reinforced concrete occurred between 1870 and 1900, with pioneering work being carried on simultaneously in Germany, America, England, and France. In his reinforced concrete Hudson River home of 1873, William E. Wards became the first builder to take full advantage of the tensile strength of steel by situating bars below the neutral axis of the beam. The inherent structural advantage of this was almost immediately confirmed by the concrete beam experiments conducted in England by the American entrepreneur Thaddeus Hyatt and the British railway engineer Thomas Rickets, whose joint results were published in 1877. Hyatt had stumbled across the principles of reinforced concrete construction by embedding glass lenses in concrete paving slabs around 1873.

Despite these international developments, the systematic exploitation of modern reinforced concrete technique was to wait upon the inventive genius of François Hennebique. Hennebique, a self-educated French builder, first used concrete in 1879. He then conducted an extensive programme of private research before patenting his own uniquely comprehensive system in 1892. Before Hennebique, the great problem in ferro-concrete had been the provision of a monolithic joint. The compound concrete and steel systems that had been patented by Fairbairn in 1845 were far from being monolithic and the same restrictions applied to the work of Hyatt and Rickets. Hennebique overcame this difficulty through the use of bars of cylindrical section which could be bent round and hooked together. Integral to his system alone was the cranking up of reinforcement bars and the binding of joints with stirrup hoops in order to resist local stress. With the perfection of this joint, the monolithic frame could be realized, leading promptly to the first large-scale application of such a system in three spinning mills that Hennebique built in the region of Tourcoign and Lille in 1896. The results were at once acclaimed a success, and Hennebique's firm immediately prospered. His partner, L.G. Mouchel, brought the system to England in 1897, building the first concrete road bridge there in 1901 and exhibiting a spectacular free-standing, helical, reinforced concrete stair at the Franco-British exhibition of 1908.

The wide success of the Hennebique firm dates from around 1898, with the regular publication of its house magazine *Le Béton armé* and the extensive use of its system in the eclectic structures of the Paris Exhibition of 1900. Despite the false facades of the Château d'Eau, constructed out of ferro-concrete by François Coignet's son, the Paris Exhibition of 1900 gave an enormous boost to concrete construction and by 1902, a decade after its foundation, the

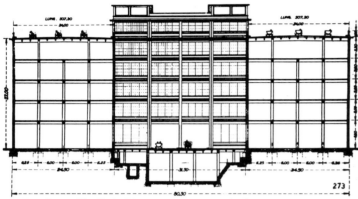

18 Matté-Trucco, Fiat Works, Lingotti, Turin, 1915-21. Section.

Hennebique firm had grown into a large international concern. Throughout Europe innumerable works were being constructed of concrete, with Hennebique acting as the main contractor. In 1904 he built his own reinforced concrete villa at Bourg-la-Reine, complete with roof garden and minaret. Its solid walls were formed out of ferro-concrete poured in place between permanent pre-cast concrete shuttering, and its almost totally glazed facade was dramatically cantilevered out from the main plane of the building. With the turn of the century, Hennebique's monopoly over his system began to wane, although his patents still had a number of years to run. In 1902 his chief assistant, Paul Christophe, popularized the system by publishing *Le Béton armé et ses applications*. Four years later Armand Considère, who had already carried out concrete research for the department of Ponts et Chaussées, headed the national committee that finally established the French code for reinforced concrete practice.

Up to 1895, ferro-concrete work in North America was inhibited by its dependence on the importation of cement from Europe. Soon after, however, grain silo and flatted factory construction commenced, first in Canada, with the reinforced concrete silo structures of Max Toltz, and then, from 1900 onwards, in the United States, in the work of the Englishman E.L. Ransome, who was the inventor of twisted reinforcement (1884). With the building, in 1902, of his 300-foot machine shop at Greensburg, Pennsylvania, Ransome became the pioneer of the monolithic concrete frame in the United States. Here he applied for the first time the principle of spiral column reinforcement in accordance with the theories of Considère. It says something for the technical precociousness of Frank Lloyd Wright that he began to design reinforced concrete structures at around the same time: his unrealized Village Bank project of 1901, and the E-Z Polish factory and Unity Temple, both begun in Chicago in 1905.

Meanwhile, in Paris, Perret Frères had begun to design and build their first all-concrete structures, beginning with Auguste Perret's seminal rue Franklin apartment block of 1903 and his Théâtre des Champs-Elysées of 1913. At about the same time, Henri Sauvage explored the expressive "plastic" potential of this new monolithic material in his set-back apartments in the rue Vavin, completed in 1912. By this date the reinforced concrete frame had become a normative technique, and from now on most of the development was to lie in the scale of its application and in its assimilation as an expressive element. While its first use on a megastructural scale was in Matté-Trucco's 100-acre Fiat Works, built in Turin in 1915, its appropriation as an expressive architectural element came with Le Corbusier's Maison Dom-Ino proposal of around the same date. Where the one clearly demonstrated that flat concrete roofs could sustain the vibration of dynamic moving loads (the Fiat factory has a test track on its roof), the other postulated the Hennebique system as a "patent" primal structure to which, after the manner of Laugier's primitive hut, the development of a new architecture would have to refer.

10 *Aerial view of Sydenham Crystal Palace*
11 *Section of nave and gallery roofs*

JOSEPH PAXTON
Crystal Palace
London, England

Built out of prefabricated and wrought-iron elements and based on a four-foot module, this 1,848-foot-long ferro-vitreous construction was erected to the designs of Joseph Paxton and Charles Fox, of Fox, Henderson & Co. Its interior volume was organized into galleries which were alternately 24 feet and 48 feet wide. The roof of these galleries stepped up by 20 feet every 72 feet, and culminated in a central nave 72 feet wide. The "ridge and furrow" roof glazing system specially devised for the occasion required 49-inch glass sheets capable of spanning between furrows 8 feet apart, with three ridges occuring every 24 feet. With the exception of the main transept (introduced for the sake of tree preservation) and the 6-foot-deep trusses spanning the nave, all the spanning and bearing elements had the same standard external dimensions. The different loads were accommodated by varying the wall thickness of the hollow cast-iron columns and by using wrought instead of cast iron to increase the spanning capacity of the standard 3-foot deep beams. Fundamentally, the ability to build such a structure derived from two technological developments which were initially unrelated. The most essential of these was the system of hot-house horti-culture perfected by J.C. Loudon early in the century. This system was first realized on a large scale by Paxton at Chatsworth, where he constructed a great palm house or "stove" for the Duke of Devonshire, be-tween 1837 and 1840. The other crucial technical innovation was the railway system itself, inaugurated by the Stockton to Darlington line of 1825. In fact the railway engineer, Charles Fox, was to detail the Crystal Palace as though it were as coherent a techno-industrial assembly as the railway network. Fox's systematic approach permit-ted the dismantling of the structure and its re-erection at Sydenham (1852-54), where it remained until it was burnt to the ground in 1936.

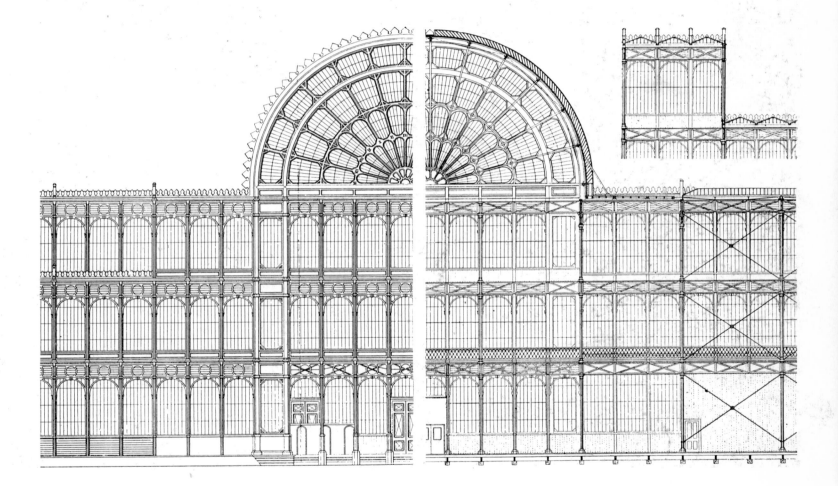

12 Above: aerial perspective
   Below: interior perspective
13 Above and below: Sydenham Crystal Palace, under construction
   Photos: Collections, The Crystal Palace Foundation of Patrick Beaver

In 1852, seven years before his death, the pioneer engineer Isambard Kingdom Brunel began to work on the execution of his finest building, the London terminal of the Great Western Railway, designed in association with the architect Matthew Digby Wyatt. The work was started at about the same time as Brunel's finest bridge, his Saltash Viaduct of 1859, which extended the broad gauge tracks of the Great Western across the Tamar river, west of Plymouth. It took the company fifteen years to decide to build a permanent terminus in London and when they eventually did so, the required track capacity had increased five times. The permanent terminus, finished in 1854, consisted of three spans of arched, wrought-iron girders covering four platforms, ten tracks and eight turntables, all of which was to be located at the rear of the Great Western Hotel, built as a separate structure to the design of P.C. Hardwick in 1854. The English approach of entirely separating the head building from the shed is even more evident here than it is in the St. Pancras terminus of 1868-74. The volume of Brunel's initial three-span shed, spanning a total width of 238 feet, was interrupted by two 50-foot transepts for the accommodation of a traversing frame, an early device for the manipulation of locomotives. These transepts and the spacing of the columns under every third girder not only provided for unexpected diagonal views, but also for a certain syncopation in the overall structure of the shed. Fox, Henderson and Co. of Crystal Palace fame, were once again the main contractors, a fact which is reflected in the use of Paxton's ridge and furrow system in the cladding the roof. The architect Digby Wyatt was retained expressly for the ornamentation of the structure, that is to say the transverse beams between the columns, the tracery of the lunettes at the end of the shed, and the vaguely Alhambric treatment of the station master's oriel. Since Owen Jones advised on the initial colour scheme of the shed, Paddington Station, with the crucial exception of Brunel and Wyatt, was detailed by the same team who had previously worked on the Crystal Palace.

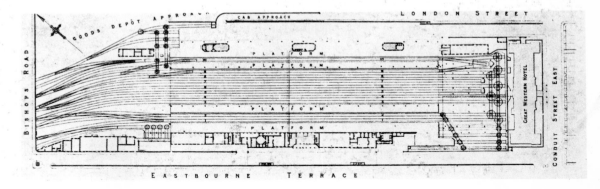

14 *View through platform*
15 *Above: view of shed structure*
   Below: plan (Paddington Station II)

16 View through transept
17 Left: column detail
    Right: vault detail

Eventually to be erected as an integral part of Haussmann's program for the modernization of Paris, Baltard's proposal for *Les Halles* passed through a number of different versions and a false start, before being finally realised in its definitive form. It was Baltard's hypothetical study for a central market in 1844 that led to his appointment, with Felix Callet, as the official architect for the site in 1845. This is also the year of Baltard's first scheme, a version of which was eventually built in 1851. Contrary to popular myth, all of Baltard's projects for *Les Halles* involved pavilions with ferrovitreous roofs. The real issue at stake for

Baltard, as for Haussmann, was the mode of expression to be used for the facades. Work on the first pavilion of the 1851 scheme, with its classical dressed stone facade, was suspended in 1853 on the occasion of Haussmann's appointment as *Préfet de la Seine*. The whole issue of the appropriate form of structure was then reopened with Napoleon III insisting, according to Haussmann, that the pavilions should be built only of iron. Baltard's third (all iron) proposal of 1853, comprising ten pavilions in all, was finally built in three stages, with the eastern section of six pavilions remaining unfinished until 1886. Two additional quadrant pavil-

ions were added to the pre-existing *halle au blé* in 1936. A typical pavilion in the central sector covered an area of 42 by 54 metres. The most innovatory feature of the whole scheme was the raising of the marketing floor 70 cm out of the ground. The purpose of this was to provide light and ventilation to the undercroft which was used for storage. However, the complimentary notion of serving this basement with a rail spur from the Gare de l'Est was never realized. When complete, Baltard's iron umbrellas, with their covered access streets, comprised a kind of city in miniature.

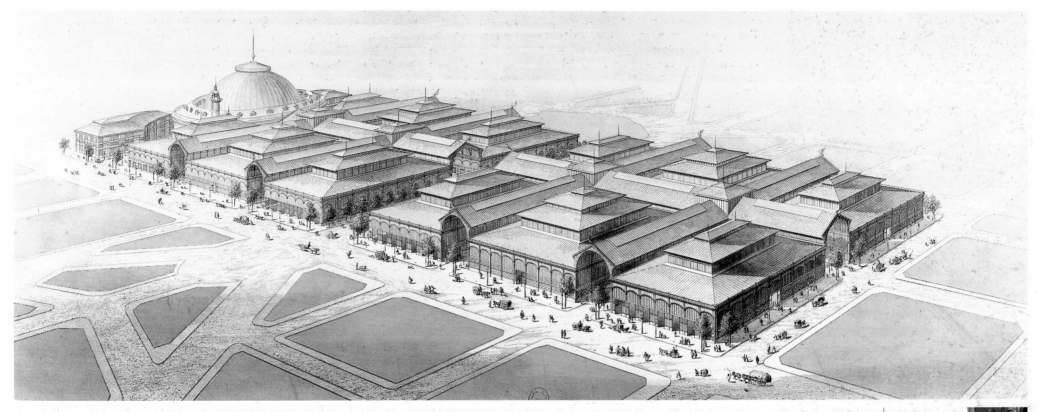

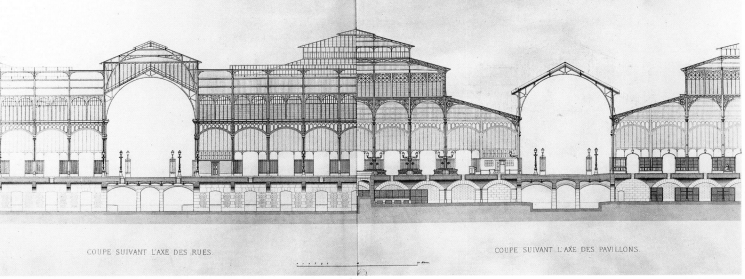

18 Facade detail
19 Above: aerial perspective
    Below: street facade
20 View of interior
21 Above: view through internal street
    Below: section
    Photos: M. Sekiya

COUPE SUIVANT L'AXE DES RUES.

COUPE SUIVANT L'AXE DES PAVILLONS.

1859

PHILIP WEBB
WILLIAM MORRIS
"Red House"
Bexley Heath, Kent, England

The Arts and Crafts, together with the English Free Style of architecture, has its origins in this joint work by Morris and Webb which took the format of William Butterfield's Gothic Revival vicarage and used its general character as the point of departure for the short-lived but influential Pre-Raphaelite domestic style. This manner received its quintessential formulation in Morris's painting, *La Belle Iseult*, which depicted his wife, Jane Burden, in an ideal, mediaevalized interior; that is to say in the kind of environment that he was to spend the rest of his life trying to recreate in terms of furniture, wall paper, tapestry and stained glass. For Webb, however, the Red House

was merely the first of a series of houses in which he endeavoured to engender an authentic ahistorical style, through the direct expression of local materials and craftsmanship. Webb adopted the Gothic Revival syntax of Pugin and Butterfield, that is, clay tiling, corbelled brick work, rubbed brick arches and circular openings, as a way of articulating an open-ended form of vernacular expression. Webb's eclectic approach varied from house to house since in theory at least, the local materials and mode of fabrication were never the same. This perennially dissatisfied and frustrated architect may be regarded as the re-interpreter of a number of regional vernaculars that

were then disintegrating just as fast as he tried to resuscitate them. Yet for all his puritanism Webb was committed, unlike Pugin, to the conscious "development" of the Gothic Revival; that is to say to the need to incorporate into its general syntax, elements drawn from later periods, such as the Georgian sash windows that are patently in evidence here. In the main, however, the Red House formulated for the first time the quintessential L-shaped Gothic Revival domestic plan with its externally expressed stair-cum-entry hall located at the intersection of the two arms of the L.

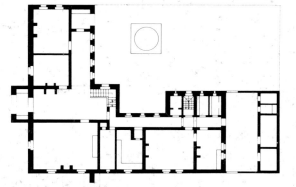

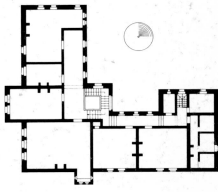

22 *View from the garden*
23 *Above: entrance hall*
   Below: first floor and second floor plans

24 *Above: ceiling above the stair hall*
   Below: interior wall of study
25 *Left, top: view through second story corridor*
   Left, middle and bottom; cabinet in the room
   Above right: salon
   Below right: fireplace in salon

Erected in honor of the Italian unification that followed the liberation of Lombardy from Austrian occupation in 1859, this 96-foot-high arcade was built as the result of a competition held in 1861. Designed by the engineer Giuseppe Mengoni, the basic structure was erected between 1865 and 1867. The 640-foot-long north/south axis of its cruciform plan links the secular Piazza della Scala on the north to the spiritual Piazza della Duomo on the south. In 1877, a triumphal arch was added to the southern end of this cruciform gallery, thereby formally terminating this covered urban link between the opera house and the cathedral.

The iconography of the inlaid mosaic concourse and the painted pendentives of the 164-foot octagonal dome, raised over the crossing, represents the union of church and state which first came into being with the triumphant nationalist revolution of 1848. The subsequent establishment of the offices of the liberal newspaper *Corriera della Serra* at one corner of the crossing only served to strengthen the political connotations of this monument. It is no accident that many of the early Italian Futurist demonstrations took place in this gallery.

As J.F. Geist has noted in his study *Passengen*, this arcade was a direct descendant of the labyrinthine passages that first appeared in Paris in the 1820s. According to Geist, Mengoni's design inaugurated the monumental phase in the development of this type; the structure being considerably higher than J.P. Cluysenaar's Galerie St. Hubert, built in 1846. The enormous scale and height of the space necessitated the introduction of a novel device for the purpose of lighting the gas lamps at the springing of the glass roof. This so-called "rat" or *Il Ratin* consisted of a gas jet mounted on wheels which, at the time of ignition, ran along a track following the perimeter of the gallery.

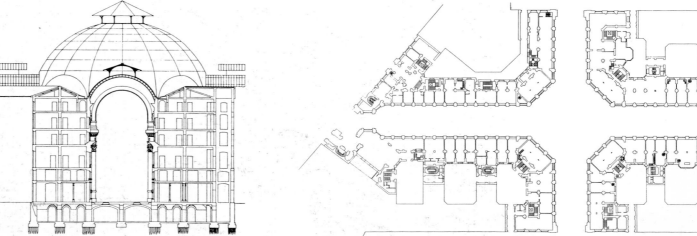

26 Above: view of the transept area
Below: section and plan
27 Piazza Duomo entrance (Photo: M. Sekiya)

After the revolution of 1789, attention had to be given to the accommodation of the young republic's national library. It was not until 1854 however that Henri Labrouste was finally charged with the task of housing the national collection in the couryard of the Palais Mazarin. Labrouste's basic concept was to create a top-lit reading room, as a *salles des imprimes,* consisting of nine square vaulted bays supported on sixteen 12-inch-diameter cast-iron columns. This main hall is top lit by oculi—one to each of the ceramic domes resting on the network of perforated, semi-circular cast-iron arches. Labrouste seems to have adopted this slender structure in order to simulate the sensation of reading out of doors; the Pompeian wall decorations serving to augment this illusion of a wind-filled tent or *velaria*. The insertion of this iron network into the courtyard of an existing palace was a logical extension of the light-weight, stone-encased, iron structure that Labrouste had already installed in the interior of his Bibliothèque Sainte-Geneviève of 1843. The enormous production of books in the nineteenth century demanded the provision of a separate book-stack or *magasin* of much greater volume than the reading space. This top-lit, four-storey, cast-iron galleried space was separated from the reading room by a full-height glass wall. The cast-iron galleries of the stacks themselves were slotted like the access decks of a ship's engine room, thereby permitting light to filter down to the lowest levels of the space.

28 Interior view
29 Above: section and plan
Below: view of the ceiling

1869-83

JOHN A. ROEBLING
WASHINGTON A. ROEBLING
Brooklyn Bridge
New York, New York, U.S.A.

The history of the 19th-century suspension bridge is as international as it is technically complex, and any honours as to its pioneers would surely have to be divided among the American James Finley, who patented a system of chain suspension as early as 1840, Samuel Brown, an Englishman, who built the ill-fated 130-metre iron-chain bridge across the Tweed in 1820, and the French engineer Marc Séguin, who built a 250-foot wire-rope bridge across the Rhône in 1825. However, it is Roebling's 1840 patent for the in-situ spinning of wire rope that has to be recognized as one of the decisive breakthroughs in modern suspension bridge tech-nology. This patent brought John Roebling a commission to build a cable-suspended, wooden aqueduct over the Allegheny River in 1845. Roebling built a number of such aqueducts before receiving two major bridge commissions in his mid-career: his 821-foot span Niagara rail bridge of 1841-55 and his 1,000-foot span Cincinnati Bridge of 1856-67; both of which were prototypes for the 1,600 foot Brooklyn Bridge, whose construction ran through two generations of Roeblings between 1869 and its completion in 1883. The twin masonry support towers of this vast span necessitated the building of foundations 78 feet below the water level and Roebling's son, Washington Roebling, became permanently crippled with caisson disease as the result of supervising this work. Of the completed bridge, Montgomery Schuyler wrote in 1891: "The designer of the Brooklyn Bridge has made a beautiful structure out of an exquisite refinement of utility, in a work in which the lines of force constitute the structure." Konrad Wachsmann was to assess its achievement in more abstract terms 70 years later, when he wrote of it as "defining a space previously un-imagined."

View from riverfront   Photo: T. Kitajima

Until the discovery of the Sheerness Boathouse, this building was always regarded as being the first multi-storey, metal-framed structure in the world. In 1825, having pioneered the mass manufacture of pharmaceutical products, Menier chose Noisiel-sur-Marne as the site on which to create his world-famous chocolate factory. In 1869, his son, Emile Menier commissioned the architect Jules Saulnier to design a new mill building to be superimposed over three turbine generators set into the river. Saulnier decided to rest his lightweight structure on the abutments of the sluice gates which took the form of four masonry piers. The structure was comprised of two exterior lattice girders running for the full height of the building and two rows of cast-iron columns running down the interior of the volume on either side of a central corridor. Both lattice girders and columns were supported on riveted, sheet-iron, tubular box beams spanning between the masonry piers, which in effect was a form of early megastructure. The three intermediate floors were formed by brick vaulted construction spanning onto riveted wrought-iron joists which in their turn were carried by the external lattice girders and the internal columns. The lattice framework on the exterior was finally filled with a thin layer of hollow brickwork whose variegated colour was coursed in such as way as to resemble alternately the letter 'M' standing for Menier and a conventionalized silhouette of a cacao tree.

32 Left: detail of entry facade
  Right: entry facade
33 Overall view

34 Detail of entry wall
35 Above: river facade
   Below left: detail of interior structure
   Below right: interior view

It is typical of the period that Eiffel's finest architectural work should be carried out in the service of Aristide Boucicaut's pioneering, *fixed price* department store first established in 1852. Boucicaut's selling methods quickly vindicated themselves and by 1872 he was able to build expanded premises for his Bon Marché store in rue de Babylone, to the designs of M.A. Laplanche. This was the complex that Boileau and Eiffel added to in 1876. The Boileau/Eiffel section of the Bon Marché store was penetrated and articulated by spectacular light wells, bridges and Baroque staircases. Equally integrated into the structure were light metal catwalks running over the high-pitched ferro-vitreous roofs covering the major voids. That Boileau was aware that such lightweight, transparent construction demanded a new architectural approach is evident from the text that he wrote for the *Revue de l'Encyclopédie d'Architecture*, in 1876. He saw that what counted now was not the play of light on solid form but rather the ambiant feeling of the illuminated space that fell into the interior voids. He wrote: "In this luminous assembly, solid architecture will play the role of a dressed stone setting; it will have to count just enough to make the interior daylight vibrate with as much intensity as possible so that the transverse graded surfaces and the semi-lit depths which surround it will appear to be as gay, resonant and well furnished as if they were in the pure daylight of the outside."

36 Rendering: interior view
37 Above, left to right:
  section showing stair elevation,
  plan of ceilings, plan of stairs
  Below: section through stairs

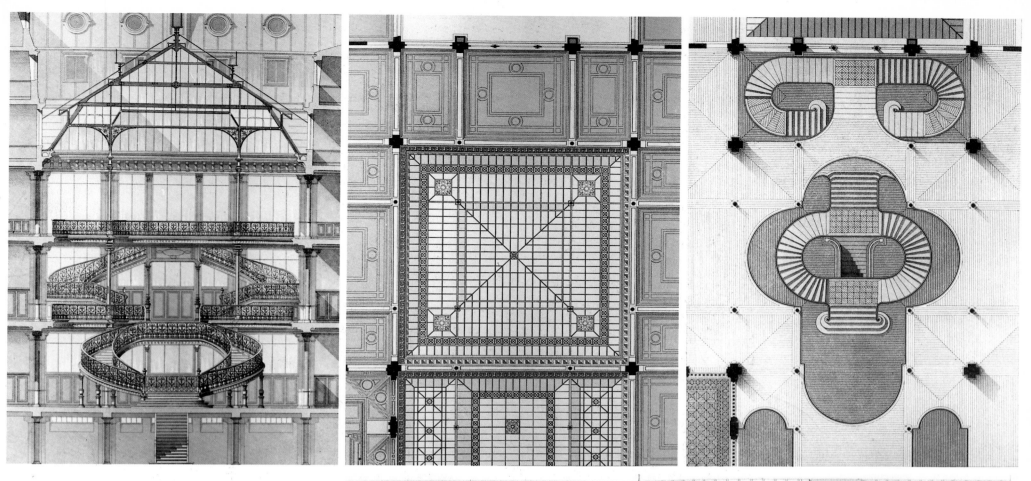

Antonio Gaudí y Cornet belonged to that generation of Barcelona architects who were strongly influenced by Viollet-le-Duc. As a member of the Catalan Art Nouveau or Modernismo movement, he followed the precepts of Structural Rationalism and tried from this anti-classical position to create an ahistorical style, with which to express both the ethos of modernity and the emergence of Catalonian Nationalism. In this Gaudí was not alone and architects such as Francisco Berenguer, Puig y Cadafalch and Doménech y Montaner, found equally imaginative ways of combining the use of masonry with dynamic structural profiles and iconographic elements drawn from either Gothic or Moorish sources. After his Casa Vicens of 1885 and his Palau Güell of 1889, Gaudí's work was to be distinguished from that of his colleagues by an indulgence in "surrealist" effects and by his unique sense of the spiritual which bordered at times on the Pantheistic. The church of the Holy Family, the design of which Gaudí assumed in 1884, was the first occasion on which he was allowed to give full expression to this sensibility. Destined to remain unfinished, this church had been inaugurated in 1882 and its undercroft built to the designs of the Gothicist architect Francisco de Paula del Villar, for whom Gaudí had previously worked in 1876 when the former was rebuilding the Montserrat lady chapel. This was the occasion on which Gaudí first encountered the mythic mountain range of Montserrat, whose volcanic pointed forms were to be refered to in the belfries of La Sagrada Familia, built in 1906. In that year the poet Joan Maragall wrote of visiting the church in the company of the architect in the following terms: "We went. Our voices passed away in the night air, like the voices of spirits beyond time. And the great bulk of the Temple construction, as yet bare of the sublime proportions which were to be added, loomed up behind us, bathed in moonlight. An open, bone-like, monstrous structure..." One can only assume that Maragall's sense of unease would have been greatly increased later on, with the uncannily realistic sculpture of Lorenzo Matamala, whose fowl, cacti, stalactites, angels and children were to swirl over the surface of the church like forces of the demi-urge itself. This vertiginous play with primaeval imagery stands in strong contrast to the elaborate abstract corbelling that supports the superstructure of the 260-foot-high belfries above.

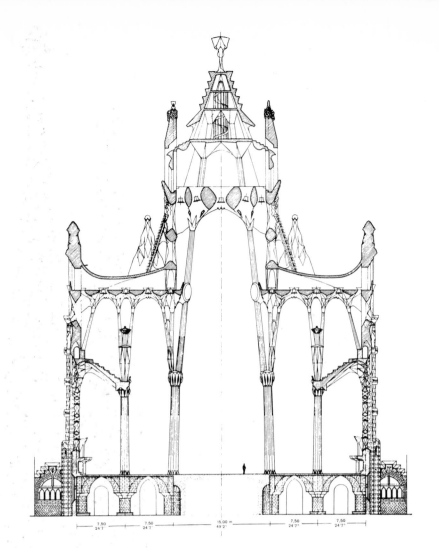

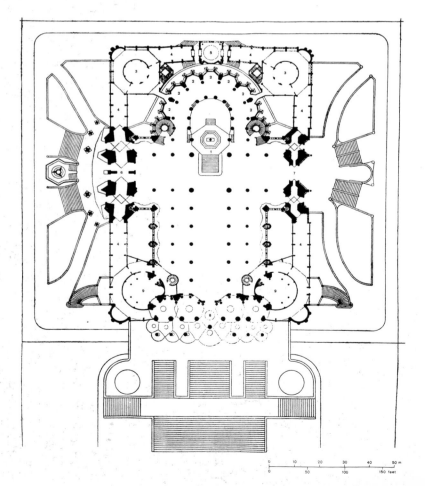

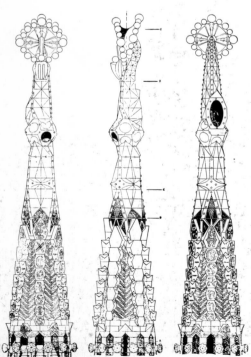

38 Left: spire elevation
    Right: section and plan
39 Overall view

40 *Above left: spires*
   Right: view of the side entrance
41 *View of the main entrance*

40

1884-90

*DANIEL H. BURNHAM
& JOHN W. ROOT
Monadnock & Kearsarge Bldgs.
Chicago, Illinois, U.S.A.*

By 1884, John Root was already at work on an early version of the 202-foot-high Monadnock Block and, faced with his client's exacting wishes that the structure should be free from ornamentation, he had started, even at this early date, to play with the idea of a single Egyptian profile to encompass the entire rise of the building—initially set at 12 floors. The fact that the Monadnock was erected during a moment of transition in Chicago construction is reflected in the additional four floors which were tacked on to its height in 1889. The whole had been originally designed as a steel frame structure; a proposition that was rejected by the clients on the grounds of the curious prejudice that such structures were intrinsically impermanent. In any event, the final work was to be a compromise; that is to say, it was a sixteen-storey, load-bearing brick structure with steel-reinforced brick piers and steel wind-bracing girders extending to the perimeter from a steel-framed central corridor. Tension straps run from this inner frame at every floor to points within five inches of the brick face, where the metal was cramped into the masonry. Battered towards its base, the Monadnock's height to width ratio of three to one was given an articulate profile as a consequence of Root's meticulous detailing, such as his rounding of the bricks about the fenestra-tion and his varying of the proportional width of the typical bay between the long and short facades. Finally, a bell-shaped cornice terminates the upward thrust of the batter in a vertical contour that resembles the Egyptian bell-shaped papyrus column found at Saqqara. Montgomery Schuyler's enthusiastic reception of the work in 1895 was echoed in Sullivan's belated appraisal of Root's masterpiece in 1923, when he wrote: "an amazing cliff of brickwork, rising sheer and stark, with a subtlety of line and surface, a direct singleness of purpose that gave one the thrill of romance."

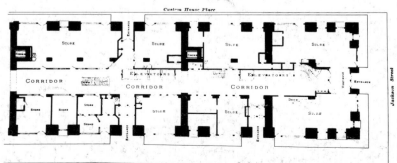

*42 Above: view of the facade
  Below: typical floor and first floor plans
43 View from the street*

The Chicago School of Architecture:
The City and the Suburb 1830-1915

19 *Development of Chicago, 1871.*

20 *Elevation of whole blocks in Chicago as carried out by Pullman.*

There in the Adler and Sullivan offices high in the Chicago Auditorium Tower I worked for nearly seven years — George Elmslie alongside — occasionally looking out through the romantic Richardsonian Romanesque arches over Lake Michigan or often, after dark, watching the glow of giant Bessemer steel converters reddening the night sky down towards South Chicago. I looked from those high-up arches down upon the great, growing city of Chicago as the Illinois Central trains puffed along the lake front.

Frank Lloyd Wright
A Testament, 1957

No adequate sketch of the rise and fall of the Chicago School of Architecture can be given without first affording an indication as to the rate at which Chicago grew from its foundation as a trading post on the basis of Thompson's original grid in 1830 to its overburdening population of nearly 300,000 by the time of the Great Fire of 1871. This boom started when a settlement consisting of some 200 houses in 1833 became a frontier town of 1,800 people in the space of a year. The population increased expotentially thereafter and by the time that George Pullman came to Chicago in 1851 to start struggling against Chicago mud (by paving thoroughfares and by raising whole streets of timber-framed houses above the ground) it was already a city of almost 30,000 people. At this date the wooden residential and commercial stock of Chicago was almost all built out of the balloon frame, invented by G. W. Snow in the late 1830s. This system of timber frame construction consisted of timber studs spaced at regular intervals nailed directly onto a sub-frame. This method of building was so standard as to constitute the first

form of Chicago construction, and it was this highly inflammable structural fabric which burnt down to the ground in the centre of Chicago in 1871.

Rail services in and out of Chicago began in 1841, and by the time of the trans-continental rail connection made at Promintory Point, Utah, in 1869, rail lines extended from the city in all directions. This rail service, complemented by extensive inland waterways, centering on Chicago, fed the city with the beef and grain surplus of the Mid-West; a surplus which sought its outlet in the East and then, via the Great Lakes, in the world at large. The building of grain elevators and the construction of the Chicago stockyard and slaughterhouse in 1865 were essential to the storage and processing of this agricultural surplus. Some idea of the magnitude of the growth in this production can be gained from the fact that the figure for hogs processed annually in Chicago rose from some 400,000 in 1860 to 1,340,000 by 1862. All of this led in the mid 1870s to the vast meat-packing undertakings of Armour and Swift and eventually in 1882 to Gustavus Swift's development of refrigerated meat storage and to the continental transhipment of meat and perishable produce in refrigerated cars. By this date, George Pullman had given up elevating the streets of the city and had become interested in improving the conditions of transcontinental rail travel, inaugurating his *Pioneer* sleeping car for such purposes in 1865. Pullman eventually triumphed over all his competitors, and from the demand for his sleeping car established the Pullman Car Co. and his ideal manufacturing city of Pullman, complete with residential and community facilities founded on the shores of Lake Calumet in 1880. This proto-linear city based

Chicago, distant view

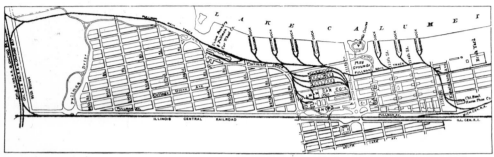

21 S. S. Beman and N. F. Barrett, the city of Pullman, 1885.

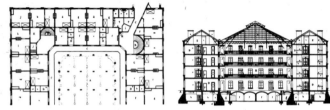

22 Godin, Familistère, Guise, France, 1859-80. Plan and cross section.

on the production of sleeping cars was the American equivalent of J.P. Godin's *Familistère* built at Guise in France from 1856 onwards. Where Godin's industrial city was a Utopian Socialist co-operative, Pullman was the benevolent, but utilitarian town of Temperance. In addition to this, the railway also brought raw material to Chicago — steel, coal, lumber and cement — the very substances out of which the city and its industries were to be built. Some notion of the rapid expansion in Chicago's own metallurgical industry may be gained from the fact that in 1860 there was only one blast furnace in the city, while by the time of the fire in 1871 there were four.

The trauma of the fire itself — which was largely a result of inadequate fire-proofing and the rapidity of urban development — effectively changed the standard method of construction and stimulated an even greater amount of building activity with the reconstruction of the burnt-out core. From 1871 to the end of the century, Chicago grew from a city of 300,000 to a metropolis of nearly 2,000,000; over two-thirds of whom had been born outside the United States. The pressure that such a rapid expansion put on land values created a demand for multi-storey construction and this demand was met, in technical terms, by the cast-iron frame (1850) and the steam elevator (1864) and soon after by the hydraulic elevator (1867). This selfsame pressure also produced the first middle-class garden suburbs of which Frederick Law Olmsted's Riverside (created outside Chicago in 1863) was a significant prototype, with its winding, picturesque wooded layout and its high-speed rail connection to downtown Chicago. It is significant for the subsequent myth of the suburb that, according to Olmsted's plan, the elite would have

been able to make the journey at leisure, on horseback, via a conveniently located bridle path.

The standard means of commercial construction in Chicago before the fire had been the supplementation of timber framing with cast-iron columns and cast-iron fronts, imported from Daniel Badger's iron foundry in New York after 1855. After the fire the first steps in arriving at a new system of fire-proof construction came from the survival of the Nixon building, which remained almost intact, because the upper surfaces of its framing members had been lined with concrete and the soffit of all the timber floors with a one-inch layer of plaster of Paris. The evident need to insulate structural members was immediately understood by all, and in particular by George H. Johnson who brought his system of hollow tile flooring to Chicago. In 1872, Johnson expanded his flooring method to include the terracotta tile covering of cast-iron columns and wrought-iron beams. From a structural point of view, Chicago construction owed its origin to the pragmatic pioneering of the French-trained engineer William Le Baron Jenney and to the theoretical work of the engineer Frederick Bauman who published, in the space of the next decade, two important seminal works: his thesis, *A Theory of Isolated Pier Foundations* of 1873 and his book, *On the improvement in the Construction of Tall Buildings* of 1882. Most of the pioneer architect-builders of the Chicago School, that is to say, Sullivan, Burnham, Holabird and Roche, received their practical training in the office of Le Baron Jenney, whose important achievements were the First and Second Leiter buildings of 1879 and 1890. The 1880s were a period of intense technical development which

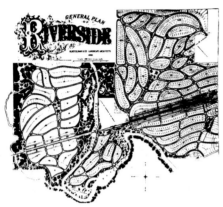
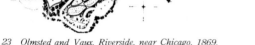

23 *Olmsted and Vaux, Riverside, near Chicago, 1869. Plan.*

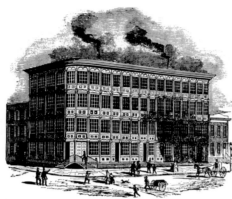

24 *Bogardus, Cast Iron Building, New York, N.Y., 1851.*

25 *Jenney, Fair Store, Chicago, 1890-91. Detail of fire-proof steel-frame construction.*

led from the masonry encasement of the free-standing, iron-columned frame, to the fully encased steel and wrought-iron frame structure of the Second Leiter building. By the time of Le Baron Jenney's Fair Store, Chicago (1890-91), the essentials of Chicago fire-proofed steel-frame construction had been perfected.

That this was a moment of technical transition in Chicago construction is borne out by the realization of the sixteen-storey Monadnock block (1889-91), designed by John Root, of Burnham and Root, as a partially load-bearing masonry structure according to the empirical principle of an increase of four inches in width for every floor over one storey in height, with a minimum width of twelve inches for the first floor. Despite the 72-inch masonry walls established at its base, the Monadnock is partially iron framed by virtue of the wrought-iron wind-bracing provided in the form of a portal frame constructed about its central access corridor. Although this made the Monadnock the first wind-braced structure in the world, the brilliance of its achievement resides finally in its formal resolution rather than its technical innovation. Of this, John Root was only too conscious when he wrote: "To lavish upon (modern multi-storey buildings) profusion of ornament is worse than useless . . . Rather should they by their mass and proportion convey in some large elemental sense an idea of the great, stable conserving forces of modern civilization." The very last of Root's works, his fifteen-storey Reliance Building (1891-95) detailed by Charles Atwood, and his twenty-storey Masonic Temple of 1892, both completed by Burnham's office after Root's untimely death in 1891, testify to his exceptional capacity as a formal

innovator. Nothing as bold or decisive was to be done with the high-rise structure until Louis Sullivan's Guaranty Building, erected in Buffalo in 1894.

After a temperamental and rather restless education (first at M.I.T. in 1872, then with Frank Furness in Philadelphia and Le Baron Jenney in Chicago (1873) and finally, a year at the École des Beaux-Arts, Paris in 1874) Louis Sullivan came back to Chicago in 1875, where he began to work for his friend and mentor John Edleman, of Johnson and Edleman. Sullivan's first task with this firm (with which he seems to have stayed for over two years) was a large piece of interior decoration, and it was here that he first demonstrated his ability to invent and develop a unique form of ornament. Sullivan then entered Dankmar Adler's office in 1879, at the time of an enormous building boom, and became an equal partner in the firm in 1881. The first works of this partnership were not only decidedly utilitarian but also rather pedestrian in their architectural treatment. Their arrival as architects of consequence came with their gaining large public commissions, and with Sullivan's mastery of the Richardsonian syntax, first evident in his Standard Club, Chicago (1887-88) and in the stripped and denuded form of the seven-storey Walker Warehouse, Chicago (1888-89). But it is the Auditorium Building, acquired by Adler as a commission in 1886, which finally served to establish the national reputation of the firm. The first and second stages of this eleven-storey multi-use building, occupying the best part of a Chicago city block, testifies to the tentative way in which Sullivan first began to adapt the Richardsonian syntax; the first scheme, with its mansard roofs and curiously eclectic facade,

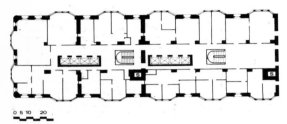

26 *Root, Monadnock Block, Chicago, 1891. Typical floor plan.*

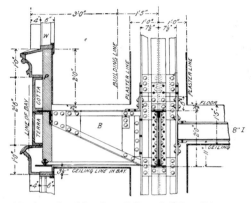

27 *Atwood and Burnham, Reliance Building, Chicago, 1890/1894-95. Cross section of window bay.*

being closer to the facade treatment of Richardson's Marshall Field Wholesale Store, opened in Chicago in 1887, a year after Richardson's death. Aside from being the largest of a series of speculative theatre developments in Chicago, the Auditorium demonstrated that an office building, a hotel, and an opera house could be elegantly combined within less than a city block, with the offices facing on to the street, the hotel on to the lake and the auditorium placed in the interior of the block. The auditorium itself was a technical *tour de force* and represented the triumph of Adler's considerable skills as an engineer. With the aid of flexible partitions suspended from the ceiling it was capable of varying its seating capacity from 4,237 to 6,000, while its stage was equipped with an elaborate hydraulic turntable whose segments could be adjusted to form platforms with different configurations, a device which was well in advance of comparable stages then existing in Europe. The acoustics of the space soon attained world renown, while its huge volume was cooled in the summer by feeding air into the hall over large blocks of ice. Building such a massive structure on Chicago's marshy soil tested Adler's ingenuity as a master of concrete raft foundations, while Sullivan, for his part, had ample occasion to demonstrate his prowess as a master of decoration in the interior of the auditorium, in the foyers, and in the restaurant located on the roof of the hotel.

Sullivan's reputation rests, however, not on the Auditorium Building, but rather on the masterly way in which he tried to confront the economic and technical realities of high-rise construction. Sullivan described the real causes for this building type with remarkable lucidity when he wrote:

So in this instance, the Chicago activity in erecting high buildings finally attracted the attention of the local sales manager of Eastern rolling mills; and their engineers were set at work. The mills for some time past had been rolling those structural shapes that had long been in use in bridge work. . . . Thus the idea of a steel frame which should carry all the load was tentatively presented to the Chicago architects.

The passion to sell is the impelling power in American life. Manufacturing is subsidiary and adventitious. But selling must be based on a semblance of service — the satisfaction of a need. The need was there, the capacity to satisfy was there, but contact was not there. Then came a flash of imagination which saw the single thing. The trick was turned; and there swiftly came into being something new under the sun. . . . The architects of Chicago welcomed the steel frame and did something with it. The architects of the East were appalled by it and could make no contribution to it.

A paragraph later, Sullivan was to write of his failure to civilize the sky-scraper in the following terms:

In Chicago the tall office building would seem to have arisen spontaneously, in response to favoring physical conditions, and the economic pressure as then sanctified, combined with the daring of promoters.

The construction and mechanical equipment soon developed into engineering triumphs. Architects, with a considerable measure of success, undertook to give a commensurate external treatment. The art of design in Chicago had begun to take on a recognizable character of its own. The future looked bright. The flag was in the breeze. Yet a small white cloud no bigger than a man's hand was soon to appear above the horizon. The name of this cloud was eighteen hundred and ninety-three. Following the white cloud was a dark dim cloud, more like a fog. The name of the second cloud was Baring Brothers.

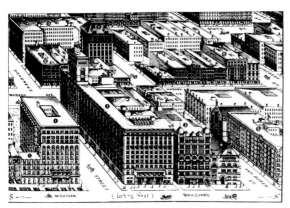

28 Chicago; Auditorium Building (no. 2) surrounded by downtown development in the mid-1890s.

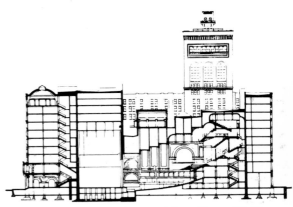

29 Adler and Sullivan, Auditorium Building, Chicago, 1887-89. Longitudinal section.

During this period there was well under way the formation of mergers, combinations and trusts in the industrial world. The only architect in Chicago to catch the significance of this movement was Daniel Burnham, for in its tendency toward bigness, organization, delegation, and intense commercialism, he sensed the reciprocal workings of his own mind.

The important high-rise structures of Sullivan's career are the Wainwright Building, St. Louis (1890-90), the Guaranty Building, Buffalo (1895) and finally the Schlesinger and Mayer department store (later Carson, Pirie, Scott) of 1899. Each of these works seems to have been a different stage in a continuous process of evolution; the first being, in the main, the trial application of pre-cast terracotta decoration to a four square brick-pilastered and steel-framed facade, the second being the brilliant resolution of this formula into a technical and aesthetic whole and the third, his last major work, being an altogether less decorative approach to the frame — a paradoxical manifestation perhaps of Sullivan's growing scepticism as to the capacity of modern society to produce an architectural culture which would be comparable to that of antiquity.

In his attempt to create an authentic culture for the United States, Sullivan (like Richardson before him) was obsessed with the Romanesque, while Wright, following their lead, also looked for inspiration in exotic and remote civilizations: in Pre-Columbian architecture and the architecture of Japan. Sullivan's own feeling for the exotic tended towards the near East and he finally settled for the Islamic. This much is evident from the Getty and Wainwright tombs which he designed in Chicago and St. Louis in 1890 and

1892 and from the ornament with which covered the entire surface of the Guaranty Building, the distribution being very similar to the repetition of an abstract but sacred ideogram over the entire surface of a mosque. At times Sullivan seems to have seen his ornament as a mystical force growing out of the very substance of the building; at other times he saw it as the organic expression of the function of the structure, as in the ornament to the Guaranty cornice which swirled around the circular attic windows in such a way as to suggest the organic flow and return of the plumbing and the elevator winding gear.

Sullivan's star began to wane with Daniel Burnham and Frederick Law Olmsted's Columbian Exposition, staged in 1893 — the so-called "White City" built around an artificial lagoon on the shores of Lake Michigan. Sullivan's last real contribution to Chicago came with the exotic form of his Transportation Building of 1891, built for this otherwise exclusively Beaux-Arts exhibition. With its Golden Door, its decoration of winged angels and its hindu-style kiosks situated on either side of the main entrance, it spoke rather hesitantly of some hypothetical ideal civilization. Two years after the Exposition opened, Sullivan, always the inveterate, temperamental and unstable figure, broke with his partner, Adler, and with this single quixotic gesture the heroic phase of his career came to an abrupt close.

Wright, who had left Sullivan's employ as early as 1893, was already an established figure by the time of realizing his famous Oak Park Studio in 1895. By that date he had already achieved two important commissions, the Sullivanian Winslow House (1893) and a pioneer example of perimeter block

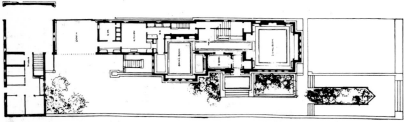

30 *Wright, Isidor Heller House, Woodlawn Avenue, Chicago, 1897. First floor plan.*

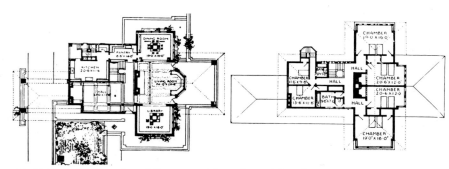

31 *Wright,* Ladies Home Journal *House, 1901. First and second floor plans.*

housing in Chicago, his Francisco Terrace apartments of 1895. The essential rudiments of Wright's Prairie Style, that is, the use of "tartan" gridded plans, the stressing of string courses and low-hipped eaves, the grouping of fenestration into horizontal bands and the provision of out-riding walls, were already latent in these works and were further refined in his Heller and Husser houses built in Chicago in 1897 and 1899. By this date, Wright was already attempting to evolve a universal format for the middle-class family home and this he effectively achieved, in a codifiable form, with his *Ladies Home Journal* houses of 1900, entitled "A Home in a Prairie Town" and "A Small House with Lots of Room in it," both of which closely resembled his Hickox and Harley Bradley houses built in Kankakee, Illinois in the same year. In the next few years Wright evolved this syntax into two separate but closely related forms: a T-shaped or cruciform, pyramidal house, with a pin-wheeling asymmetrical plan for the accommodation of the family, and a flat-roofed, frontal, pyloned, almost windowless prism enclosing a symmetrical plan for the accommodation of public institutions; this last being first projected in his Village Bank project of 1901 and his Yahara Boat Club proposal of 1902.

This differentiation of format between the domesticity of building and the civic nature of architecture became crystallized in the *annus mirabilus* of Wright's early career, the year 1904, when he designed three masterpieces, one after another: the Larkin Company office building for the Martin Mail Order concern, and the Martin House, both built in Buffalo in 1904, and the Unity Temple realized in Oak Park, Illinois at the end of 1906. Of these, the Larkin Building was clearly the most significant, for its formulation of the office building as an idealised workplace.

Throughout his life, Wright professed an almost mystical belief in the sacrament of work, evident in his self-conscious, Whitmanesque work song, "I'll Live, As I'll Work, As I am!" With his Unitarian background, he seems to have been determined to bring the workplace under the rubric of religious form. Thus, apart from the similarity of the *parti* adopted in the Larkin Building and the church, the arrangement and revetment of the top-lit Larkin interior reveals the same ecclesiastical spirit as is to be found in the Unity Temple. And while the church is the more ornately finished of the two, the Larkin interior archieves a similar sacramental atmosphere through the provision of improving inscriptions; Wright's much beloved mottoes which were incised into the spandrels of the uppermost gallery. Such phrases as "Ask and it shall be given you. Seek and ye shall find. Knock and it shall be opened unto you." More imperative moral precepts were inscribed above the sculptured fountains at the entrance to the building on two plaques by the sculptor Richard Bock, bearing the words: "Honest labor needs no master. Simple justice needs no slaves," and "Freedom to everyman and Commerce with all the World."

Like Richardson and Sullivan, and with the same initial success that Richardson had experienced in the East, Wright and his team of craftsmen and designers posited a totally new form of culture for the emerging egalitarian, commercial society of the American Mid-West. That he sought, like the European *Jugendstil* architects of his generation, to create a total work of art or *Gesamtkunstwerk* is evident from the fact that he designed and detailed

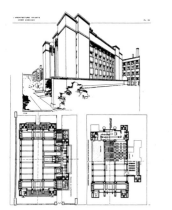

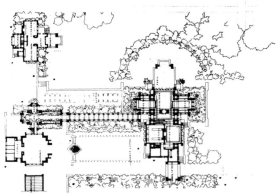

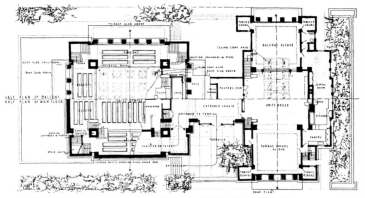

32 *Wright, Larkin Building, Buffalo, 1903-04. First floor, typical floor and perspective.*

33 *Wright, Darwin D. Martin House, Buffalo, 1904. First floor plan.*

34 *Wright, Unity Temple, Oak Park, Chicago, 1904-08. First floor plan.*

virtually every piece of equipment and revetment used in the furnishing of his works. Thus, from the Martin House, to the Larkin Building, to the Unity Temple, the grammar remained constant while the inflection changed. But the limits of this approach, as elsewhere, became evident where the normative technology of an industrialized society rudely asserted the values of a truly universal reality which was incapable, by its very nature, of conforming to the fragile aesthetic precepts of an ahistorical and hermetic art form. Hence, Wright's disgust with the Martin family when, having designed the Larkin office furniture and equipment, they refused to let him re-style the telephones.

Despite Wright's heroic assertion, made at the end of his Hull House lecture of 1901 — *The Art and Craft of the Machine* — that architecture would be capable of imbuing the modern city with a soul (he depicted Chicago as a mammoth mechanism), the abrasive nature of industrial reality and the fundamentally fragile form of the city in an uprooted society led Wright to project his public buildings as *introverted,* windowless structures, where the representative and significant space-form was constituted by the interior rather than by the facade of the Renaissance. In this respect there is an unbroken line of development in Wright's public work, from the Larkin Building of 1904 to the Johnson's Wax Administration Building, built at Racine, Wisconsin in 1936. The same cannot be claimed, however, for his much more varied domestic work, although even in this case one could say that the opposite was true; namely, that the Prairie house, at least up to 1915, always opened up its interior to the "paradise-garden" of the Mid-Western suburb.

This was the concept of the suburb that Wright's followers inherited after his abrupt departure from Chicago in 1909, when the scandal of his private life became public knowledge. After the precipitous closure of his Oak Park Studio in the following year, the phenomena of the Chicago School became two separate architectural cultures; on the one hand, the official Beaux-Arts ruling taste of Daniel Burnham and the City Beautiful Movement, which became finally consolidated with the publication of Burnham's Plan for Chicago in 1909; and on the other, the unofficial, counter-culture of the Prairie School, in part Sullivanian, in part Wrightian, as practiced by the followers of both men between 1909 and 1915, this date being the point at which middle class, Mid-Western taste began to favour for its domesticity the Neo-Colonial historical mode. The Prairie School lasted for barely fifteen years (1900-15), starting with the earliest independent works by Sullivan's protégé, George Elmslie. The Wrightian wing of this "school" included Wright's disciple and co-initiator of the Prairie House, Robert C. Spencer, and other architects who at one time or other were assistants in the Oak Park Studio, including John van Bergen, George Dean, William Drummond, Marion Mahony (Wright's renderer) and last but not least Walter Burley Griffin. Aside from Elmslie, the Sullivanian wing of the school included William Purcell, Richard Schmidt and Hugh Garden.

The complex, uneven, and sometimes clumsy work of Griffin was at times as refined as the best work of Wright, particularly when he was assisted by his wife Marion Mahony. Griffin attempted to reconcile, albeit inadvertently, the

35 Burnham, Plan for Chicago, 1909-12.

36 Griffin, Plan of Canberra, Australia, 1913.

waning radical culture of the Prairie School with the more normative precepts of Burnham's City Beautiful movement. This much is already evident in Griffin's prize winning plan for the Australian capital of Canberra (1912-13) which was every bit as axial in the layout of its arterial network and its disposition of public monuments as Burnham's paradoxical proposal for the Haussmannization of Chicago of 1909. In both instances the grid remained; in Canberra in the form of suburban "lungs" extending for a certain distance on either side of the main arteries; in Burnham's Chicago Plan as the existing fabric of the city, now to be rationalized by the superimposition of Baroque boulevards. From the point of view of diagonal cross city movement, the orthogonal street grid is of course inefficient, and it says something for the soundness of the Haussmannian principle that many of the *percements* proposed by Burnham in his plan came to be eventually implemented as elevated freeways. From a cultural point of view, however, this realization had no relation whatsoever to Burnham's nostalgia for the Baroque street.

The Chicago School in the four stages of its development, from the pioneering work of Le Baron Jenney and the lucid formulations of Root, to the exotic idealizations of Sullivan and the suburban projections of Wright, may be seen as a continuous, if disjunctive development lying uneasily between the ready acceptance of Richardson's Romanesque in the late 1870s, and Burnham's efforts after 1893 to impose a normative Neo-Classical style on the public architecture of the United States. In summing up the achievements of the Chicago architectural avant-garde in the late 1890s, Leonardo Benevolo wrote:

But the results attained could be neither standardized nor diffused, and the only consistent way of abstracting a general norm from them, when changed economic and functional needs made this necessary, was to go back from the single experiments to common cultural premises, though it was precisely the original element of these experiments that was lost during this operation; what was left was, of course, the basic eclecticism, and the necessary lowest common denominator could be none other than classicism.

HENRY HOBSON RICHARDSON
J.J. Glessner House
Chicago, Illinois, U.S.A.

Built a decade after his somewhat uncharacteristically Shavian, Watts Sherman House built at Newport, R.I. in 1874, this is probably the most memorable of Richardson's domestic works. Its design came toward the end of his career and was finalized only one month before his untimely death in 1886. The most unusual aspect of the house is its U-shaped plan which while fronting on to the building line of the adjacent streets flanking the site, opens onto a sheltered courtyard to the rear of the lot. Since the Michigan Central Railroad passed quite close to the house, Richardson adopted this unusual arrangement in order to afford as much silence and privacy as possible. For this reason the street elevations, faced in massive blocks of rough-cut grey granite, are largely left blank save for the essential small-scale fenestration elements and entrances. All the principal rooms are lit, in the main, from the garden court; the garden facade being faced in red brick, with limestone lintels. Ironically known at the time as Richardson's "granite hut" it was to offend the local dignitaries such as George Pullman who lived in the same street. Apart from its evident hermetic attitude, the most curious thing about the plan was the narrowness of the servant's corridor serving the principle spaces. This feature seems to have arisen as a result of the site shape and the *parti* adopted.

The brooding, cryptic mediaeval aura of the Glessner House is redolent with the romantic sentiment of the period. This much is also confirmed by a letter that Glessner (one of the founders of International Harvester) wrote towards the end of his life about the building of the house: "We slept in this house for the first time on December 1, 1887, and never in the old house after that. The fire on the hearth typified the home, so we carried the living fire from the hearthstone in the old home at Washington and Morgan Streets, and with that started the fire on the new hearth, accompanied by a little ceremony..."

Glessner's awareness of the volatile and difficult context in which he was building is born out by another passage in the same letter: "I think there is the desire in us all to receive the family home from the past generation and hand it on to the next... Rarely can this be accomplished in this land of rapid changes. Families have not held and cannot hold even to the same localities for their homes generation after generation..." It is against this feeling of rootlessness that Glessner sought Richardson's assistance in building a domestic "monument," in a syntax that was possibly more appropriate to a jail than a house and it is ironic, to say the least, that the Glessner House could have been added to Richardson's Allegheny Court House and Jail of 1884, without altering a single detail.

Above: entry
Below: first floor plan

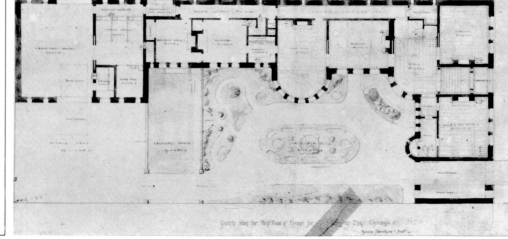

54 Above: entry facade
  Below: courtyard facade
55 Above right: entry hall
  Below left: detail of stairs
  Below right: dining room
  Photos: T. Kitajima

JOHN EISENMANN
GEORGE H. SMITH
Cleveland Arcade
Cleveland, Ohio, U.S.A.

Terminated on its two ends by nine-storey, stone-faced, office buildings and designed in a Richardsonian style by Smith, the Cleveland Arcade is a ferro-vitreous, top-lit gallery some 300 feet long, 60 feet wide and 100 feet high. Three balconies, a mezzanine and a lower concourse give access to three tiers of offices and two tiers of shops. Together with the offices the whole development has a depth of 378 feet, with office frontages extending for 130 feet and 180 feet on the two avenues at either end. These facades, facing Euclid and Superior Avenues respectively, together with the office space they house, are faced in dark obsidian, pressed brick and Pennsylvania sandstone.

After training as an engineer at the University of Michigan in 1871, Eisenmann carried out advanced engineering studies in the technical high schools of Munich and Stuttgart, graduating from the latter in 1878. According to Geist, Eisenmann's stay in Germany would have enabled him to become familiar with the latest techniques of arcade construction. Both from a technical and formal point of view, Eisenmann's solution to the roof of the arcade is remarkable, for the main trusses are pin-connected, three-hinged, arched trusses; their bottom chords effectively establishing the space of the nave. These 50-foot-span, wrought-iron trusses; with their 23-foot rise, seem to spring from 44 cast-iron, griffin-headed gargoyles flanking the perimeter of the void. The triangular top chord supports a continuous glass monitor 20 feet wide by 10 feet high. It is interesting to note that the tradition of the arcade as a spontaneous "political" arena was to be continued even in America and on a number of occasions the Cleveland arcade was put to political use, particularly when the National Convention of Republic Clubs held its convention there in 1895, filling the arcade with over 2,000 people.

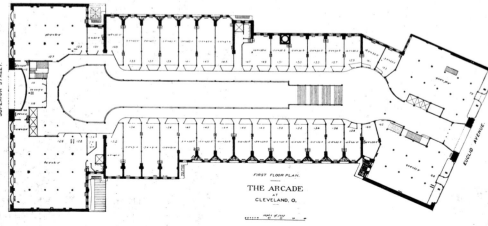

FIRST FLOOR PLAN.

THE ARCADE
AT
CLEVELAND, O.

56 Above: lower concourse
  Below: plan
56-57 Interior view

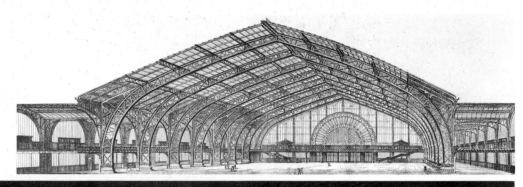

1889
FERDINAND DUTERT
VICTOR CONTAMIN
Machinery Hall
in Paris International Exhibition
Paris, France

It is tempting to see this structure in conjunction with the Eiffel Tower as being, respectively, the female and male symbols of this large and spectacular exhibition built to celebrate the centennial of the French Revolution of 1789. Both structures were in any event equally dedicated to display; Contamin's *Galerie des Machines* exposing the prized artifacts of an industrial civilization and Eiffel's tower making available to a large public the breathtaking prospect of Paris from the air. As an exhibiting machine Contamin's building was the culmination of four generations of such *Galerie des Machines*, successively built in Paris for the exhibitions of 1855, 1867 and 1878. Almost identical in structural/spatial concept to Hector Horeau's unrealisable submission for *Les Halles Centrales* of 1849, this 380-foot-wide, three-pinned arch, easily out distanced the span of W.H. Barlow and R.M. Ordish's 240-foot-wide shed built at St. Pancras, London in 1876. The important innovation here was the articulated ground pins of the arches, since both St. Pancras and the Horeau structures had been based on the principle of the arches being embedded into the foundations. The Contamin device — derived in part from the hinged support principle employed in Eiffel's Pont Garabit of 1884 — produced zero bending at the ground plane and thereby resolved the forces at each joint into horizontal and vertical thrusts. Erected and glazed in the space of a year, Contamin's shed was a huge "tent" of blue and white translucent glass covering a clear space of 800 by 380 feet and held in place by 10-foot-deep, wrought-iron, lattice arches; steel, at that date, still being extremely expensive. Beneath this canopy, mobile platforms running on rails, shuttled some 100,000 people a day above the latest examples of industrial machinery laid out at their feet; a mechanical panorama to be viewed solipsistically, so to speak, from the vantage point of a mobile exhibiting machine.

Above: interior perspective
Below: detail of interior structure
Photo reproduced from
Geschichte der Modernen Architektur *by J. Joedicke*

1889
GUSTAVE EIFFEL
Eiffel Tower
Paris, France

Right: overall view
Below: diagram of horizontal force

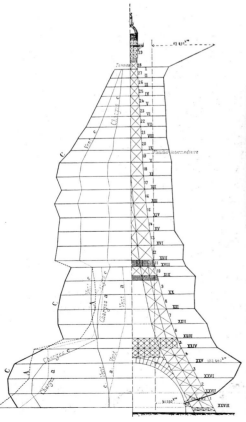

This 1,000-foot-high, parabolic viaduct pylon (without its viaduct), was the culmination of Eiffel's heroic career as an international engineer of almost Verne-like stature. Spain, Portugal, Switzerland, Hungary, Rumania, Russia, South America, the Philippines, Indochina, Egypt and even Panama: wherever the railway infrastructure of European colonization went, Eiffel followed it. The first project for the Tower was made in 1884 by two young Swiss engineers, Nouguier and Koechlin, who had previously worked for

Eiffel on the design of the 550-foot-span Garabit Viaduct completed in Massif Central in the very same year. Soon after the initial presentation of the tower, it was decided to use it as one of the main features of the exhibition of 1889. The tower was constructed at a remarkable rate; the foundations were in by June 1887 and the first 200-foot-high platform achieved by March 1888. Exactly a year later the entire structure comprising some fifteen thousand prefabricated steel parts was complete. The

Tower was amply supplied with elevators: four inclined systems serving the 200-foot level, and two more continuing the relay to the 370-foot level, with a vertical shuttle carrying the more intrepid visitors to the apex. By this system, 2,350 visitors could gain access to the summit every hour. It was typical of Eiffel's working method that the guide rails for the elevators should first have been used as tracks for the climbing cranes, with the aid of which the tower itself had been erected.

The unique work of an otherwise conservative career, this daring and unusual office building owes as much to the remarkable vision of Wyman's patron Louis Bradbury, a self-made mining tycoon, as it does to an autodidact architect's exceptional talent. Both Bradbury and Wyman were pre-occupied by the quasi-Fourierist promise of achieving a utopian future in America, as this had been partially described in Edward Bellamy's *Looking Backwards* of 1877. Bellamy's description of a commercial structure in his utopian novel reads like an account of the Bradbury Building: "...a vast hall full of light, received not alone from the windows on all sides but from the dome, the point of which was a hundred feet above... The walls were frescoed in mellow tints, to soften without absorbing the light which flooded the interior."

The light court of the Bradbury Building, comprising four tiers of iron-framed office floors set on top of a stone clad concourse level, was similar to that of the Chamber of Commerce built in Chicago, in 1889, to designs of Baumann and Huebre. The Bradbury court however, was much larger, measuring 50 feet wide by 120 feet. Aside from its resemblance to Godin's *Familistère*, built at Guise in 1860, the Bradbury Building is unique not only for its dramatically projecting stair and lift towers, but also for its glazed hydraulic elevators giving access to the various office floors. These constructions serve to animate the volume of the court movement; a lively effect compounded of light filtering through the stair landings and of the oscillation of the elevator cabins. By way of contrast, the exterior of the building is traditional, being built of a mixture of sandstone and dressed brickwork.

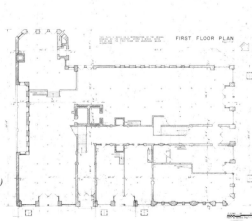

60 *Above: interior view*
  Below left: first floor plan
  Below right: detail of the railing (Photo: T. Kitajima)
61 *Left, top to bottom: northwest elevation, section,*
  isometric of central court
  Right: interior view

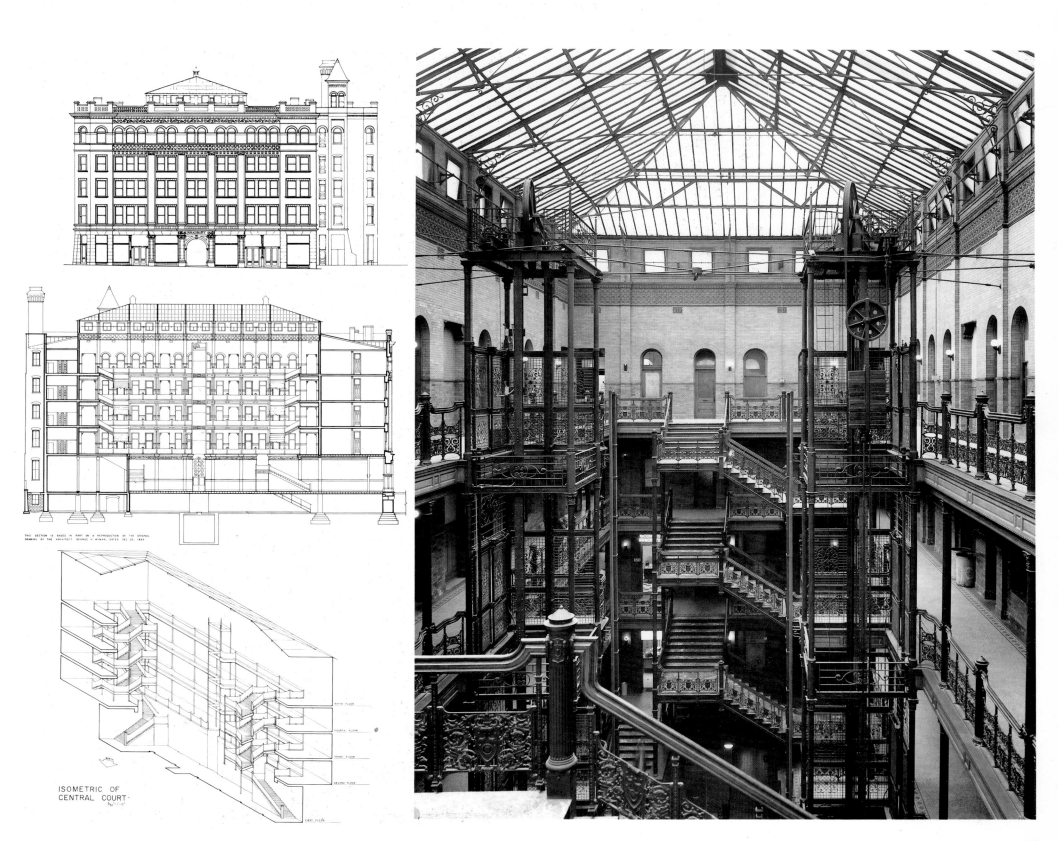

THIS SECTION IS BASED IN PART ON A REPRODUCTION OF THE ORIGINAL
DRAWING BY THE ARCHITECT GEORGE H. WYMAN, DATED DEC 25, 1892.

FIFTH FLOOR

FOURTH FLOOR

THIRD FLOOR

SECOND FLOOR

FIRST FLOOR

ISOMETRIC OF
CENTRAL COURT·

Neither Sullivan nor Le Baron Jenny can be credited with the invention of the skyscraper, if by such a term one simply means the achievement of a multi-storey building of great height, since this had already been achieved in Root's Monadnock Block, Chicago of 1884-92. Sullivan and Atwood are to be credited, however, with their independent evolution of a format and a syntax appropriate to the high-rise steel frame. The eleven-storey Wainwright Building represents Sullivan's first attempt at a truly multi-storey format, in which the device of the suppressed transome taken from the facade of Richardson's Marshall Field Store, Chicago of 1888, is used to impart a decidedly vertical emphasis to the building's overall form. Unlike Atwood, Sullivan created a representative mask for the steel frame which deliberately made no formal distinction between the masonry "pilasters" and the steel reinforced piers carrying the principle load. The two-storey base of the classical tripartite composition is faced in fine red sandstone set on a two-foot-high string course of red Missouri granite. While the middle section consists of red brick pilasters with decorated terracotta spandrels, the top is rendered as a deep overhanging cornice faced in an ornamented terracotta skin to match the enrichment of the spandrels and the pilasters below. This creation of an exotic, all red architecture can be seen as anticipating Frank Lloyd Wright's Larkin and Johnson Wax Buildings of 1904 and 1936 and even as presaging Louis Kahn's vision of an architecture "unbroken, flowing white and gold." However the Wainwright as a totality is undeveloped. As Bush-Brown has written, "Even the light court (of the U plan) which might have been graceful, does not capitalize upon the facade's pier and spandrel motif..."

Above: view of the facade
Right: first floor plan
Photo: T. Kitajima

DANIEL H. BURNHAM & CO.
AND CHARLES B. ATWOOD
Reliance Building
Chicago, Illinois, U.S.A.

The four initial floors of the fourteen-storey Reliance Building, designed by Charles B. Atwood of Daniel Burnham's office and the structural engineer E.C. Shankland, were erected in 1890. This the first comprehensive achievement of the system now known as Chicago construction was repeated innumerable times in Chicago in the building boom that lasted from 1890 to 1893. It consisted of a riveted steel-frame superstructure, hollow-tile flooring on steel joists, plaster fire-proofing, perimeter bay windows filled with plate glass, steeltrussed wind bracing and bedrock concrete caissons sometimes extending for as much as 125 feet beneath the footings. As Carl Condit has written of the Reliance Building: "The relatively small area of the plan, four by seven bays with a span of 12 feet, the height of 200 feet, and the astonishing proportion of glass in the total wall area made careful provision for wind bracing a necessity. To meet this requirement Shankland introduced columns of two-storey length and plate-and-lattice truss girders of 24-inch depth set between and bolted to all peripheral columns. The use of columns double the normal length was one factor in the record speed with which the steel of the upper ten stories was erected. The job required 15 days from July 16th to August 1st, 1895." Atwood's remarkable ability is evident in this structure, with its elegant bay-window fenestration, arranged in syncopated, vertical shafts and its white glazed facing tiles and its thin projecting cornice which to the shame of all concerned, owner and city alike, has long since been dismantled in the name of security and so far never replaced.

Right: overall view
Below: plan

Built for a totally committed client, with whom Frank Lloyd Wright later collaborated (in 1896) on the production of an ideological, almost religious text entitled the *House Beautiful*, this structure represents Wright's initial conception of the sacramental home and his first steps towards the evolution of the Prairie Style. Certain features of this style, finally formulated at the turn of the century, are already visible in the flat Roman brickwork, in the low-hipped roof with its overhanging eaves, and in the use of extended ornamental surfaces for the unification of the fenestration into a horizontal band. At this date, however, Sullivan is still a strong influence, as is evident from the style and articulation of the ornament, obviously borrowed from Sullivan's Getty Tomb of 1890. Sullivan is also present, from a stylistic point of view, in the inglenook alcove built into the entry hall as the spiritual centre of the home; the form of the screen being derived directly from Sullivan's Schiller Theater of 1891-92. The general organization of this house is somewhat eclectic and Wright at this juncture is obviously still caught between the symmetrical ideal of the classical Italianate house and the asymmetrical irregular format of the Shingle Style house, this being related to the Arts and Crafts/Gothic Revival domestic form. Thus the street front of the Winslow House is symmetrical while the rear is totally irregular. The scale and placement of the ornament on the front relates to Sullivan's use of Islamic prototypes and is further evidence of the way in which non-Western "exotic" cultures became the basis for the effort that Wright and Sullivan were to make in developing an appropriate architectural culture for the New World.

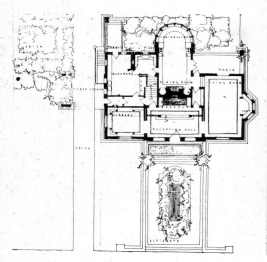

64 *Left: ground floor plan*
   Above right: rear view
   Below right: stable facade
65 *Above: main facade*
   Below: view toward inglenook

With the thirteen-storey Guaranty Building Sullivan challenged the classic format of bottom, middle and top which up to then had been brought to the treatment of most tall office structures, including his own Wainwright Building of 1891. In a work that was exactly contemporaneous with Charles Atwood's Reliance Building, Sullivan attempted a comparable two part composition, where the two lower "mercantile" floors are combined into a stereometric four square base and the upper eleven office storeys are modelled as a continuous "fluted" mass culminating in a concave attic floor, which doubles at the same time as a terminating cornice. Sullivan's seminal essays of the time, his *Ornament in Architecture* of

1892 and *The Tall Office Building Artistically Considered* of 1896, articulate the expressive strategy adopted in both the Wainwright and the Guaranty Buildings. The last of these texts, reveals the rationale behind the sculptural form of the Guaranty cornice, of which Sullivan wrote, "... at the top of this pile, is placed a space or storey that, as related to the life and usefulness of the structure, is purely physiological in its nature — namely, the attic. In this, the circulatory system completes itself and makes its grand turn ascending and descending. The space is filled with tanks, pipes, valves, sheaves and mechanical et cetera that supplement and compliment the force originating plant, hidden below ground in

the cellar." This vitalist, organic approach to the expression of industrial civilization found its compliment in Sullivan's attitude to ornament of which he wrote in 1892: "The ornament, as a matter of fact is applied in the sense of being cut in or on, or otherwise done; yet it should appear when completed, as though by the outworking of some beneficient agency it had come forth from the very substance of the material..." This is of course exactly how the ornament appears on the Guaranty Building, where it permeates the entire *public* surface of the structure, both inside and out, like a ubiquitous tatoo.

66 View of the facade
67 Left, from top: detail of ornament, 12th floor plan, first floor plan
Photos: T. Kitajima

68 *Overall view*
69 *Above left: view toward the altar*
    Above right: view toward the entry
    Below: plan

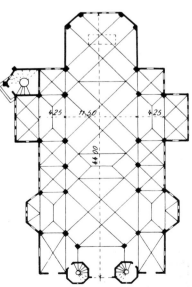

A student of both Henri Labrouste and Viollet-le-Duc, Anatole de Baudot was concerned throughout his career with developing a non-classical form of architecture, to be derived in an absolute sense from the logic of its structure and the mode of its construction. A unique means of achieving this ideal of a tectonically determined language came from his collaboration with the engineer Paul Cottacin who, in 1889, had patented an extraordinary system of wire reinforced construction, in both brick and concrete, under the title *Travaux en ciment avec ossature metallique*. Cottacin's system, first tentatively applied by de Baudot in the construction of reinforced cement floors in his Lycée Victor Hugo, erected in Paris between 1894 and 1896, consisted of a wire network capable of distributing loads throughout extremely thin reinforced cement members, such as the three-inch-thick slab separating the nave of his Montmartre church from its apse. The commission of this church around 1894 presented de Baudot with the opportunity for using Cottacin's system in order to realize a new and totally integrated mode of expression — referential to the Gothic but in no way duplicating it. The two men developed an elegant skeleton comprising twenty-six 1 foot 8 inch by 1 foot 8 inch reinforced concrete columns, set diagonally to the axis of the 38-foot-wide nave and continuously bonded by rod and wire reinforcement into the arches and vaulted slab roofs that they carried above. This same reinforcement also bonded the superstructure into the reinforced brick load bearing side walls and facings — Cottacin's *briques enfilées*. Such an approach meant that the facings and ceramic decoration were not so much applied as bonded in. In 1899 when the skeleton was complete, work on the site was interrupted by the municipality, who asserted that the conditions of the building permit had been infringed. They effectively challenged the stability of this extremely slender, 80-foot-high structure, and even though the municipality lost their case, Cottacin was unjustly replaced as site engineer when work was resumed in 1902. In fact neither of the two men were to enjoy a wide practice after this unique work was brought to completion, Cottacin being overshadowed by the success of the Hennebique system, and de Baudot being reduced after 1900 to entirely theoretical studies in which (in anticipation of the Italian engineer, P.L. Nervi) he explored the possibilities of creating wide span, reinforced concrete, folded slab structures.

Guimard's reputation was universally established by his Castel Béranger, built as a multi-storey version of *le style Guimard*, which he had already started to evolve in his Hôtel Jassade of 1893 and his École du Sacré-Coeur of 1895. Guimard's point of departure was initially the work and thought of Viollet-le-Duc, but increasingly, after 1895 Guimard turned to Victor Horta's interpretation of this structuralist approach. In 1896, after visiting Brussels in the previous year. Guimard organized an exhibition featuring Horta's work and wrote of his *maître Belge*; "All the architects I showed your work to (and I took pleasure in telling them that you are the only architect I know) pay homage to your talent."

Never entirely resolved as a total composition the Castel Béranger is nonetheless an important transitional work in Guimard's career. The stem and branch-like character of both the interior furnishing and the exterior ironwork stand in a curious and brittle contrast to the articulate, architectonic but disjunctive elements that make up the cumbersome mass of the building's exterior. With 36 apartments, each different from the next, the Castel Béranger is a curious compound of rational planning and non-rational intent and expression. Guimard

was to exploit its completion as an occasion for promoting *le style Guimard*. To this end he staged an exhibition of the building and its contents in the Salon du Figaro in 1899, while simultaneously publishing a book of the work under the title, *L'Art dans l'habitation moderne. Le Castel Béranger*. More acerbic than his flamboyant country houses of the turn of the century and located in the fashionable, fast-growing suburb of Auteuil, the Castel Béranger gave Guimard a prime opportunity with which to demonstrate the synthetic subtleties of his style, in which urban and rustic references could be judiciously mixed together.

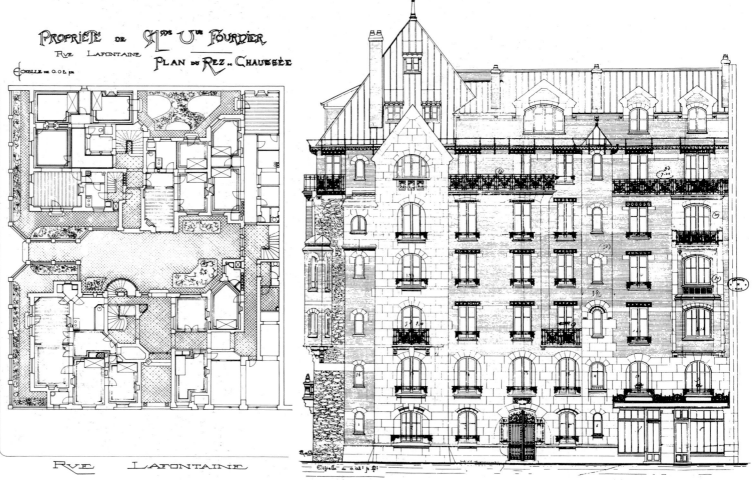

70 *Above left: ground floor plan*
   Above right: elevation on rue La Fontaine
   Below: elevation on rue La Fontaine
71 *Above left: entrance gate*
   Above right: entrance hall
   Below: view of the side elevation (Photo: M. Sekiya)

3 The Structure and Symbolism of the Art Nouveau 1851-1914

For the private citizen, for the first time the living-space became distinguished from the place of work. The former constituted itself as the interior. The counting-house was its complement. The private citizen who in the counting-house took reality into account, required of the interior that it should maintain him in his illusions. This necessity was all the more pressing since he had no intention of adding social preoccupations to his business ones. In the creation of his private environment he suppressed them both. From this sprang the phantasmagorias of the interior. This represented the universe for the private citizen. In it he assembled the distant in space and in time. His drawing-room was a box in the world-theatre.

Digression on *art nouveau*. The shattering of the interior took place around the turn of the century in *art nouveau*. And yet the latter appeared, according to its ideology, to bring with it the perfecting of the interior. The transfiguration of the lone soul was its apparent aim. Individualism was its theory. With van de Velde, there appeared the house as expression of the personality. Ornament was to such a house what the signature is to a painting. The real significance of *art nouveau* was not expressed in this ideology. It represented the last attempt at a sortie on the part of Art imprisoned by technical advance within her ivory tower. It mobilized all the reserve forces of interiority. They found their expression in the mediumistic language of line, in the flower as symbol of the naked, vegetable Nature that confronted the technologically armed environment. The new elements of construction in iron — girderforms — obsessed *art nouveau*. Through ornament, it strove to win back these forms for Art. Concrete offered it new possibilities for the creation of plastic forms in architecture. Around this time the real centre of gravity of the sphere of existence was displaced to the office. The de-realized centre of gravity created its abode in the private home. Ibsen's *Masterbuilder* summed up *art nouveau*: the attempt of the individual, on the basis of his interiority, to vie with technical progress leads to his downfall.   (Walter Benjamin, *Paris: Capital of the Nineteenth Century,* 1935)

The Art Nouveau, which, as the name would suggest, was not initially an architectural movement at all, had its origins in England. The first hint of this development came with Dante Gabriel Rossetti's rediscovery of the illustrated art of William Blake, the English revival of Blake dating from Rossetti's purchase of Blake's *Notebooks* in 1847. This was followed by James McNeill Whistler's importation of Japanese taste into England with his painting, "Princesse du Pays de la Porcelaine" of 1863. Prior to this, Whistler had been studying painting in Paris in the mid-1850s, at the same time as the engraver Félix Bracquemond discovered the Japanese woodcut; a revelation which was to be a prime source of inspiration for the culture of the Art Nouveau. As far as architecture and design were concerned, the impulses stemming from Blake and Whistler remained relatively dormant until 1875, when Whistler and his architect E.W. Godwin started to create the English Aesthetic interior; first in the "antithesis" of the blank façade to Whistler's own house, built in Tite Street, Chelsea in 1877, and afterwards in the interiors that they created first for Whistler and then for Oscar Wilde in the same street. In both cases the interior was finished with *tatami* mat floors, off-white walls, panels lined with gold leaf paper, white lacquered furniture and the occasional surface rendered in sulphur yellow or light pink. This unencumbered bare background was relieved by pottery, flower arrangements, light fittings, prints, cushions, etc. —

37 Dresser, "Force and Energy" (1870) and a stained glass window (1873).

38 Liberty & Co., Ltd., London. Publicity 1900.

39 Le Corbusier, Villa Fallet, La Chaux-de-Fonds, Switzerland, 1903.

the formula that was to be reinterpreted by C.R. Mackintosh and the Glasgow School in their graphic art and object design of the late 1890s. Similarly, the Japanese pastiche pieces that Godwin designed for Whistler established the prototype for all subsequent Art Nouveau furniture. Whistler seems to have regarded Japanese art as an as yet uncompromised form of expression with which one might revitalize the perennial bourgeois nostalgia for the effable beauty of the lost classical world. His "Symphony in White, No. IV, The Three Girls" of 1879, presents a Japanese interior as an ideal setting for an Hellenic image of beauty, the picture depicting three girls in Biedermeier clothes carrying bamboo parasols. This curious cultural synthesis was explicitly declared in his Ten O'Clock Lecture of 1885, in which he stated: "The story of the beautiful is already complete — hewn in the marbles of the Parthenon — and broidered, with birds, upon the fan of Hokusai — at the foot of the Fuji-Yama."

The third, and the more pragmatic, origin of the Art Nouveau in England was closely tied to the activity of William Morris and to the Arts and Crafts movement. This movement had been anticipated in its turn by the official wing of the English design reform movement which, in 1848, began to respond critically to the double challenge offered by a vastly increased productive capacity and a sudden expansion in the world market for finished goods. This didactic impulse first manifested itself as a public policy in the Great Exhibition of 1851 — that is, in the first international exhibition of applied art objects that was staged in Paxton's Crystal Palace — and then in the reaction to the evident low standard of the objects exhibited, on the part

of a group of artists and civil servants who were attached, in various ways, to the Department of Practical Art; namely, Henry Cole, Richard Redgrave, Owen Jones, M.D. Wyatt, Lewis Day, John Bell, William Dyce, and the German émigré architect Gottfried Semper, whose critique of the Exhibition, given under the title of *Science, Industry and Art,* was published in Germany, in Braunschweig in 1852. The reformist intent and the groundwork for the Great Exhibition had been established by this group prior to 1851, through the art objects they produced after 1847 in Felix Summerly's Art Manufactures, (the pseudonym for Henry Cole's art workshops) and through the ideas they advanced in the *Journal of Design and Manufactures,* edited by Redgrave after 1849. In 1851, Henry Cole and his circle established the South Kensington Museum for the express purpose of improving the quality of design, and in 1857 official Schools of Design were attached to this institution, an educational innovation which eventually became the Royal College of Art. However, the most memorable figures of this circle were neither Cole nor Redgrave, but rather the architect Owen Jones, whose influential *Grammar of Ornament* was published in 1856 (going through nine editions by 1910) and the designer Christopher Dresser, who taught at the Schools of Design after 1859, and who published in that year his famous text *Unity in Variety*, in which he first referred to the "lines of life" as being the basic energetic structural order underlying all plant form. The third figure of consequence, at this time, was Arthur Lasenby Liberty who, having been a dealer in Japanese art since 1862, started, on Morris's advice, his own famous furnishing store and design firm of Liberty's in 1875.

40 Mackmurdo, title page for "Wren's City Churches," 1883.

41 Mackmurdo, Century Guild Stand, Liverpool International Exhibition, 1886.

42 Voysey, "Cereus" wallpaper, 1886.

The importance of Dyce, Dresser and Jones in the development of Art Nouveau architectural ornament can hardly be overestimated, particularly Jones's book, The *Grammar of Ornament*, which featured mostly ornament of non-western origin, i.e. Persian, Egyptian, Indian, Chinese, Moorish and Celtic, etc. It also contained a number of plates by Dresser demonstrating how ornament may be derived from the conventionalization of plant forms. Where Dresser was clearly an influence on Gustave Serrurier-Bovy and Henry van de Velde, Owen Jones had his greatest impact around the turn of the century, notably in inspiring the works of High and Late Art Nouveau. First among such works was Wright's Prairie Style of 1900 and then somewhat later, the earliest houses designed by Le Corbusier in La Chaux-de-Fonds, above all, his first house, the Villa Fallet of 1903, its decoration having been derived from the flora and fauna of the Jura region.

The influence of William Blake passed beyond the limits of the Pre-Raphaelite sensibility, that is to say, beyond the paintings of Rossetti and Burne-Jones, with the pioneering designs of the architect Arthur Heygate Mackmurdo, who introduced Blake-like, curvaceous, linear motifs into his furniture and graphic design between 1881 and 1883, and who, at the same time, began to develop a totally unrelated ahistorical architectural style around 1886, first with his Century Guild and Cope Brothers' exhibition stands built for the Liverpool International Exhibition of that year and then with the remarkable house, Brooklyn, built in Private Road, Enfield in 1887. With its absolutely plain, white, roughcast walls and rhythmic pilasters, Brooklyn not only dispensed with the Shavian trappings of

Mackmurdo's early houses, but also adopted the abstract shallow surface modelling first seen in English domestic work with Godwin's house for Whistler of 1877.

The fruit of Mackmurdo's daring endeavours in the separate fields of graphic decor and architectural design was to be harvested by his articled pupil, Charles Annesley Voysey, and then, in turn, by Voysey's major follower, the Scottish architect Charles Rennie Mackintosh. There is little doubt that the work of these two remarkable artists constitutes the most fertile contribution of British architecture to the evolution of the early modern movement. Equally competent in almost all fields of design, both men were to synthesize complete styles and to produce "total works of Art" (*Gesamtkunstwerk*) of the highest caliber. After their major achievements, that is to say, after Mackintosh's Glasgow School of Art of 1897, and his three important houses designed in the years 1899 to 1903, and after Voysey's finest house, Broadleys, built overlooking Lake Windermere in 1900, the energy of the Art Nouveau, which Swinburne had recognized as the "flame-like impulse of the idea," passed to the Continent. From the mid-1890s on, this impulse began to appear in Europe in the Viennese *Sezession* of Joseph Maria Olbrich and Josef Hoffmann, in the Jugendstil of Otto Eckmann, Peter Behrens and Henry van de Velde. The Art Nouveau strictly speaking manifested itself at the same time in the work of Victor Horta and Hector Guimard, and finally in the Catalan *Modernista* of Antonio Gaudí, Francisco Berenguer, Luis Domènech and Puig y Cadafalch.

No two men could have been more opposite, and still have influenced each

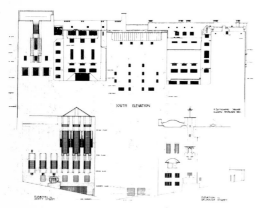

43 *Mackintosh, Glasgow School of Art, Glasgow, 1897-1909. Elevations.*

44 Poster for the Glasgow Institute of the Fine Arts (1896) by Herbert McNair, Margaret and Francis Macdonald.

45 *Mackintosh, project for the* Haus eines Kunstfreundes. *1901.*

other, than Voysey and Mackintosh; the one in essence puritanical and religious in almost everything he did, the other equally pure as far as the basic form was concerned, but sensuous and "pagan," with regard both to ornament and symbolic content. Voysey, without being a radical-socialist, was still tied to the fundamentally moralistic and insular attitude of Morris, while Mackintosh was drawn by circumstance and inclination, to the more cosmopolitan and Symbolist stance of the Continent, where the work of the Glasgow Four — that is, himself, Herbert McNair, and Francis and Margaret Macdonald — had been enthusiastically received. Their debut at Liège in 1897 led to their exhibiting in Munich in 1898 and 1900, and to their participation in the Eighth *Sezession* Exhibition held in Vienna in 1898. In 1902 they were given a certain amount of recognition in their own country, through being commissioned with the Scottish section of the Turin Exhibition of Decorative Arts of 1902.

Jan Toorop's highly graphic *The Three Brides* of 1892, published in the first volume of *The Studio* in 1893, and the art and editorial policy created by the graphic artist Aubrey Beardsley in his proto-symbolist magazines, *The Yellow Book* and *The Savoy* of 1894 and 1896 respectively, created the climate in which the linear, *repoussé* graphic art of the so-called Glasgow "spook" school came into being. Translated architecturally into off-white walls, white lacquered, elongated Voyseyesque furniture, spidery wire light fittings and pewter hardware, embellished with silver and violet glass, this style reached its apotheosis in Mackintosh's *Haus eines Kunstfreundes* of 1901. This project was the prototype for Mackintosh's Hill House, Helens-

burgh, of 1902-03. At the same time is formed the point of departure for Hoffmann's Palais Stoclet of 1905. For Robert Delevoy, the hall of Hill House is the masterwork of Mackintosh's career, "where light, colour openwork partitions, cage-type lamps and light furniture combine in a spatio-dynamic composition that anticipates Russian Constructivism and Dutch de Stijl." The same prophetic claim could be made for the last significant works that he built in Scotland: the Glasgow School of Art Library (1907-09) and the Cranston Tea Rooms (1907-11).

Benjamin's contention that the Art Nouveau was a compensatory narcissistic fantasy reserved solely for the inner domestic realm, finds confirmation in the fact that Art Nouveau architecture attained its most fluid expression in the interior. More often than not the exterior was nothing but a bare sculptural mass incised with linear decoration. If the English Gothic Revival was the architectural paradigm which lay under the work of Voysey and Mackintosh, the French Gothic equivalent, namely the parallel, but more intellectual "structural rationalism" expounded by Viollet-le-Duc in his text *L'Entretiens sur L'Architecture* of 1863-72, supported the work of Hendrik Petrus Berlage, Victor Horta, Guimard and Gaudí. In this respect Horta came closest to achieving the structurally rationalist ideal while gaining immediate renown as the first Art Nouveau architect, with his Hôtel Tassel, Brussels, of 1893. He depended for his invention not only on Viollet-le-Duc's precept of revealing structural procedure, but also, at least as far as the exterior was concerned, on a Baroque masonry tradition dating from Louis Seize. Nevertheless, behind the superficial symmetry of the Tassel stone facade, the

46 *Illustration from Viollet-le-Duc's*
Treizième Entretien, *Paris, 1872.*

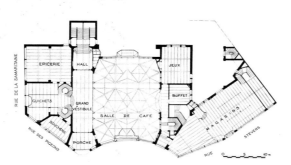

47 *Horta, Maison du Peuple, Brussels, 1895-98. First Floor plan.*

48 *Guimard, Castel Béranger, Auteuil,*
Paris, 1894-98. Elevation.

interior was totally disrupted by the intrusion of a structural iron frame, used here for the first time in a private house in order to liberate or (as Benjamin would have no doubt have put it) to destroy the spatial confines of the interior. While this iron frame supported the top-lit octagonal space in the centre of the house, the main plant form to be found in the architecture of this "winter garden" was the iron tendrils of a progressive technology — a kind of new nature. Stairways led from this inner hall to fractured floor levels on every side, thereby breaking with the notion of planning floor by floor. This split level interior was to anticipate Adolf Loos's invention of the *Raumplan* by seven years.

Departing from the ironwork inventions depicted in *L'Entretiens*, Horta developed a private and public syntax of architecture. The private thematic was essentially the language of wrought iron; the "whiplash" form whose inflected tentacles extended from the balustrading and latticework of the stair hall to enrich the floors, walls, ceilings and chandeliers of the entire interior with cryptic arabesques. The public version, on the other hand, served to articulate the Tassel House elevation, where the structure of the iron bay window erupted through the architraves of the classic masonry facade. Apart from this, the Tassel House, like Horta's masterwork the Maison du Peuple (built for the Belgium Union of Socialist Workers in 1897), repressed the implicit eroticism of the interior in favour of a new structural language in which stone cornices were carved to receive iron, and iron capped to carry stone; a total architectural syntax in which wide metal spandrels were provided for the accommodation of large areas of glass. And yet, as Leonardo

Benevolo has put it, Horta "did not wish to provide the inhabitants of his houses with accommodation that was too inconvenient or too committed . . ." He sought "a coherent and technically irreproachable manner of composition," one which would be compatible with the building industry and the urban scene of his time. Benevolo writes, "He was the most exquisite of the *art nouveau* architects, but in a way also the most old fashioned, the nearest to an architect of the past."

This particular combination of conservatism and technical innovation distinguishes Horta's work from that of his Parisian follower Hector Guimard, who, while equally committed to the ideas of Viollet-le-Duc, was somewhat less adept at the structural and decorative use of iron. Guimard was at the same time much less conservative, his initial reputation being made by his fantastic re-interpretation of the French Rococo furniture. Like Mackmurdo, Guimard's early output was divided between his architecture, which he modelled in principle after Anatole de Baudot's structurally rationalist Saint-Jean-de-Montmartre church started in 1897, and his furniture and interior decoration, which was even more distorted than Horta's Neo-Rococo, and clearly influenced in this respect by the sculptural and linear arabesques of the Glasgow Four. Once again, the erotic display of energized, almost animate, form was reserved for the interior, while Guimard's earliest architectural creations, his École du Sacré-Coeur (a realization of an illustration from *L'Entretiens*) and his Castel Béranger, both erected in Paris in 1895, displayed a much more articulate formal language, based upon construction and the laws of statics. While the Castel Béranger

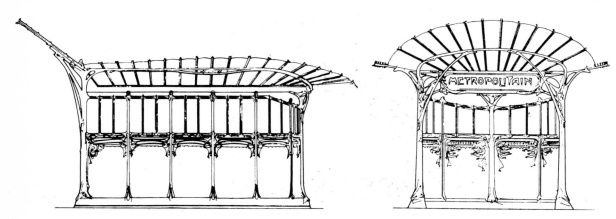

49 Guimard, Métro entrance, Paris, 1900. Elevations.

exemplified Viollet-le-Duc's thesis that an unprecedented architectural code could be created out of the articulation of constructional logic, Guimard's subsequent work attempted to render the free-form of his furniture at an architectural scale. This came first with the fantasmagoric and "national romantic" Castel Henriette built at Sèvres (1899-1900), then in his short-lived, Humbert de Romans auditorium, Paris (1897-1901) and finally in his Coilliot ceramic shop completed in Lille in 1900, where, in imitation of a monumental wooden gable, the masonry superstructure was carved into forms that were ultimately more appropriate to wood. This architectonic conflict with regard to the match between a given material and its form — the inherent conflict that is, between Alois Riegl's theory of the will-to-form or *Kunstwollen* (1893-1901) and the real exigencies of technical production — was resolved by Guimard in his cast-iron prefabricated modular stations erected for the Paris Métro system after 1900.

The impulse to re-articulate a latent national culture, always present in the English Arts and Crafts movement from Webb onwards and evident in most of the Continental exponents of the *art nouveau* (sometimes to the point of an artificial regionalism, such as appeared with the École de Nancy), was never more active as a cultural drive than in the school of Barcelona, which followed the precepts of Viollet-le-Duc in an attempt to re-discover a fundamentally Catalan expression. The architects Puig y Cadafalch, Doménech y Montaner, Berenguer and above all Gaudí, tried to create a *Modernista* which would express the contradictory nature of the ascendant culture of Barcelona. Thus the *Modernista* tried to produce an architecture that was modern but

traditional, industrial but landed, Spanish but Catalan, isolated but cosmopolitan, socialist but patrician, Gothic but Moorish, Christian but Pagan, and finally maritime but mountainous. The sea in question was of course the ancient Classical basin of the Mediterranean; the mountain the nearby range of Montserrat - the volcanic outcrop (or serrated mountain) sheltering the monastery of Montserrat at its base. This mediaeval structure in which Gaudí had his apprenticeship as an architect was at one time the legendary site of the Holy Grail (celebrated in Wagner's opera *Parsifal*) and the location of the Black Virgin, the patron saint of Catalonia. This mystical, and for Gaudí, haunting conjunction first found expression in Gaudí's earliest house, his *mudejar* or Neo-Moorish, corbelled and tile-faced residence built between 1878 and 1883, for the tile manufacturer Vicens in the suburbs of Barcelona. Just before completing this work, Gaudí's pantheistic yet religious development began with his assumption in 1884 of the responsibility for completing the Holy Family church in Barcelona. Nothing could be more exemplary of the manner in which the Gothic Revival was translated into the "structuralism" of the Art Nouveau (cf. Mackintosh's Glasgow School of Art) than the three stages through which the structure of the Sagrada Familia church passed between 1898 and 1918. This remarkable development, as David Mackay has recently shown, was largely due to the important role played by Gaudí's lifelong friend and architectural assistant, Berenguer, Gaudí achieving no work of consequence after Berenguer's death in 1914.

The capacity of Berenguer for creating an architecture of structural logic manifested itself most strongly in his independent work designed for Gaudí's

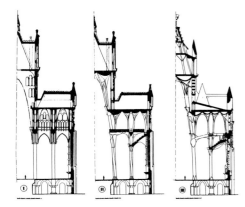

50 *Gaudí, Sagrada Familia Church, Barcelona.*
Comparative sections showing the evolution of the form
of this structure between 1898 and 1914.

51 *Gaudí, Casa Vicens, Barcelona, 1883-85.*
Tabicade multi-ply arch in the garden screen.

patron Eusebio Güell Bacigalupi, notably the Güell wine cellars and chapel built at Garraf in 1888. The same lucid, consequential thinking about structural form is evident in the intricate stone corbelling on the interior to the East facade of the Sagrada Familia (detailed by Berenguer) and in Berenguer's co-operative building erected at Santa Coloma de Cervello in 1911. The three stages of the transformation of the Sagrada Familia nave show how it passed from being an almost neo-Gothic structure with vertical columns and paraboloid arches, to being, in 1915, an almost entirely vaulted construction with helical piers similar to those used in Gaudí's Colonia Güell, under construction from 1898 to 1914. The 1918 scheme for the great church shows an even more arborescent conception with vaults rising out of inclined helical piers. There is an uncanny resemblance between the final form of this vaulted structure — arrived at through the use of a funicular model — and the illustration of a modified basilica form, as this had appeared in Viollet-le-Duc's *L'Art Russe* of 1870.

To a great extent Gaudí's attempt to achieve an authentic Catalan architecture depended on the extensive use of the traditional Catalan vault, which first appeared in his work in the Casa Vicens of 1878 and comprised therein a simple vault or *boveda tabicada* made out of two layers of bonded 6×12 inch tiles. Rather than use *voussoir* arches Gaudí generally achieved his spans by employing such vaults together with corbelled brick abutments. While Gaudí has often been claimed as a structural rationalist for his elimination of buttresses and his system of balancing counter thrusts, it is questionable whether his work is to be regarded as rational from the point of view of building production.

No *Modernista* architect contrasts so strongly with Gaudí in this respect as Luis Doménech y Montaner, whose publishing office designed for Montaner y Simon was finished in Barcelona in 1885. The continuously glazed upper storey and the regular rhythm of the arched facade were to establish Doménech as the most rational architect of the *Modernista* school, a reputation which he was to consolidate with his St. Paul Hospital (1902-12) and his Palace of Catalonian Music (1905-08), both built in Barcelona. And yet, as Oriol Bohigas has remarked, Doménech was restricted from taking rationalism to its logical conclusion, by virtue of his commitment (like Morris and indeed like Gaudí himself) to the revival of craft. His hospital, while rationally organized into pavilions (see Guadet's *Eléments et théorie de l'architecture* of 1902), was anachronistic and archaeological in terms of its architecture. Nevertheless, Doménech came closer than any other *Modernista* architect, to the role played by Otto Wagner, not only in respect of his commitment to the cause of Catalonian independence (comparable to Otto Wagner's commitment to the Austro-Hungarian Empire) but also in his determination to combine traditional architectural elements with advanced engineering technique, even if the referent in each case was entirely different: Neo-classical in the case of Wagner and mediaeval in the case of Doménech.

Doménech's determination to revitalize the Catalonian masonry tradition, and to rival the "great spaces" that it created in the 15th century, found its ultimate expression in his *Palau de la Musica Catalana*. While this building does not equal the cryptic lyricism that permeates most of Gaudí's work, it

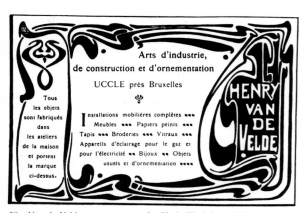

52 Van de Velde, announcement for Uccle Workshop, 1895.

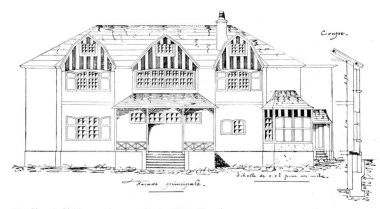

53 Van de Velde, own house at Uccle, 1896. Elevation.

nonetheless achieves, through the vivid iconography of its murals by Luis Bru and its sculpture by Miguel Blay, a much more explicit representation of the triumph of Catalonian nationalism just five years before Catalonia gained its partial independence with the Mancomunitat decree of 1913. The contradictory, dependent yet autonomous status claimed by Catalonia seems to be reified in the interior of this auditorium where sculptural groups on either side of the proscenium refer to the respective musical traditions to which the house is dedicated. A tree representing the revival of Catalonian folk music surges upwards beside Anselm Clave's bust on one side, while on the other, the European classical tradition, symbolized by a Doric portico, embraces the bust of Beethoven and supports on its entablature the cloud-swept forms of Richard Wagner's Valkeyries. The narrow-vaulted, iron-ribbed ceiling supported on laminated, riveted girders, the continuous glass curtain wall on three sides of the auditorium together with the Tiffany-like, inverted, glass cupola hanging from the centre serve to make this one of the most daring tectonic works of the period.

Like Peter Behrens, the Belgian architect and theorist Henry van de Velde began his career as a painter in 1881 when he first enrolled in the Academie des Beaux-Arts at Antwerp. He followed this initiation into fine art with two years in France (1884-86), where he made contact with a circle of Impressionist painters and Symbolist poets. On returning to Antwerp in 1886, van de Velde participated in the founding of the cultural circle *Als ik kan* and a year later he joined an association of young Neo-Impressionist painters including among their number Théo van Rysselberghe. From 1889 onwards

he was part of Octave Maus's circle *Les XX* which turned him away from Neo-Impressionism towards applied art and the flowing expressive graphic line of Paul Gauguin. Thus van de Velde's famous mural tapestry "The Angel's Watch" of 1891, exhibited in the *section d'art artisanal* of the *Les XX,* was already Gauguinesque. The contact between *Les XX* and William Morris's protégé, Walter Crane, had the effect of making van de Velde acutely aware of Morris's social commitment. Meanwhile in 1890, he became involved with the journal *Van Nu en Straks* for which he devised a totally new form of typography, and three years later he gave up painting altogether to concentrate on illustration.

Van de Velde seems to have found his essential point of departure as an applied artist on seeing the Liège artist, Serrurier-Bovy's somewhat Godwin-like furniture of the early 1890s; in particular, a writing desk supposedly inspired by English taste, which Serrurier-Bovy exhibited at an exhibition organized by *Les XX* in 1894. Serrurier-Bovy had previously worked in England in the circle of E. W. Godwin and Christopher Dresser, and took the oriental and organic (biological-botanical) preoccupations of the English Aesthetic Movement back with him to Belgium. As Robert Schmutzler points out it is quite likely that Dresser's linear designs, such as his "Force and Energy" of 1870, would have had an influence on van de Velde's own development of a "form-force" aesthetic. The effect of Serrurier-Bovy on van de Velde was in any event instantaneous, and van de Velde's furniture designs — dating from the setting up of his studio and workshop in Uccle in 1895 — are obviously influenced by Serrurier-Bovy. Modelling his career after

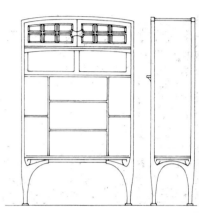

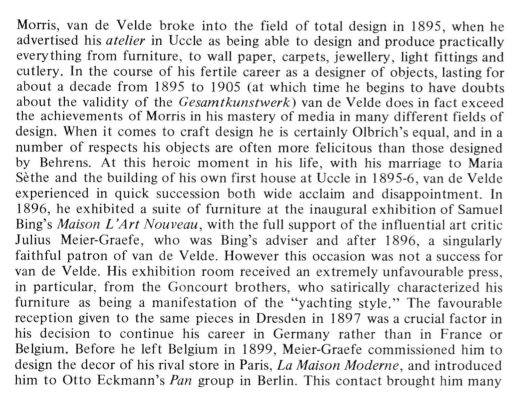

54　Van de Velde, Esche House, Chemnitz, 1903. Elevation.

55　Van de Velde, design for book cupboard, 1904.

Morris, van de Velde broke into the field of total design in 1895, when he advertised his *atelier* in Uccle as being able to design and produce practically everything from furniture, to wall paper, carpets, jewellery, light fittings and cutlery. In the course of his fertile career as a designer of objects, lasting for about a decade from 1895 to 1905 (at which time he begins to have doubts about the validity of the *Gesamtkunstwerk*) van de Velde does in fact exceed the achievements of Morris in his mastery of media in many different fields of design. When it comes to craft design he is certainly Olbrich's equal, and in a number of respects his objects are often more felicitous than those designed by Behrens. At this heroic moment in his life, with his marriage to Maria Sèthe and the building of his own first house at Uccle in 1895-6, van de Velde experienced in quick succession both wide acclaim and disappointment. In 1896, he exhibited a suite of furniture at the inaugural exhibition of Samuel Bing's *Maison L'Art Nouveau*, with the full support of the influential art critic Julius Meier-Graefe, who was Bing's adviser and after 1896, a singularly faithful patron of van de Velde. However this occasion was not a success for van de Velde. His exhibition room received an extremely unfavourable press, in particular, from the Goncourt brothers, who satirically characterized his furniture as being a manifestation of the "yachting style." The favourable reception given to the same pieces in Dresden in 1897 was a crucial factor in his decision to continue his career in Germany rather than in France or Belgium. Before he left Belgium in 1899, Meier-Graefe commissioned him to design the decor of his rival store in Paris, *La Maison Moderne*, and introduced him to Otto Eckmann's *Pan* group in Berlin. This contact brought him many

German commissions, including the Hohenzolern Craftwork Shop (1899), Haby's Barber Shop (1901), Habana Tobacco Co. (1900), Esche House, Chemnitz (1902), the Folkwang Museum, Hagen (1901-02) and the restroom at the Dresden Exhibition of Applied Arts of 1906 which effectively closed the High Jugendstil phase of his career. In 1897, van de Velde's commitment to the *Gesamtkunstwerk* had included even the design of his wife's kimono-like dresses, so that the fall and decor of her clothing would harmonize with the "form-force" aesthetic of the house. At this moment in his career van de Velde regarded the design of the environment as having a direct impact upon the moral sensibility and well being of society. After his polemical essays of the mid-1890s — *Déblaiement d'art*, 1894, *L'art futur*, 1895, and *Aperçu en vue d'une Synthèse d'art,* 1895 van de Velde projected his Uccle house as an organic whole including hardware, furniture, light fittings, carpets, curtains, china, glassware and silver. In all of this van de Velde intended a structurally rationalist *Gesamtkunstwerk*, based on the frank revelation of the process of construction and manufacture. However the outcome was somewhat different, as he himself acknowledged in 1962: "Whether it was a matter of the works of German, Austrian or Dutch artists, we were all more attached than we thought to a kind of romanticism which would not allow us to consider form 'without ornament,' we were too much painters, too much wedded to literature, to glimpse the necessity of abandoning ornament and decoration . . . the temptations and subconscious insinuations of romanticism prompted us to bend and twist our structural schemes and present them as ornaments acting as structural elements, or as

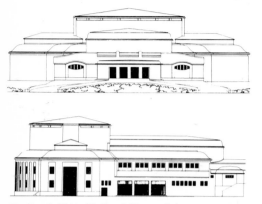

56 *Van de Velde, Werkbund Theatre, Cologne, 1914. Elevations.*

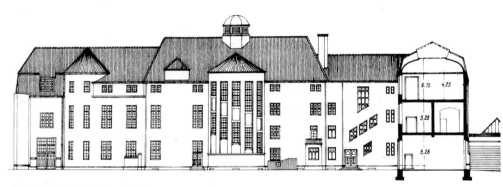

57 *Van de Velde, Weimar Art School, 1904-11. Elevation.*

structures inbred with the rhythms of a linear ornament." In this same passage van de Velde makes an acute distinction between his own "structurally dynamic ornament" and the whiplash forms of Horta.

Van de Velde's final entry into architecture around 1903 seems to have been influenced equally by Nietzschean thought and by Theodor Lipps's neo-romantic aesthetic theory of empathy, advanced in 1893. While van de Velde had been subject to the influence of Nietzsche since the 1880s, the specific import that the Apollonian-Dionysiac opposition might have had for visual culture only became apparent to him with Lipps's theory of empathy of 1893-97, and with the specific application of this theory to architecture in Wilhelm Worringer's *Abstraction and Empathy* of 1908. Worringer's distinction between Classic-Apollonian abstraction and Gothic-Dionysiac empathetic form seems to have ultimately had a classicizing influence on van de Velde's architecture after 1908. Van de Velde's feeling for an *Ur-classicismus* came to the fore with his meeting with Elisabeth Forster-Nietzsche and his 1910-14 proposal for the Nietzsche monument at Weimar. His final project for this commission consisted of a temple, a sculpture by Maillol and a sports stadium located within an heroic landscape. As Gunther Stamm has written: "The individual parts of the outlay, the formalistic aspects of the architectural elevations, and Maillol's statue were believed to express adequately Nietzsche's notion of the *Ubermensch*. The evocative qualities of the design create an irrational experience on the part of the beholder." By this date, van de Velde had moved away from the comparatively simple minded moralistic reformism of Morris's socialist vision.

In 1902, van de Velde was invited by the Grand Duke of Saxe-Weimar to start an institute at Weimar for the express purpose of improving the standard of local handicraft production. This move obviously paralleled the foundation of the Artists' Colony at Darmstadt, six years before, under the patronage of Ernst Ludwig. On van de Velde's initiative, a series of small ateliers were established for the aesthetic and technical training of craftsmen from local craft industries. Van de Velde taught the rudiments of his "structurally-dynamic ornament" as part of this programme. In 1904, with the progressive involvement of the Prussian Ministry of Trade, it was decided to develop the programme into a full-blown arts and crafts school and in 1906 van de Velde designed a new building for the *Kunstgewerberschule*, which was officially opened under his direction in 1908. Like the Weimar Bauhaus, which was to be its successor, van de Velde's five year curriculum was organized about a first year foundation course, with a second year given over to object design, and the later years to working at a more architectural scale. In 1909, van de Velde was forced to concede that his school was unable to produce works of the standard attained by the AEG under Behrens's direction and from this date forth he was to become involved in the controversy as to the proper policy to be adopted by the State. Should it follow Hermann Muthesius's advocacy of standardization and encourage normative or typical design suitable for machine production? Or, should it still cling to the reformist principles of William Morris and put all its efforts behind the resuscitation of local culture? In the last analysis van de Velde, like Philip Webb, gave his full support to the continued protection of local handicraft and art. He realized that the level of competition offered by industry would only have the effect of eventually eliminating craftwork. The ideological conflict underlying this matter came to a head in 1914 in the famous Werkbund Exhibition debate of that year. On this occasion van de Velde led the opposition against Muthesius's eleven point programme for the establishment of type forms or *Typsierungen* in every range of artistic object so as to facilitate the production of that which Muthesius quite frankly called "export art." In his response to this premature advocacy of an almost Neo-classic typology, van de Velde argued that: ". . . nothing good and splendid . . . was ever created out of mere consideration for exports. Quality will not be created out of the spirit of export. Quality is always first created exclusively for a quite limited circle of connoisseurs and those who commission the work. These gradually gain confidence in their artists; slowly there develops first a narrower, then a national clientele, and only then do foreign countries, does the world slowly take notice of this quality. It is a complete misunderstanding of the situation to make the industrialists believe that they would increase their chances in the world market if they produced *a priori* standardized types for this world market before these types had become well tried common property at home. The wonderful works being exported to us now were none of them originally created for export: think of Tiffany glasses, Copenhagen porcelain, jewellery by Jensen, the books of Cobden-Sanderson, and so on."

The impasse suggested by these challenging words, uttered on the eve of the First World War in opposition to Muthesius's programme of standardization, betray, despite their confident tone, a lack of conviction in the Werkbund project for the collective upgrading of craft production and the cultural integration of the machine; principles which van de Velde had at one time embraced. As Fritz Schumacher wrote, van de Velde was a socialist in theory but an individualist in practice. This much seems to be borne out by his idiosyncratic Werkbund Theatre, built for the Cologne Werkbund Exhibition of 1914; its tumuluslike form being determined according to the Lippsian thesis that aesthetic experience depends upon the identification of the psyche with the form of the object.

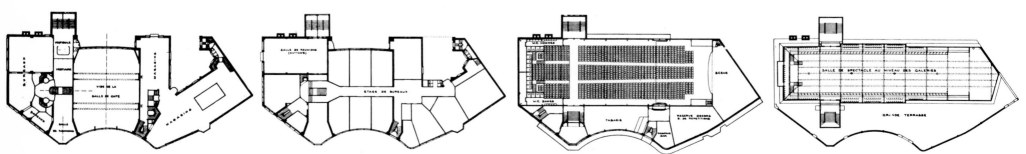

84 *Above: theatre interior*
   Below: plans from left; 1st floor, 2nd floor, 3rd floor, 4th floor
85 *Left: section*
   Right: main facade
   Photos reproduced from Victor Horta *by F. Borsi & P. Portoghesi*

This structure, commissioned by Emile van de Velde and built for the Belgian Worker's Socialist Party, was the only work in which Horta attempted to demonstrate the precepts of Viollet-le-Duc at a truly public scale. While his department stores of the turn of the century may also be regarded as public buildings, they did not really afford the same scope for the totally integrated use of different kinds of structures to house a variety of spaces, each one having a different scale. The ground floor of the Maison du Peuple was given over to co-operative stores, ticket offices, a playroom and large café in the center of the composition; this last being 65-foot deep, 55-foot wide, and 25-foot high. Above this the first floor was allocated to offices and the second to an auditorium. In this building Horta exploited a native brick and stone vernacular (the building was erected with the help of donated union labor) to create an architecture of revealed construction. Thus, the brick work was consistently modelled so as to receive the stone, and the stone, in turn, carefully shaped so as to receive iron and glass. The reticulated ceiling of the café was designed to distribute the load of the upper floor onto four twin columns situated on either side of the space. This structurally articulated public volume was a large scale version of the foyers of Horta's bourgeois town houses of approximately the same date. Whether the Maison du Peuple, built on a restricted site, was quite as successful as its reputation, was challenged many years later by the old socialist Camille Huysman just prior to the building's demolition in 1964. Huysman who had been a member of the original building committee argued that the placement of the auditorium on the second floor had been a fundamental error. The elevation of this public volume without the provision of an elevator naturally made public access to the auditorium somewhat difficult and Huysmans went on to assert that the acoustics of the space itself had been unsatisfactory.

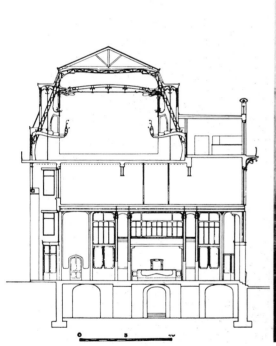

This town house built in the fashionable Avenue Louise for Armand Solvay, nephew of Ernst Solvay, the industrial chemist, social reformer and founder of the Solvay industrial empire, was a much more formal work than Horta's Tassel House of the previous year. Due to the formality of its plan, with its hall and double staircase opening off a built-in *porche cochère*, the Hôtel Solvay was in some respects a return to Horta's Louis XV manner. The programme was allocated as follows: a kitchen in the basement with ancillary services, a carriage underpass leading to the stables in the garden, a business reception suite on the ground floor and a first floor salon occupying the full 50-foot width of the frontage and overlooking the avenue. This space was complemented by a large dining room facing the garden while the upper floors were occupied by bedrooms, etc. Without doubt the most remarkable feature in the interior of the house was a large mural by Théo van Rysselberghe on the double stair landing; its violet, red, blue and russet color scheme making a rich combination with the green marble of the stairs and the polished mahogany of the glazed partitions separating the salon from the stair hall. On visiting this house while under construction in 1895, Hector Guimard was supposed to have been disappointed to learn that his much revered *maître belge* intended to furnish the interior with wall papers and fittings drawn from the English Arts and Crafts. For Guimard, presumably, this would have compromised the essential urbanity of the work.

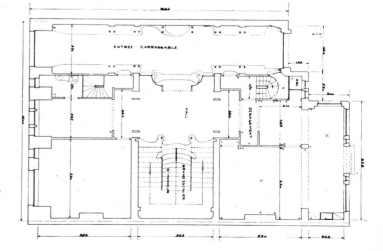

Above left: street facade
Above right: detail of the stair
Below: plan

HENRY VAN DE VELDE
Bloemenwerf House
Uccle, Belgium

Like Morris, van de Velde, an accomplished Post-Impressionist painter, abandoned fine for applied art in 1895 with the building of his own house at Uccle, near Brussels; a structure which at once established the main tenets of his elusive and enigmatic style. Possibly no other work from the early modern movement illustrates so directly Alois Riegl's concept of the "will to form" as this continentalized version of the Arts and Crafts house. Like Behrens's house in Darmstadt of approximately the same date, this is van de Velde's first architectural work and the somewhat awkward angles on the interior testify to the fact that it is the work of an amateur. The almost symmetrical plan of the house — a rectangle with clipped corners — is subtly distorted to the right as one faces the main entrance. Unlike the Gothic Revival form of Webb's Red House, the scheme is organized about a central double height entrance hall with an asymmetrical staircase ascending from left to right. The distorted but symmetrical hexagonal plan is further displaced by the dynamic form of the stair pushing the internal volume toward the right and van de Velde consciously reflected this movement in the dining room bay window and in the projecting stairs extending into the garden. The ground floor comprises a study, a bedroom, a bathroom, a large studio, a dining room and a kitchen — these last two spaces opening directly off the main hall. The upper floor and attic are given over to bedrooms, bathrooms, etc., planned around a central landing looking down into the entry. The house makes references on its exterior to both the English Arts and Crafts tradition and the Flemish, agrarian vernacular. Thus, while the Voyseyesque white walls were punctuated by louvred shutters, the narrower vertical boarding on the gables was painted black in order to give the top of the house that characteristically English, Yeoman, half-timbered effect (cf. Richard Norman Shaw's Leys Wood, Sussex of 1869).

The craft studio which van de Velde set up in conjunction with the furnishing of this house was in many respects the proving ground for his own version of the total work of art, with van de Velde designing absolutely everything with which the house was furnished, including the cutlery and even the clothing worn by his wife Maria Sèthe. Her kimono-like dresses (a form adopted so as to permit freedom of movement) were decorated with serpentine linear motifs designed to as to harmonize with both the body and the "form-force" aesthetic of van de Velde's interior. Although van de Velde maintained an equally rigorous expression throughout, there is a discernible split here between the syntax adopted for the utensils and the furniture, and the formal order of the architecture, for where the former tended to be organic, graphic, flowing, linear and light, the latter was inorganic, disjunctive and angular.

Above: overall view
Below: plans

Photo: Archives d'Architecture Moderne, Brussels

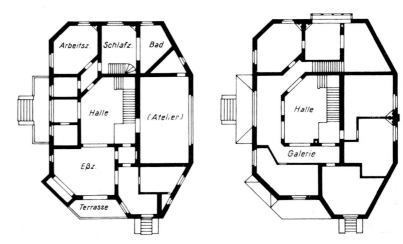

1897-1904
KARL GÉRARD
HENRY VAN DE VELDE
PETER BEHRENS
The Folkwang Museum
Hagen, Westphalia, Germany

In 1896, Karl Ernst Osthaus, at the age of 22, inherited the private means with which he was able to fulfill his ambition of founding of a didactic museum in which the arts and natural sciences might be exhibited side by side, together with examples of advanced industrial design. As he wrote to an associate at the time of founding the Folkwang Museum; "...culture can only develop where art and life are united... why can't the same be true of the joyless products of industry?"

Osthaus intended to demonstrate the unity of life and art by living amid the cultured milieu of his museum and in 1897 he commissioned the Berlin architect Karl Gérard to design him a three-storey structure comprising a dining room and a kitchen with ancillary spaces on the ground floor, living accommodation on the second, and a top-lit exhibition gallery and music room above. While Gérard's Neo-Renaissance design was historically eclectic on its facade, it sported a more dynamic and open structure on its interior, which was comprised of a system of cast-iron columns, supporting brick arches. In 1900 Gérard was relieved of having anything more to do with the commission and Osthaus asked the Belgian architect van de Velde to take over the design of the interior. Van de Velde's initial move was to clad the internal iron armature and brick spans in a plaster sheath, profiled and contoured in accordance with the principles of his "form-force" aesthetic. This rendering enabled van de Velde to impose his own sculptural and calligraphic signature on the upper and lower halls of Gérard's original design, and these organic plaster profiles were matched by the more brittle, yet equally sculptured expression, that van de Velde adopted for the balustrades to the main staircase and its upper gallery. This part glyptic, part architectonic expression found its focus in Georg Minne's five kneeling figures arranged radially about the perimeter of a cylindrical basin in the centre of the space. While the principal rooms were all furnished with exhibition cases, chairs and tables designed by van de Velde, the *tour de force* was the music room, in which a bookcase, a chair, a corner table and a sofa were symmetrically arranged in two identical but mirrored halves about a central door. These rather different forms were united by an undulating wooden panel whose dynamic contour stemmed from the transom of the door itself, the whole symmetrical assembly looking like the leading edge of an insect's wing.

In 1904, Osthaus commissioned Peter Behrens to create a lecture space within the ground floor of the museum. Contemporaneous with the pavilions that Behrens built in Oldenberg in 1905, this space took on an almost liturgical form, comprising two cubic volumes, terminated in by half cylinder and capped by a hemisphere. Nothing could have been further from van de Velde's vitalist attitude than this cold, brittle, Neo-Quattrocento interior, executed in a highly mannered linear style that was to characterize Behrens's work throughout the next decade.

88 *Exhibition area*
89 *Above: upper hall*
   Below left: detail of stair railing
   Below right: close up view of columns

After having been largely confined to the interior and decorative art work produced by the so-called Glasgow Four — that is to say to the decorative style created by himself, Herbert McNair and the Macdonald sisters — Charles Rennie Mackintosh emerged as an architect of world stature with his winning competition design for the Glasgow School of Art, projected in a manner that was close to the late Gothic Revival style of G.E. Street. Following the precepts of the English Gothic Revival, Mackintosh designated the main body of the school as a loose-fitting envelope with the bulk of the studio space being stacked on four floors. This mass, which effectively read as two storeys from the street side, was fragmented and complex towards the rear of the building where the museum and library were located in the short arms of the E plan. The granite faced, asymmetrically arranged street facade with its high, wrought-iron braced studio windows was complimented by the architecture of the return facades, pierced by small openings and stepping down in stages towards the rear of the site. The first of these, built as the eastern end of the building, was treated in a traditional Gothic Revival manner complete with finials, gables, turrets and incised windows. This would have been repeated on the Western side had it not been for Mackin- tosh's radical re-design of the second stage in 1906. The art school is thus a record of Mackintosh's stylistic development from 1897 to 1907. The difference between the Voyseyesque entry hall of the first stage and the double-height oriels to the library of the second (a motif patently influenced by Norman Shaw's New Zealand Chambers of 1876) reflects the full range of Mackintosh's development by this date. In decorative terms, this may be seen as a transition from a linear and curvaceous expression to a much more geometric and crystaline manner, anticipatory of the Art Deco house that he was to design for Bassett-Lowke.

90 *Main entry facade*
91 *Left: library facade*
  Above right: detail of the entry facade
  Below right: decorative motif of the railing
92 *Above left: view of the library from mezzanine*
  Above right: detail of library furniture
  Below left: ground floor and first floor plans
  Below right: sections
93 *Above left: view of gallery*
  Above right: main stairs
  Below left: board room (Mackintosh room)
  Below right: fireplace in the board room

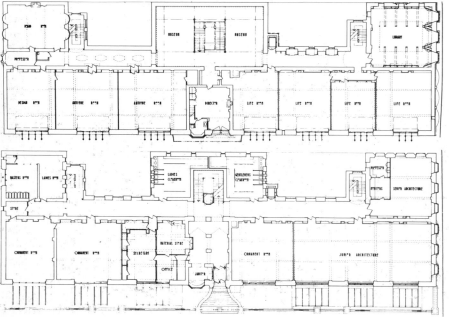

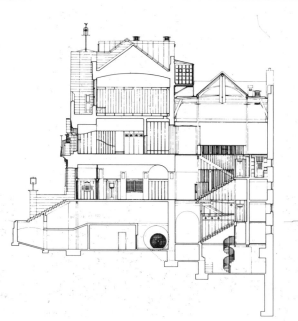

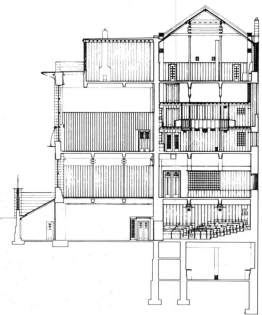

1898
CHARLES F. A. VOYSEY
A.C. Briggs House, "Broadleys"
Lake Windermere, England

94 Perspective with inset plans
95 Above: view across carport
   Below left: bay windows
   Below center: interior view of bay windows
   Below right: stair details
   Photos: T. Kitajima

GROUND PLAN

DINING RM 22·9×17·0   KITCHEN 18·0×17·0   SERVANT ROOM 14·0×13·0

HALL 35'×27·6'

DRAWING ROOM 20'×20·6'

VERANDAH

ENTRANCE COURT

BROADLEYS · WINDERMERE
FOR A · CVRRER · BRIGGS ESQ

FIRST FLOOR PLAN

No 2   No 3   SPACE OVER HALL   No 4 17·6×17·0
No 1   No 5   No 6   No 7

PLAY ROOM 23'×17'

Throughout almost a quarter of a century of practice (1895-1919) Voysey's domestic syntax remained essentially unchanged: lean, slate-covered roofs with wide overhanging eaves, carried on thin and delicately curved wrought-iron gutter brackets; white, "roughcast" rendered masonry walls with stone window trim and horizontal string courses; fenestration grouped into horizontal bands divided by the vertical accents of battered buttresses and chimney stacks. All of these features are present in this quintessential "yeoman" house built on a bluff overlooking Lake Windemere; a work which in many respects may be regarded as a condensation of Voysey's domestic style. The typical L-shaped Gothic Revival plan with its exposed staircase in the inner angle is here

reduced to the simplest possible terms (cf. Butterfield's early vicarages of the 1840's or Philip Webb's more irregular Red House of 1859). It is significant that Voysey's characteristically battered buttress occurs here only once, at the apex of the L, as though he has already embaced the proto-rationalist strategy of reserving certain rhetorical features for unique situations. By the same token, the semi-circular belvedere to the terrace and the three semi-circular bay windows looking out over the lake may be seen as anticipating the controlled "expressionism" of architects like Erich Mendelsohn. Throughout his long and successful career as a domestic architect, Voysey maintained his independence and kept himself somewhat removed from both the "crafty-ness" of the

Arts and Crafts movement and the "artiness" of the Art Nouveau. Neither traditional nor *avant-garde*, his somewhat subterranean influence on the formation of the so-called International Style remains as indisputable as it is enigmatic. While lacking the manipulative brilliance of either Lutyens or Shaw, his influence on his contemporaries was equally powerful. It is clear that the work of Olbrich and Mackintosh would have been quite different had it not been for the sharp sensibility of Voysey and C.H. Townsend, and it is even possible that the young Frank Lloyd Wright may have been influenced by his achievement. If, as Allen Brooks has suggested, Robert C. Spencer's "farmhouses" of 1900 did indeed anticipate Wright's first *Ladies' Home Journal* house of

the same year, then the case can be made that even the Prairie Style owes something to Voysey; for, clearly, Spencer's work of this date was decidedly Voyseyesque. And while Voysey's spatial planning was rarely brilliant, his interiors were nonetheless subtly articulated with bright, ceramic-tiles fireplace surrounds and bleached oak wainscotting. Above all they were naturally lit in unexpected and interesting ways and this, together with their "enriched" plainness seems to have made them a model for Alvar Aalto's domestic work. To what else can the bamboo-screened stair of Aalto's Villa Mairea (1939) be indebted save to the battered stair-screen in Voysey's own house, The Orchard, built at Chorley Wood, Hertfortshire in 1900?

This compositional duality is probably the finest of a series of artists' studios designed by Paul Hankar and built in Brussels between 1890 and the turn of the century. Trained under Henri Beyaert and heavily influenced by the English oriental, aesthetic manner of E.W. Godwin and Christopher Dresser, Hankar produced rather unique Art Nouveau houses whose strong geometric organization pointed towards the crystallization and eventual demise of the famous whiplash form. With its horseshoe shaped arches, elaborate grill-work and general air of Balkanized *chinoiserie* this is an atypical work for its date in the city that was once justly known as the capital of Art Nouveau. The work of Hankar may be distinguished from that of most of his contemporaries by his preference for strong earth colours and his penchant for painted ceramic tiles and elaborate wall decoration, this last being invariably executed by his friend, the painter Adolphe Crespin. At the same time the discipline with which he articulated the structural elements of his buildings indicates how strongly he had been influenced by Viollet-le-Duc. However, his contribution when compared to that of Horta's, appears to be less hierarchic and flamboyant. Nothing, for instance, could be further from Horta than the simple audacity of his facades or the straightforward and economic arrangement of his interiors. Hankar, like others of his generation, thought of architecture as the synthesis of the plastic arts and to this end he was involved in the furnishing of the private houses that he built.

Right: main facade
Below: ground floor plan

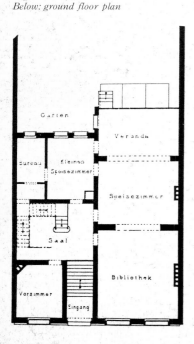

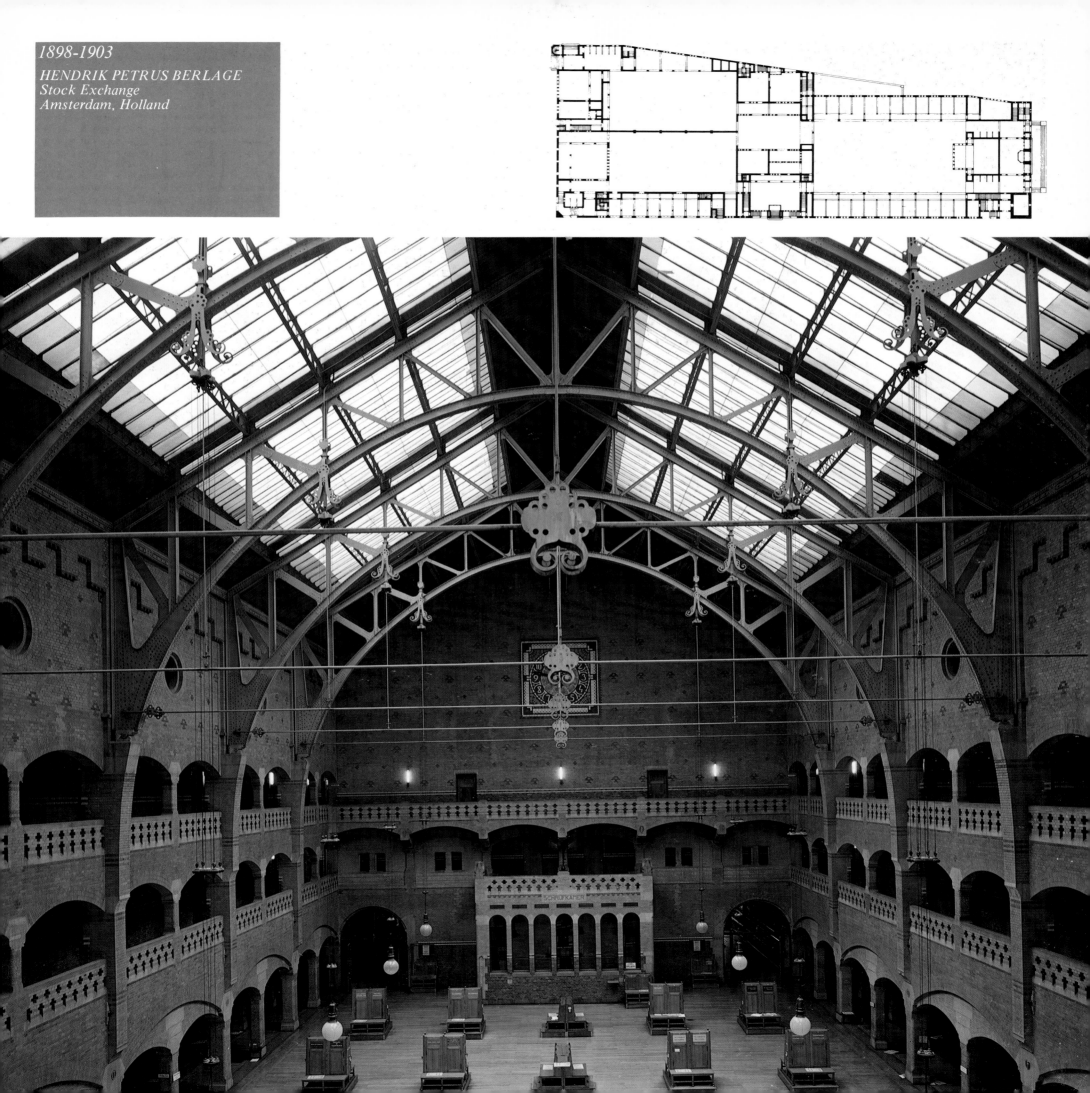

1898-1903
HENDRIK PETRUS BERLAGE
Stock Exchange
Amsterdam, Holland

Developed over the span of eighteen years, Berlage's Stock Exchange (finalized in 1898) gradually changed from the awkwardly eclectic National Romantic design of his unsuccessful competition entry of 1885 to a highly articulate and seminal expression in unadorned brickwork. In probably no other work of the turn of the century (not withstanding the brilliant achievements of such Art Nouveau architects as Horta, Gaudí, Guimard, etc.), are the principles of Viollet-le-Duc brought to such a consequential and logical form of expression.

Treated as though they were internal "agoras," the three main exchange halls are top-lit and flanked by galleried auxiliary accommodation on their sides (the offices required for the brokers, notaries, etc.). These brick walls and the one plain brick wall separating the grain and share exchanges are stiffened and articulated by brick piers which in their turn carry the steel and wrought-iron trusses by which the glass roofs are supported. The procedure and manner in which these trusses distribute their loads to the ground via pad stones and corbels, and

the way in which these are then combined with brick, relieving arches and stone columns at their bases, amounts to a constructional language which is as rich and inflected as the structure of a Gothic cathedral. As Mies van der Rohe was to remark, Berlage attained a medieval standard of architectonic logic and precision without indulging in any kind of pathetic nostalgia for a medievalized world (cf. Pugin). Furthermore, as in most of Berlage's urban work, the building made a powerful contribution to the fabric of the city, asserting its

precisely proportioned mass as a strict delineation of the pre-existing street space. As in the mediaeval town this was to use building mass as the agent by which the outside rooms of the city acquire their palpability and definition.

97 Above: ground floor plan
Below: produce exchange hall
98 Left: overall view
Right: view toward the produce exchange hall
99 Produce exchange hall

In 1897, led by the painter Gustav Klimt, and with the tacit support of their master Otto Wagner, the architects Josef Maria Olbrich and Josef Hoffmann joined forces with their contemporary, the painter-designer Koloman Moser, to found the Viennese *Sezession*. In the following year the *Sezession* Exhibition building was erected in the Ringstrasse to the designs of Olbrich. Its crowning element, based on a sketch by Klimt, was incribed with the slogan: "The time our art, the art our freedom." Planned as a covered courtyard structure, the building provided for gallery space on all sides of a large top-lit rectangular exhibition hall in the centre.

The general form of the crowning element sketched by Klimt included, in vague outline, both the battered pylons and the gilded laurel motif with its dedication to Apollo. This last was rendered by Olbrich as a perforated metal dome, suspended between four pylons and set above profiled planar masses whose severity recalled the work of the English architects, C.F.A. Voysey and C.H. Townsend. An equal but opposite symbol of vitality occurred on the cover of the first issue of the *Sezession* magazine *Vers Sacrum*, which depicted an ornamental shrub whose vital roots were bursting through its tub into the earth beneath. A comparable opposition was obviously intended by the iconography of the building wherein the crowning laurel of Apollo was to be countered by the fertile force of the unconscious, as this was represented above the entrace in the form of the Medusa frieze, flanked by the Owls of Minerva. These birds, designed by Moser, were supposed to mediate between the Apollo and the Medusa, and thereby to watch over the fortunes of the arts within.

100 *View across street*
101 *Above left: laurel dome (Photo: M. Sekiya)*
    Above center: section
    Above right: ground floor plan
    Below left: detail of main facade
    Below right: detail of side facade

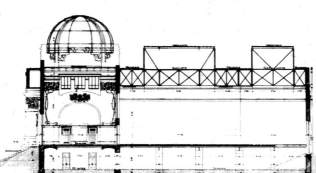

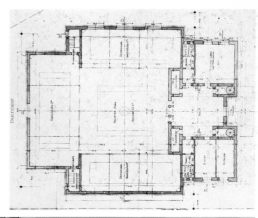

DER·ZEIT·IHRE·KVNST
DER·KVNST·IHRE·FREIHEIT·

This traditionally planned basilica church is in essence a masonry shell erected around a riveted and plated, wrought iron and steel structure whose principle lines of support are 19 feet apart. The steel trusses supporting the roof of the nave span 32 feet, while the aisle trusses, which extend over the side chapels and the bounding masonry walls have an effective span of 16 feet. While the need to keep costs to the minimum certainly influenced the decision to employ such a structure, the ideological factor cannot be discounted since this institution was in-tended to serve a working class community whose principal livelihood lay in maintaining the railway infrastructure (the building is situated close to the Gare Montparnasse). This much seems to be born out by the iconographical programme of the building, the chapels along the entire length of one side being decorated with murals successive-ly depicting the patron saints of metal-lurgists, carpenters, joiners, artists and art workers, etc. Possibly this appeal to craft-work in general explains the somewhat discordant use of timber for the balcony rails to the mezzanine. With the exception of this elegant use of a lightweight metal skeleton, Astruc's career was undistin-guished. Unlike Georges Chedanne, author of the famous steel-framed office building on the rue Réaumur, Paris, Astruc seems to have been unaware of the necessity to develop an architectural language that would be appropriate to riveted construction. The legendary split between engineer and archi-tect was never more dramatically expressed than in this unique but rather eccentric work.

102 *Left: main facade*
  Right: view through nave toward the altar
103 *View across nave*

The Ernst Ludwig House, completed for the first exhibition of the Darmstadt Artists' Colony of 1901, and named after its patron, the Grand Duke of Hesse and Darmstadt, was undoubtedly the most "progressive" building that Olbrich designed during his nine year residence in Darmstadt; progressive in the sense that its bare walls anticipated the rational tradition in modern architecture. Consisting of eight studio/living spaces, four on each side of a common meeting hall, it was the Darmstadt Colony's main public building, around which a number of individual artist's houses were built. These houses, with the exception of Behrens's own house, were all designed by Olbrich. With its high, blank, horizontally fenestrated facade, shielding north lights to the rear, and its ornate, recessed circular entrance flanked by giant figures carved by the sculptor Ludwig Habich, it was the ultimate monumentalization of themes that Olbrich had broached in the Vienna *Sezession* building of the previous year. Once again the combined influence of Voysey and Wagner is evident in the profiling and organization of the facade.

Olbrich had come to take up residence here as "court architect" in Darmstadt in 1899. Shortly after, he was joined by six other artists, who made up the founding group known as *Die Sieben* (The Seven), who were then charged with creating an exhibition to be staged under the title *Ein Dokument Deutscher Kunst* of 1901. On the occasion of the opening of this exhibition, a mystical ceremony took place on the steps of the Ernst Ludwig House in which a prophet descended the steps from the studio entrance to receive the gift of a "crystal," which, like the transformation of carbon into a diamond, symbolized the way in which ordinary materials may be turned into art.

Above: entrance facade
Below: Mathildenhöhe, Darmstadt, site plan

LOUIS H. SULLIVAN
Carson, Pirie, Scott & Co. Building
Chicago, Illinois, U.S.A.

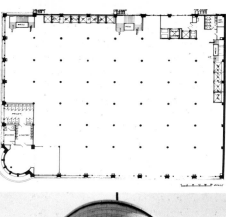

Originally built for the established firm of Schlesinger and Mayer, the first three-bay, nine-storey phase of this department store was erected in 1899, and the second, twelve-storey increment on the corner of Madison and State Streets between 1903 and 1904. The southernmost five bays along State were added in 1906 by D.H. Burnham. Located in downtown Chicago at an important commercial junction, this store was purchased soon after completion by the prosperous firm of Carson Pirie and Scott and it is still owned and managed by them. Sullivan's building finally comprised a seven by eight bay loft volume with each structural bay measuring approximately 22 by 20 feet. Like other large commercial structures by Sullivan, the interior of the building is devoid of architectural interest. It is simply commercial floor space with a thick service wall and elevator bank stacked along the inner wall. The real significance of the building resides in its decoration and in its terracotta faced skeleton frame, the proportions of which uncannily anticipated the later Chicago School of Mies van der Rohe. At street level, however, a continuous ornamented, two-storey high, cast-iron facade imparts a public finish to the display front and the corner rotunda, the swirling ornamental relief over the entrance being similar to the organic decoration that Sullivan published in 1924 in his *A System of Architectural Ornament According with a Philosophy of Man's Powers*. This is Sullivan's penultimate work in Chicago, his very last contribution to the city being the rather inconsequential Krauss Music Store, completed in 1922, two years before his death. Like the Reliance Building, this structure was originally capped by a thin slab cornice. In the State Street phase of 1903, Sullivan slightly reduced the height of the top three floors of his otherwise extremely abstract facade in order to impart a diminishing effect to the upper part of the structure (cf. Sullivan's Auditorium Building). This formula was faithfully followed by Burnham when he added the last increment along State Street. It is interesting to note, however, that he did not follow the refinement of recessing the uppermost storey.

Above left: typical floor plan
Above right: detail above main entrance
Below: view across street

106 Overall view
107 Bottom left: wall detail
  Above right: detail of awning
  Below right: detail of glazing

Since he did not enter the Compagnie du Métropolitan competition of 1898, Guimard gained the only public commission of his career largely through the patronage of his friend, Adrien Bernard, president of the Conseil Municipal de Paris. Due to a conflict over which authority should have the rights of exploitation, Paris was late in equipping itself with an underground train system. It is interesting to note that London was to place its transit below ground as early as 1863, while New York and Vienna were to follow suit with the advent of electric traction in 1877 and 1898 respectively. Constructed like the Crystal Palace out of interchangeable, prefabricated cast iron and glass parts, Guimard created his métro system in opposition to the ruling taste of French classical culture. As early as 1886 Charles Garnier, architect to the Opéra, had already declared his opposition to anything other than masonry for such purposes and the struggle over the public form of the métro was still going on eight years later when out of deference to Garnier, Guimard's métro entrance for the Place de l'Opéra was rejected in favour of Cassier Bernard's innocuous Neoclassical design. Away from the operatic shrine of the bourgeois city, Guimard's system flourished, emerging overnight like the manifestation of some organic force, its sinuous green cast-iron tentacles erupting from the subterranean labyrinth to support a variety of barriers, pergolas, maps, hooded light fittings and glazed canopies (see Place Dauphine and Place des Abesses for the remaining exotic entrances which are still intact). These surrealistic "dragonfly's wings" — to quote a contemporary critic — received a mixed, not to say chauvinistic, press, the verdigris colour of their iron supports being regarded as German rather than French. This imaginative attempt to render the Orphic myth in modern terms was to be complemented later by the astringent technical forms of the elevated section of the métro, built to the designs of the architect Jean Camille-Formigé and the engineer Louis Biette. Such structures were close in form and spirit to the viaducts that Otto Wagner had already designed for the Stadtbahn in Vienna.

An exceptional work by any standards, this house is all the more remarkable for being the first work of a painter turned architect. Before coming to Darmstadt in 1899, Behrens had had at least ten years experience as a painter, during which he had participated in the foundation of the Munich *Sezession* in 1893. Resident in the Darmstadt as a member of the Artists' Colony from 1899 to 1903, Behrens was the only artist of the *Die Sieben* (The Seven) to design his own house, together with its interior, including the furniture, the light fittings, the chinaware, the cutlery and many of the wall and ceiling decorations. In retrospect, much of this work now has the appearance of being derivative: the dining room furniture in particular is obviously close to the style of Henry van de Velde. The house is organized about a dining and music room on the raised ground floor, with a kitchen and ancilliary services in the basement, and the main bedrooms and studio space above. While this format was quite typical for a small bourgeois house, its internal and external expression was un- usual, particularly for its combination of features drawn from the English Arts and Crafts movement (cf. the work of Richard Norman Shaw), with elements such as the high-pitched roof drawn from the German vernacular. At a detail level, there was Behrens's identification with Nietzsche's *alter ego Zarathrustra,* evident in the radiant crystal image which dominates the decor of the music room and appears even more forcibly as an heraldic emblem embossed in metal on the front door.

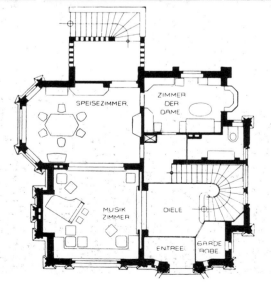

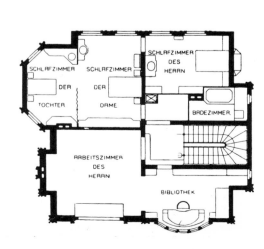

Above left: view through vegetation
Above right: main entrance
Below: first floor and second floor plans

VICTOR HORTA
A l'Innovation Department Store
Brussels, Belgium

Conceived as a large three-floor shopping hall on the well-established commercial frontage of the rue Neuve, Horta was to treat the facade of this department store as though it were a replica of the section, cut across the three-storey-high "nave" of the central space together with the galleried side aisles which constituted its basic volume. Horta directly embodied the wrought iron and steel arch and its adjacent spans in the fenestration of the facade, softening and deepening this profile with an identical silhouette projected in front of the structure and the glass skin. As in his Van Eetvelde house of 1898 this device imparted a certain depth and sculptural substance to an otherwise flat facade. In this instance the recessed plane was a curtain wall comparable in its scale to Henri Gutton's *Grand Bazar* completed in the rue de Rennes, Paris in 1906. With the exception of these two stores and Frantz Jourdain's *La Sammaritaine, Magasin No. 2,* 1905-10, the metallic structural frame of the late nineteenth-century department store was rarely expressed on the exterior and certainly never with the simplicity and audacity that characterized Horta's *A L'Innovation*. However, the purity of this remarkable concept was compromised in 1922 when the internal structure was replaced by a reinforced concrete frame; an up-grading of the fire resistance of the structure which did little to save it from its eventual destruction by fire in 1967.

Above: section
Below: street facade
Photo reproduced from
Victor Horta *by F. Borsi & P. Portoghesi*

1902
RAIMONDO D'ARONCO
Central Pavilion
International Exposition
of Decorative Arts
Turin, Italy

A leading member of the belated Italian Art Nouveau movement, D'Aronco was fortunate enough to be commissioned with both the Central and the Music Pavilions for the Turin Exposition of 1902. However, like many other members of the so-called *Floreale* movement who had been trained in the Beaux-Arts manner, D'Aronco never really felt at ease with the sinewy asymmetrical forms of the Art Nouveau, and in his everyday practice he tended to revert to Sommaruga-like parodies of classical compositions. The Turin pavilions seem to have been the more resolved and dynamic works of his somewhat awkward *Floreale* career. The central pavilion, with its high clerestory lit dome linking single-storey exhibition halls to either side, may have been based on C.R. Mackintosh's unrealized auditorium scheme for the Glasgow International Exhibition of 1901, for the *parti* is clearly based on the same basic theme of a radially buttressed domed hall. Beyond this similarity, the prime influence was evidently the Viennese *Wagnerschule* and above all the works of Wagner and Olbrich. D'Aronco clearly knew Olbrich's *Sezession* building of 1898, and Wagner's Academy of Fine Arts project of the same year. We find the same evocative angels around the perimeter of the dome with their arms stretched skyward bearing laurels, the same linear Wagnerian decor falling vertically from abstracted laurel wreaths, ranged as circular discs about the perimeter of the central form. The terminals of D'Aronco's buttresses are likewise transformed into Egyptoid pylons, reminiscent in their form and decor of the crowning element of Olbrich's *Sezessionbau.*

Main facade
Photo reproduced from The Anti-Rationalists,
edited by N. Pevsner & J. M. Richards

1902-03
CHARLES RENNIE MACKINTOSH
"Hill House"
Glasgow, Scotland

Derived partly from the long standing Scottish baronial tradition and partly from C.F.A. Voysey's white rendered, slate-roofed houses of the 1890's and from James McClaren's essays in the Scottish vernacular (his rural building at Fortingall, Perthshire of 1891), the Hill House in Helensburgh, built for the publisher William Blackie on a site overlooking the Firth of Clyde, was Mackintosh's second free-standing domestic work, the first being William Davidson's house, Windyhill, completed at Kilmacolm in 1901. Both of these works adopted the same L-shaped Gothic Revival Plan (cf. Philip Webb's the Red House of 1859) as their *parti*, comprising a main block with a service wing at right angles. These houses and the highly influential *Haus eines Kunstfreundes* (House of an Art Lover) that Mackintosh designed in 1901 for Alexander Koch's competition of this name, are part of a series which employ the same basic syntax: grey harled walls, steeply pitched slate roofs with shallow eaves, protruding semi-circular stair towers, simple pierced window openings with square gridded fenestration, spots of sparkling ornament and battered chimneys, reminiscent of the work of Voysey. Unlike Voysey, the harling (rough cast rendering) is invariably returned into the window surrounds, thereby achieving a stark geometrical effect; a transition that is decidedly softened in Voysey's work through the use of stone surrounds and cills. The placement of these openings is more precisely determined in Hill House than in Windyhill, so that this house for Blackie, decorated and furnished throughout with Mackintosh's own furniture (some of which he designed specifically for this house) is altogether the finest example of his domestic style at the turn of the century.

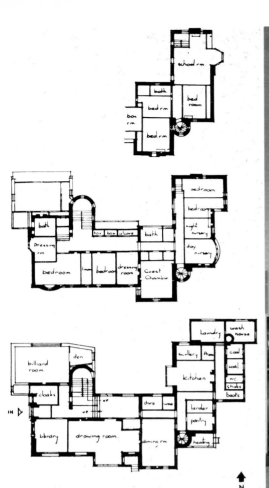

111 Overall view
112 Above left: stairs in entry hall
 Above right: entry hall
 Below left: bed alcove
 Below right: fireplace in drawing room
113 Above left: plans from top; attic, first floor,
 ground floor
 Above right: bed room
 Below right: alcove in drawing room
 Photos: T. Kitajima

Initially formulated in 1902, Pennsylvania Station was the last great New York monument to be designed by Charles Follen McKim. While construction began in fairly good time for a large structure, such were the engineering and logistical problems encountered in erecting this complex interchange, that it was not completed until 1911, one year after McKim's death.

This commission was occasioned by the perfection of electrical rail traction which facilitated the underground entry of suburban and main line trains into Manhattan. In competing for the westward bound traffic with New York Central, the Pennsylvania Railroad finally decided to construct a tunnel under the Hudson River and to build in consequence a major terminus uniting its own network with the New York City subway infrastructure and the Long Island railway system.

The extraordinary ingenuity involved in integrating all these systems has been well described by Leland Roth: "The tracks of the Pennsylvania road were to be at the lowest level, with the Long Island tracks the southernmost of the subterranean train-yard. These tracks were to lie below the tubes of the planned subways to the east and west of the station. The subway stops at each end of the station were to be connected by a long concourse that also led directly to stairs down to the Pennsylvania and Long Island trains. Above this subway concourse was the main waiting room floor, itself still one storey below street grade."

McKim's architectural solution to this multi-layered concourse was to take the two block Manhattan site and to enclose it in a "thick-wall peristyle" thereby establishing an outer perimeter of Tuscan pilasters and columns. Where this wall was merely a shell containing ramped vehicular access or office accommodation it was flanked by two-storey-high pilasters; where it had to permit and announce monumental pedestrian entry it became a free-standing colonnade. Naturally, the greatest extent of this inter-columnation was on Seventh Avenue, where the station front faced the core of the city, but similar porticos occured at mid-block, on the north and south of the central axis and at the western end of the terminus.

The building was conceived as a vast cruci-form "gateway," with a large sunken waiting hall in its center, which modelled after the Baths of Caracalla, gave rise to three large coffered vaults, whose tripartite, pitched roof external silhouette was the emblematic "sign" of the terminus when seen from a distance.

The entry progression towards the center when arriving by train was as follows, first one rose by stairway towards the sub-grade concourse, which was roofed by exposed lattice steel arches and vaults; then one entered into the central waiting hall and finally climbed a grand stairway to the arcade level from which opened the lunch-room and the dining room and a gallery of shops leading out to the Seventh Avenue portico.

An ingenious system of ramped and sunken carriageways permitted passengers to be dropped off at the central waiting room level, from whence they would proceed directly to main concourse and by stairs to the sunken platforms beneath. The demolition of this terminal in the mid-sixties can only be regarded as a fundamental loss to the architectural heritage of New York.

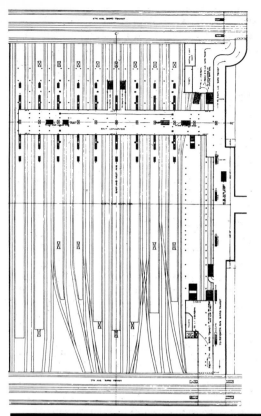

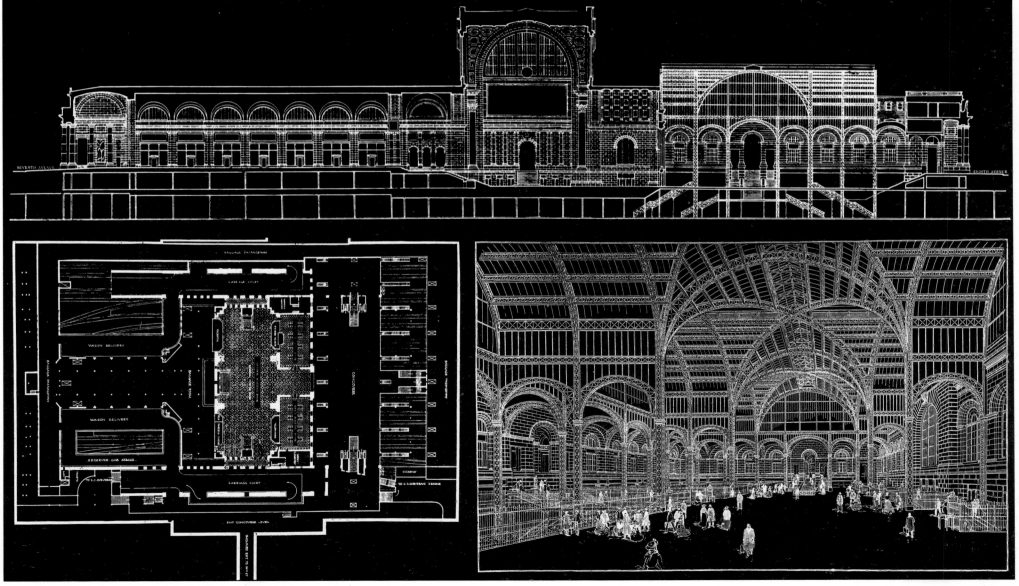

114 View of the concourse
115 Above: exit-concourse level plan
Center: section on east-and-west axis
Below left: waiting-room level plan
Below right: The concourse

AUGUSTE PERRET
Apartments, 25 bis rue Franklin
Paris, France

This apartment building with which Perret established his reputation is to be regarded as one of the canonical works of 20th-century architecture, not only for its explicit and brilliant use of the reinforced concrete frame (the Hennebique system) but also for the way in which its internal organization was to anticipate Le Corbusier's later development of the free plan. Perret deliberately made the apartment partition walls non-structural throughout and their partial removal would have yielded an open space, punctuated only by a series of free-standing columns. As it is, each floor is organized with the main and service stairs to the rear (each with its own elevator) the kitchen to one side and the principal rooms to the front. These last are divided up from left to right into rooms assigned to smoking, dining, living, sleeping and reception. It is interesting to note that the male and female domain of the bourgeois residence, namely the *fumoir* and the *boudoir* occupy the projecting bays of the facade. While the frame *per se* is clearly expressed (despite its ceramic tile facing), Perret has treated reinforced concrete here in the same way as one would have normally dealt with wood. His consciously classic insistence on trabeation and the translation of wooden tectonic elements into lithic forms, that is to say, his rejection of the more plastic nature of concrete served to give this work a somewhat *retarditaire* appearance. Nonetheless from a technical standpoint this building was well in advance of its time, including the use of glass bricks for the stair towers to the rear. Moreover, Perret, by virtue of being the architect of his family contracting concern, was always able to achieve levels of technical perfection which were to elude his contemporaries who chose to work in the same material.

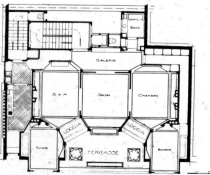

Street facade and second floor plan

117 Street facade
118 Detail of entrance facade

After being cut in 1895 as a *percement* linking Notre-Dame-des-Victoires and Saint Denis, the rue Réaumur was rapidly developed as a commercial street, serving the textile trade, between 1897 and 1905. In 1898 the city organized a competition for the design of typical facades for the new street and many prominent architects were eventually included among the prize winners, including Guimard, Lavirotte, Hermant, Montarnal and Le Voisvenel, the last three going on to build versions of their designs in the street itself. As far as we know Chedanne did not enter the competition but nonetheless applied in 1903 for permission to erect the building that has long since been known as *Le Parisien*, so named after the newspaper company that occupied the premises for many years. The fact that the permit was granted for a very different structure may indicate that Chedanne was not the sole author of the building, particularly since he was then already occupied in designing a department store for Galleries Lafayette built between 1904 and 1906. More articulate than Jourdain's *La Samaritaine* of the same date and more complex than Horta's *A L'Innovation* of 1901, *Le Parisien* confronted the street with a riveted- and plated-steel facade in which a dialogue was established not only between the load-bearing elements and the non-load-bearing fenestration with its corrugated-steel sheet spandrels, but also between the primary and secondary systems of vertical support. The primary system carries the spandrels according to an evident Palladian order of A:B:A:B:A:B:A, while a secondary system picks up the arrises of the bay windows on the top floor and conducts these loads back to the paired columns at the ground. As recent commentators have remarked the plastic quality of this structural system anticipates in some respects the gigantic megastructural works which have recently emerged in America from the school of Mies van der Rohe.

4 Otto Wagner and the Wagnerschule 1894-1912

58   *The Vienna Ring (1859-72) based in part on the prize winning designs of Ludwig Forster.*

Taken as a whole, the monumental buildings of the Ringstrasse expressed well the highest values of regnant liberal culture. On the remnants of a *champ de Mars,* its votaries had reared the political institutions of a constitutional state, the schools to educate the élite of a free people, and the museums and the theaters to bring to all the culture that would redeem the *novi homines* from their lowly origins. If entry into the old aristocracy of the genealogical table was difficult, the aristocracy of the spirit was theoretically open to everyone through the new cultural institutions. They helped to forge the link with the older culture and the imperial tradition, to strengthen that "second society," sometimes called the "mezzanine" where the bourgeois on the way up met the aristocrats willing to accommodate to new forms of social and economic power, a mezzanine where victory and defeat were transmuted into social compromise and cultural synthesis.

Carl Schorske
Fin-de-Siecle Vienna, 1979

In 1894 Otto Wagner succeeded Karl von Hasenauer as professor of architecture in the Academy of Fine Arts in Vienna. One Year later at the age of 54, he published his first theoretical work, *Moderne Architektur.* This was followed in 1898 by the first publication of the work of his students, given under the title *Aus der Wagnerschule.* Having been educated in Berlin by C.F. Busse, one of Karl Friedrich Schinkel's prime pupils, Wagner's architectural allegiances were divided between the rationalism of the *Schinkelschuler* and the more rhetorical manner of those last great architects of the Ringstrasse, Gottfried Semper and Hasenauer, whose State Museums, Burgtheater and Neue Hofburg were under construction in the Ring throughout the last quarter of the century. In 1892 Wagner won two major commissions which

were to transform his career and establish his reputation as a public architect; these were the creation of the Viennese metropolitan railway system known as the *Stadtbahn* (1894-1902) and the building of a system of embankments, sluice gates and control towers in connection with the regulation of the Danube Canal (1894-1907).

Wagner's polytechnical background made him acutely aware of the technical and social realities of his epoch. At the same time, his romantic and progressive character was drawn towards the radical activity of his talented pupils — to the anti-academic art movement co-founded by his assistant Joseph Maria Olbrich and his most brilliant pupil Josef Hoffmann, who had graduated with a Prix de Rome in 1895. These men were not only influenced by the work of Charles Rennie Mackintosh but were also equally captivated by the exotic vision of two young Viennese painters, Gustav Klimt and Koloman Moser. Under the leadership of Klimt, the architects Olbrich and Hoffmann and the painter Moser banded together in their opposition to the Academy and in 1897, with Wagner's blessing, they founded the Vienna *Sezession.* In the following year Wagner declared his sympathies for the *Sezession* through facing the facade of his pseudo-Italianate Majolika House in brightly coloured faience tile, arranged in floral patterns. A year later, in 1899, he scandalized the establishment by becoming a full member of the *Sezession.*

In 1898, Olbrich built the *Sezession* building, apparently after a sketch by Klimt, who was to remain the prime mover of the revolt. From Klimt came the battered walls, the axiality, and especially the laurel motif with

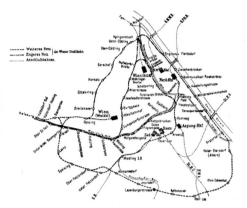

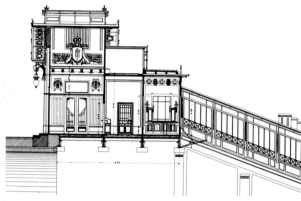

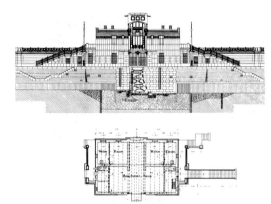

59　The Stadtbahn, Vienna, 1894-1902.

60　Wagner, Karlsplatz Station, Vienna, 1898-99. Section.

61　Wagner, Kaiserbad Sluicegate House, Danube Canal, Vienna, 1906-07. Longitudinal section through canal.

its dedication to Apollo. This last was rendered by Olbrich as a perforated metal dome, suspended between four short pylons and set above planar masses whose severe modelling recalled the work of such British architects as Charles Francis Annesley Voysey and Charles Harrison Townsend. A comparable symbol of organic vitality occurred on the cover of the first issue of *Ver Sacrum* which showed an ornamental shrub whose vital roots were depicted bursting through its tub into the earth beneath. From this symbolic point of departure — ever subject to the influence of Klimt's pan-eroticism — Olbrich began to evolve a style of his own.

This evaluation took place largely in Darmstadt, where Olbrich had been invited by the Grand Duke Ernst Ludwig in 1899. Later in that year he was joined by six other artists, the sculptors Ludwig Habich and Rudolf Bosselt, the painters Peter Behrens, Paul Bürck and Hans Christiansen, and the architect Patriz Huber. Two years later, this Artists' Colony exhibited its life-style and "habitat" as a total work of art, under the title *Ein Dokument Deutscher Kunst*. The exhibition was opened in May 1901 by a mystical ceremony called *Das Zeichen* (The Sign), which took place on the steps of Olbrich's Ernst Ludwig House. In this ceremony, an "unknown" prophet descended from the golden portal of the building to receive a crystalline form as a symbol of base material transformed into art, just as carbon may be changed into the brilliance of a diamond.

The Ernst Ludwig House, built in 1901, was undoubtedly the most progressive work that Olbrich designed during his nine-year residence in Darmstadt. Consisting of eight studio living spaces, four on each side of a common meeting hall, it was in effect the colony's initial focus, around which a number of individual artists' houses were eventually built. With its high, blank, horizontally fenestrated facade, shielding north lights to the rear, and its ornate, recessed circular entrance flanked by giant statues carved by Habich, it was the ultimate monumentalization of themes that Olbrich had broached in the *Sezession* building.

Between this "pan-erotic" masterpiece and the final classicization of his style in 1908 — the year of his premature death — Olbrich continued his search for a non-historicist expressive mode. Throughout the last decade of his life he created works of exceptional originality, culminating in his cryptic and brooding *Hochzeitsturm* or Wedding Tower, which, with the adjacent exhibition buildings, was completed on the Mathildenhöhe in Darmstadt for the *Hessischen Landesausstellung* of 1908. With its pyramidal compositon, the Mathildenhöhe complex built on top of a reservoir was in effect a "city crown" whose form anticipated the symbolic centre of Bruno Taut's *Stadtkrone* of 1919. Girded by a series of tiered concrete pergolas, it was drawn by Olbrich as a mountainous labyrinth of dense foliage, whose colour would change with the seasons from green to russet brown. In contrast to the serenity of the plane-tree garden in which it stood, it rose from the ground like a brooding mystical mountain.

Olbrich's leadership of the Darmstadt colony was challenged for a while by Peter Behrens, a graphist and painter, who had come to Darmstadt from the Munich *Sezession* in 1898. He emerged as an architect with the building and furnishing of his own house at Darmstadt in 1901. In their rivalry as

62 Olbrich, sketch for the Secession Building, Karlsplatz, Vienna, 1898.

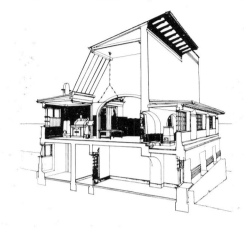

63 Olbrich, Ernst Ludwig House,
Mathildenhöhe Colony, 1899-1901.
Perspective/section through a typical studio.

Gesamtkünstler to the house of Hesse-Darmstadt, it was Olbrich rather than Behrens who was to be the brilliant designer of objects, while in their architectural careers outside Darmstadt, it was Behrens who became the more powerful creator of form. Above all, it was he who initiated their common return to the crypto-Classicism that characterizes the work of Olbrich's final years, his Tietz department store and the mansion that he built for the cigar manufacturer Finhals; both works being completed in Düsseldorf in 1908.

In 1899 Josef Hoffmann began to teach at the applied art school attached to the Austrian Museum for Art and Industry in Vienna; a school which had been founded, in accordance with Gottfried Semper's educational programme, some thirty-five years before. A year later, he replaced Olbrich as the designer of the elite Hohe Warte suburb on the outskirts of Vienna, building four villas there between 1901 and 1905. With his first work on this site, designed in the manner of English Free Architecture, for Koloman Moser, he succeeded Olbrich as the prime architect of the *Sezession.* By 1902, however, Hoffmann was already beginning to embrace a more planar and Classical mode of expression, based on the post-1898 work of Otto Wagner.

By the time of the Vienna *Sezession* Exhibition of 1900, at which Mackintosh's work was shown in Austria for the first time, Hoffman had already arrived at a furnishing style of refined rectilinear form. This was his initial move away from the obsessive curvilinearity of his Apollo shop built in Vienna in the previous year. By 1901, he was preoccupied with a graphic,

abstract figure-ground form of design. "I am particularly interested in the square as such," he wrote, "and in the use of black and white as dominant colours because these clear elements have never appeared in earlier styles." Together with Moser and other Secessionists, he became interested in the craft production of decorative and applied art objects, along the lines of C.R. Ashbee's Guild of Handicraft. By 1902, with his setting for Klinger's Beethoven statue, exhibited in the Secession Building, he had arrived at his own abstract style, in which certain contours or proportions are emphasized through the use of projecting beads and clusters of small squares. A year later, with the backing of Fritz Wärndörfer, the Hoffmann/Moser *Wiener Werkstätte* was started for the design, production, and marketing of high-quality domestic objects.

The last issue of *Ver Sacrum* was published in 1903 and with its demise the high period of the *Sezession* was over. In 1904, Hoffmann and Josef August Lux started to edit a new periodical, entitled *Hohe Warte,* named after the garden suburb on the outskirts of Vienna. From the outset it was dedicated to the propagation of "back to nature" garden city values, and later, in less liberal times, it became the garden city platform of the Austrian National Socialist movement. Unlike Hoffmann, Lux was quick to react against its chauvinistic exaggeration of folklorish values, resigning his editorship in protest against its *Heimatstil* policy as early as 1908.

By 1903, Hoffmann had reinterpreted the style of his master, particularly in his design for the Classical and austere Purkersdorf Sanatorium, which was to have such an influence on Le Corbusier's post war development.

64 *Illustration from* Die Großstadt. *Central quarter in Wagner's future metropolis.*

Two years later, Hoffmann began to work on his masterpiece, the Palais Stoclet, built in Brussels between 1905 and 1910. Like Auguste Perret's Théâtre des Camps-Elysées of 1912 the abstracted Classical decor of this work paid veiled homage to the Symbolist aesthetic of the Belle Epoque. Unlike Perret's theatre, however, the Palais Stoclet was essentially atectonic: its thin white marble facing with metal seams had all the mannered and handcrafted elegance of a *Wiener Werkstätte* object, rendered at a large scale. Of its conscious denial of structure and mass Eduard Sekler has written:

A strongly linear element is introduced by these articulated metal bands but it has nothing to do with 'lines of force', the way linear elements did in the architecture of Victor Horta. At the Stoclet house, we have lines which occur equally along horizontal and vertical edges – they are tectonically neutral. At the corners . . . where two or more of these parallel mouldings come together, the effect tends towards a negation of the solidity of the built volume. A feeling persists as if the walls had not been built in a heavy construction, but consisted of large sheets of thin material, joined at the corners with metal bands to protect the edges.

These bands, which issue from the apex of the stair tower, where four male figures support a Secessionist dome of laurels, are vaguely reminiscent of Wagner's stylized cable mouldings, and as these cascade down over the corners they serve to unite the whole building through the continuity of the seam.

Wagner's mature style dated from his sixtieth year, with the completion of his Vienna Stadtbahn network in 1901 – designed with Olbrich. Not a trace of the Italianate style of his first Wagner Villa of 1886 remains in his *Die Zeit*

telegraph office of 1902, or in his Kaiserbad Dam Works of 1906, both of which seem to relate in their engineered elegance and punctilious revetment to the atectonic style of Hoffmann. Yet the dematerialization of the Palais Stoclet had already been anticipated by Wagner's own masterwork, his Imperial Post Office Savings Bank built as much for the reality of the present as for some remote Symbolist utopia. To a similar end his *Großstadt* plan of 1910, with its hierarchy of neighbourhoods was projected as a rationally planned and realizable future. His description of this projected metropolis was devoid of all sentimentality when he wrote in 1911:

The allusion to tradition, sentiment, picturesque appearance, etc., as a basis of housing for modern man has simply lost its actuality for today's tastes. The number of inhabitants of the big cities who prefer to disappear in the masses as a "number" is considerably larger than the number of those who want to daily hear a "good morning" or "how did you sleep" from the hypocritical neighbours surrounding their private residences.

Equally realistic in all his public work, Wagner built with great technical precision for a bureaucratic state which he thought would last for ever. Thus crowned by an honorific pergola, hung with laurel wreaths and flanked by winged Victories whose arms are raised skyward, the Post Office Savings Bank stood for the republican benevolence of the Austro-Hungarian Empire at the height of its power.

However, like the Palais Stoclet, the Post Office Savings Bank can also be seen as a gargantuan metal box, an effect due in no small measure to the thin polished sheets of white sterzing marble that are anchored to its facade with aluminium rivets. Its glazed canopy frame, entrance doors, balustrade and parapet rail are also of aluminium, as are the metal furnishings of the banking hall itself. Faced in ceramic, lit from above and resting in its turn on a suspended concrete floor, studded with glass lenses for the illumination of the basement, this hall existed until very recently in the purity of its original form. Its unadorned, riveted steel work was of the same order as the industrial lighting standards and aluminium heating cowls which stood, at regular intervals, around its perimeter. Of the difference between this and the directly engineered forms of the mid-nineteenth century Stanford Anderson has written:

The details of an engineered building are not placed before us in the *sachlich* manner of nineteenth-century exhibition halls of railway sheds; the concept of an engineered building is revealed to us instead through the building's own modernist symbols of exposed industrial materials, structure and equipment.

In other words what Wagner achieved with this work was the modernist equivalent of the classical notion of *tectonic,* carried out exclusively in industrial materials.

By 1911, the "classicization" of the *Sezession* was complete, and for all his continuing interest in the evolution of an appropriate *Heimatstil,* Hoffmann represented Austria at the Rome International Art Exhibition of that year with a pavilion whose design was patently crypto-classical. This atectonic

work saw its echo one year later in Behrens's St. Petersburg German Embassy completed in 1912. In such a climate it fell to Wagner to close the *Sezession* as it had begun, with the vigour of his extremely austere yet elegantly proportioned second Wagner Villa, built in Hütteldorf in 1912. In this lucidly planned house, lyrically decorated by Moser and influenced to an equal degree by the pupils of the *Wagnerschule* and the recently published works of Wright, Wagner was to spend the last six years of his life.

There is little doubt but that the Post Office Savings Bank is the masterpiece of Wagner's late career. This prize winning design in a limited competition of 37 entries held in 1903 was built in two phases, the first in 1904-06 and the second in 1910-12. The remarkable quality of the building largely derives from the sparkle and reticulated brilliance of its revetment which consists, in the main, of thin profiled sections of white sterzing marble held in place by aluminium bolts. The granite facing to the rusticated base is secured in a similar way; however, in this instance the bolts are countersunk below the surface of the stone. This precision engineering approach permeates the entire structure both inside and out and reaches its apotheosis in the central top-lit banking hall. Here, the obscured glass lay light roof, the riveted steel superstructure, the bracketed light fittings, the cylindrical hot-air registers and the continuous glass block floor are orchestrated into a brilliant "machinist" whole, which is relieved by the standard wooden chairs and benches built to Wagner's Neo-classical design. One senses in this "standardized" interior, the ideal of the total work of art (*Gesamtkunstwerk*) on the threshold of being reduced to the terms of a universal culture based on engineering form. On the other hand the specific rhetorical appeal of this building resides largely in its fusion of traditional and synthetic materials; in Wagner's mixing of majolica tiles, white marble linings and black glass. This is Wagner's famous *Ausgleich* or compromise between old and new at the level of materials. The same sensibility appears in the aluminium acroteria, employed by the architect as the revetment to the cornice and the attic storey. From this rooftop tribune, festooned with aluminium wreaths, Othmar Schimkowitz's winged angles with their arms raised in benediction reflect the mythical benevolence of Robert Musil's *Kakania*. In retrospect they may be seen as the last gesture of nineteenth-century liberalism, for within six years of the building's completion Wagner was dead and the Austro-Hungarian Empire was dissolved.

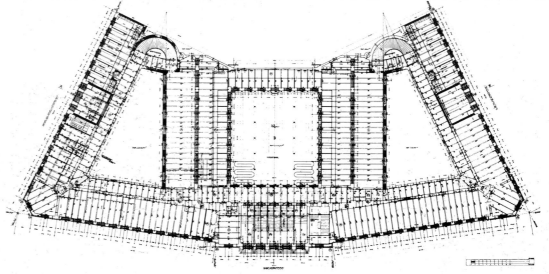

124 *Above: main facade*
   Below: first floor plan
125 *Central banking hall*

Designed for the Larkin Company (Martin Mail Order Co.), this was Wright's first attempt at rendering the work place as a sacramental realm. Its non-hierarchic, open planned office accommodation was stacked for three floors above the ground, on either side of a central top-lit "nave" running the full length of the building. The visual inter-penetrability of this section, repeated in innumerable structures since then, was ideologically and plastically enriched by improving texts incised into the balcony upstands which faced onto the central space. "Whatsoever ye would that others should do unto you, do ye so unto them," etc. Like the Unity Temple, to be built in Chicago's Oak Park some two years later, this was the public version of the Prairie Style designed by Wright down to the last detail including the light fittings and the furniture. The limits of this *Gesamtkunstwerk* approach came exactly at that point where the Martin Co. refused to allow Wright to re-style the telephones.

As introspective as any of Wright's public structures (and some of his private ones as well) the most articulated facade of this building occurred on its interior, and in this one respect it is typologically related to both the arcade and the department store. This reinforced concrete frame and brick faced structure with its high exterior upstands raised in order to accommodate built-in filing cabinets was to become the precedent for Mies van der Rohe's first attempt at formulating the modern office structure as a type in his office building of 1922. The Larkin Building was equally pioneering in the realm of services, Wright being quick to realize that one would have to air condition such a large enclosed space. To this end he installed a built-in ducted system for cleaning and heating the air (after 1909 it also cooled it in summer). The used air was finally exhausted via ducts built into the stair towers. The exclusion of these service elements from the main body of the building anticipates Louis Kahn's mid-twentieth century principle of always articulating the "servant" from the "served" elements.

126 View of exterior
127 Left: first floor plan
*   Right: view of interior*
Photos: © The Frank Lloyd Wright Foundation

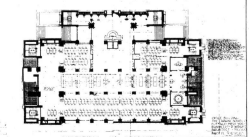

127

Derived in part from an abortive commission that Wright received from his pastor uncle in 1897, this "four square building for a four square gospel" was eventually built for another Unitarian community in Oak Park. Even then its realization was hardly smooth as Wright chose to build the entire structure out of reinforced concrete, and his pioneering of this material caused many delays and difficulties. Out to bids in March 1906 it was not finally occupied until 1908. The core of this building is the temple itself which was conceived as a Greek cross inscribed within a square. The center of this cross is capped by a skylight; the volume itself rising for three stories with a mezzanine level and full gallery around three sides of the square plan. As Grant Carpenter Manson has written: "The spatial effect of this manipulation of levels is surprisingly close and intimate: no member of the congregation feels himself to be either much lower or higher than the speaker. This close relationship, plus the great simplicity of decoration in the room and its astonishing brightness, conspire to give a grand sense of the meaning of Unitarianism and its total lack of pomp and circumstance."

However true this may be, there is little feeling of austerity in this interior which may be regarded as the quintessential sacred space of Wright's fictitious Prairie Culture. As in his Hardy House, built in Racine, Wisconsin in 1905, Wright was able to animate the bare planar masses of this structure, through the simple applications of wooden battens, whose rhythmic beat was echoed in the cruciform pendant light fittings suspended in the space. The highly abstract nature of this entire composition, comprised of interpenetrating plans throughout, clearly anticipated the Dutch Neoplastic movement by some twenty years. On the other hand the actual complex was structured according to a more or less traditional hierarchy, the high blank mass of the church, unrelieved save for its clerestory windows, is complemented by the lower and more informal and open order of the adjacent meeting room. The entrance as in most of Wright's work of this period is discretely hidden from view. Like the Larkin Building designed a few months previously, the Unity Temple also pioneered the integration of services, incorporating such features as internal roof drainage and a plenum heating/"air-conditioning" system incorporated into the four hollow concrete piers supporting the cruciform structure of the roof.

128 *Exterior view*
129 *Above: interior of the temple*
Below: ground floor and first floor plans

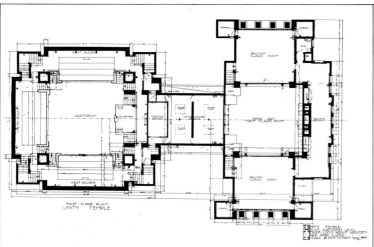

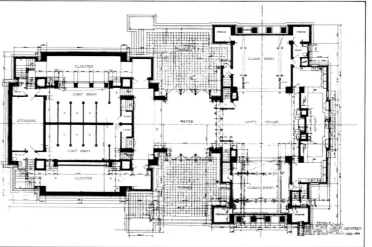

This ambitious utopian project was the juvenile masterpiece of one of two star pupils who emerged from the École des Beaux-Arts around the turn of the century, the other being Auguste Perret. Both men were greatly influenced by the academic, elemental approach to composition, preached and practised by their master, Julien Guadet, whose *Eléments et théorie de l'architecture* had been published in 1902. Having won the Prix de Rome in 1899, Garnier's hypothetical industrial city was the result of his four-year period of independent study at the French Academy in Rome. Set on the side of a river valley in the Lyons region, this industrial city of 35,000 was intended to function not only as a regional centre but was also to demonstrate the precepts of an ideal socialist society: that is to say, it had no church, barracks, police station, law courts or prison. Within the gridded parkscape of the city, Garnier projected a comprehensive and varied housing typology, in accordance with a hypothetical building code regulating density, light, and ventilation. The principal representative institution of the city was the central assembly building projected as a political centre, comprising a cluster of union meeting rooms and a number of auditoria. Like the *agora*, of which it was intended to be the modern counterpart, Garnier's assembly building was depicted as being peopled by shadowy figures, dressed in scant, classical (Biedermeier) clothing. Their equally plain houses were to be made out of reinforced concrete and were to be without the elaboration of cornices and mouldings. Just as simple and innovative from a technical point of view were the engineering methods to be employed in achieving the industrial structures, above all the projected covered shipyards of the city, the form of which Garnier took from Contamin's *Galerie des Machines* of 1889.

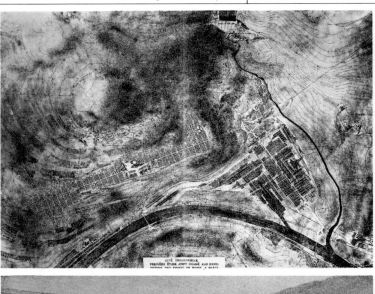

Top left: plan
Top right: factory
Middle left: furnaces
Middle right: residential quarters
Bottom left: station
Bottom right: assembly rooms

Greatly modified between the time of the open competition in 1904 and the beginning of its construction in 1910, the changes which Saarinen made to his original design reflect a fundamental change in the "ruling taste" of the period. Saarinen's successful competition entry had been rendered in his own version of the Finnish National Romantic manner centred about a pinnacled tower. In many respects, this design was a re-working of the language used in his National Museum built in Helsinki in 1902 and in his own house built as part of the Hvittrask complex designed with Gesselius and Lindgren in the same year. This media-

evalizing manner was vehemently denounced by Sigurd Frosterus who had also entered the station competition with a design that reflected the influence of his master, Henry van de Velde. Frosterus believed that a new railway station should be rationally related to railway technology and to international travel and that it should avoid the sentimental and nationalistic references so evident in Saarinen's initial design. Frosterus was strongly supported in this debate by the critic Gustaf Strengell and Saarinen's final design of 1906 reflects this criticism directly. That this was more than a passing accommodation on Saarinen's part is evident

from his subsequent work which was decidedly subject to the style of van de Velde; namely, his Molchow House built in Mark Brandenberg, Germany in 1905 and his Finnish Parliament competition entry of 1908. As far as its typological organization was concerned the Helsinki Station seems to have been modelled on the gargantuan German termini built after the Franco-Prussian war to facilitate the future mass movements of troops by rail (see Eggert and Faust's Frankfurt-am-Main terminus completed in 1888).

Overall view of the main facade

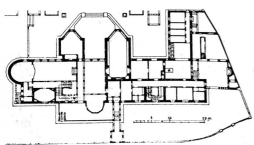

Derived in its general organization from C.R. Mackintosh's *Haus eines Kunstfreundes* competition entry of 1901, this house represents the ultimate crystallization of the *Jugendstil:* that is to say the point at which the free-flowing Pan-erotic qualities of the style became overlaid by a thin veneer of frozen gridded planes. As Eduard Sekler has pointed out, the bronze cornices which delimit these planes are cast in the form of cable mouldings, which seem to issue from the feet of the four Atlas figures at the crest of the tower. This continuous seam has the effect of stressing the planar nature of the volume at the expense of its mass, and in so doing it imparts a certain weightlessness to the entire structure. It is as though the building had literally been fabricated out of cardboard. Instead it is actually constructed of reinforced masonry and faced with thin sheets of Norwegian marble. This atectonic expression is virtually identical to that used by Behrens in his Oldenburg pavilions of 1905, and for which an equivalent exists in the double height entry hall of the Stoclet Palace, where the gallery spandrels have no apparent structural connection whatsoever to the pilasters which support them. This house was explicitly built under the sign of the *Sezession* with Athena, the muse of the movement, standing guard over the entrance and a diminutive laurel dome, taken from Olbrich's *Sezessionbau* crowning the whole composition. As the last monument of the *Sezession,* one is uncertain as to whether it should be prized for its brilliant crystallization of a particular sensibility, or alternatively, valued as the ultimate Secessionist setting for Klimt's mosaic mural "The Kiss," which adorns and patently dominates the dining room of the house. The conflict between symmetry and asymmetry evident in the opposition that occurs between front and back in Wright's Winslow House is here reversed. At the same time, this split of formal versus informal, is integrated into the whole composition. The axis dividing the dining and smoking rooms and linking the hall to the "doric" fountain in the garden is offset here on the garden side by the asymmetrical placement of the service wing. Moreover, an unrelenting formality permeates the entire house, from the checker-board "quadrat" tiles of the entry vestibule to the *Wienerwerkstatte* cutlery and tableware which Hoffmann had designed himself.

Overall view and main floor plan

This four-storey structure (Perret's first attempt at an unfaced reinforced concrete frame), his *première tentative (au monde) du béton armé esthetique,* was erected in 1905, in the same year that his father died and the family contracting firm began to trade under the name of Perret Frères. Of very similar form as an exactly contemporaneous structure erected in New York, this cul-de-sac building at the end of the rue de Ponthieu was one of the earliest mechanical stacking garages. It is ironic that such a utilitarian programme should have been given a treatment that is almost liturgical, with the central gantry bay rendered as a surrogate "nave" and the parking galleries to either side as aisles. This latent ecclesiastical feeling — to be built out literally in Perret's Notre-Dame-du-Raincy Church of 1922 — was to be further reinforced by the large decorative window spanning above the main entrance to the "nave." Aside from this ultimately Gothic reference, the pioneering importance of this work lies in its effort to bring the concrete frame under the rubric of classical form. As Reyner Banham has observed: "The facade is composed of a rhythmic *travée* of pseudo-pilasters disposed 3:5:3, the rhythm being counted off by the windows that occupy what would (in a Chicago building) be termed an 'attic frieze'." One may think of this as an early effort to humanize the normative technique of the Hennebique reinforced concrete systems, following its popularization by Paul Christophe in his book *Le béton armé et ses applications* of 1902. This much is surely evident from the modelling of the facade: the projection of the "pilasters," the recession of the spandrels, and the thin profile of the surrogate cornice terminating the composition. This syntax came to be further elaborated by Paul Guadet (Julien Guadet's son) in the house that he built for himself in the Boulevard Murat, Paris in 1910.

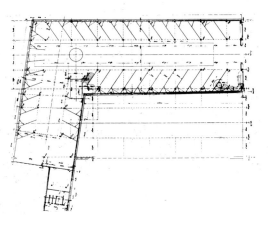

Left: plan
Center: street facade
Right: view of interior

Stimulated by his visit to England in 1894, Guimard's first essay in an exotic, rustic manner came with his quite uninhibited Castel Henriette, finished in Sèvres in 1900 and demolished 69 years later. This house, "Part fortress, part folly and part shrine," as Gillian Naylor has characterised it, may be seen as the *hameau* obsession of Marie Antoinette at Versailles taken to fantasmagoric not to say ironic extremes, so much so that the Castel Henriette verged on being a parody of itself. Guimard's country house formula with its jaunty roofs, wide overhanging eaves supported on outlandish brackets, random-rubble stonework, and precision masonry in brick, was reworked with greater control in the Castel Orgeval, built at Villemoisson in 1905 and as yet still standing. Less flamboyant than the Castel Henriette and more rustic than the near symmetrical Hôtel Nozal, in the rue de Ranelagh, Auteuil, of about the same date, the Castel Orgeval demonstrates how Guimard would modulate his domestic expression or what he called the *sentiment* of the job according to the personality of the owner. He also supposedly took into consideration the social status of the work and the general feel of the *genius loci*. Like Philip Webb and Viollet-le-Duc, but with greater self-consciousness and different expressive consequences, Guimard held the view that all authentic cultural expression must of necessity reflect the idiosyncrasies of the given region, landscape, climate, epoch, society, culture and craft.

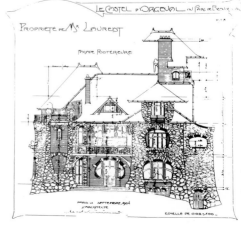

134 *Above: overall view*
  Below: garden elevation
135 *Above: view from the garden*
  Below left: detail around service entry
  Below right: detail around porch

Of approximately the same date as his Post Office Savings Bank, Wagner's St. Leopold Church was built on the crest of a hill, thereby terminating the main axis of his Lupus Sanatorium which was afterwards realized on the slope below in 1909. In as much as this was the most honorific work that he ever built, the Am Steinhof Church may be seen as the culmination of Wagner's "neo-classical" manner, as set forth in his book *Moderne Architektur* of 1895. While a church could hardly have been regarded as new programme, Wagner approached its form in an entirely new way, rendering its massive masonry as though it were the outer cladding of a lightweight metal structure. As in the Savings Bank one encounters an external finish consisting of thin sheets of sterzing marble held in place by metal rivets and once again Othmar Schimkowitz's metal angels, wreaths and acroteria are used to ornament and stress the salient features of the form. This time, however, the metalwork is copper or copper-plated iron rather than aluminium; the radial ribwork, the cupola and the cross all being verdigris picked out in gold against the verdigris of the dome. In this way, as Leonardo Benevolo has written: "... the traditional repertoire was given new life by the transposing of formal values from plastic to chromatic, from the three dimensional to the flat (Riegl would say, from tactile to optical values)." While it has none of the prophetic tone of the Post Office banking hall, the Am Steinhof Church interior is clearly the most spectacular building of Wagner's career; its flattened Soanesque "false" vault standing in surprising contrast to the high, iron framed and timber clad dome springing over the crossing above. Where the one served to intensify the black, white and gold revetment of the inner space, the other signalled its traditional silhouette across the profile of the valley.

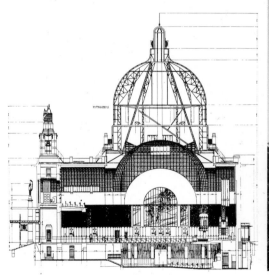

136 *View toward the altar*
137 *Left: front elevation and section*
 Right: overall view

137

In effect a joint creation by Antonio Gaudí and his young assistant, the painter/architect Jose Maria Jujol, the Casa Batlló is an elaborate transformation of an existing building. Built next to the elegant but relatively more orthodox Casa Ametller designed by Puig y Cadafalch, the Casa Batlló is one of the first buildings by Gaudí with a largely mosaic surface. This facade, created out of broken and discarded pieces of coloured ceramic is highly iridescent, fluctuating in the light, as it reflects a series of aqueous hues ranging from light blue, to yellow, ochre and white. The strange, orange and green, humpbacked and pierced roof profile which dominates the structure is in part an allusion to the mountain of Montserrat and in part a reference to the legend of St. George and the Dragon, which seems to have played a major part in the mythology of Catalonian Nationalism. The turret, which passes through the roof form, capped by a cross and enriched with the gold initials of the Holy Family, is replete with equally ambiguous symbolism: the turret corresponding to the triumphant lance of the sovereign church, and the roof profile to the back of the dragon. Similar semi-figurative interpretations can no doubt be attributed to the bone-like concrete forms which frame the *piano nobili* of the Batlló apartment, looking onto the Paseo de Gracia. Internally, the building seems to have been planned around the traditional Barcelona light court. However, in this instance the court is little more than a seven-storey, stair/lift well, divided into two connected parts and lined from top to bottom in tiles which gradate in colour from white at the bottom to sky blue at the top. An elaborate, organically profiled stair leads from the street mezzanine to the principal apartment of the Batlló family. The interior of this principal apartment is treated in an equally fluid and organic manner. An almost normative order is restored on the garden facade, where the polychrome mosaic and the repeated balcony grills culminate at roof level in a brightly coloured mural.

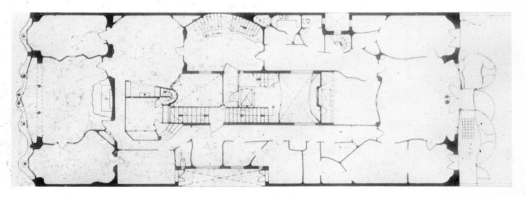

138 *Overall view from the street*
139 *Above left: roof and turret*
    Below left: light well
    Right: principal room on piano nobili
    Bottom: floor plan of piano nobili

Known locally as "La Pedrera" (the quarry), the Casa Milà, has a mountainous, undulating, sombre stone facade hung basically onto a steel frame which is totally concealed. As in the Casa Batlló and in his work on the Park Güell, the principles of Viollet-le-Duc which certainly served as his point of departure in the Casa Vicens, have now been totally abandoned. The object and aim is essentially plastic and fantasmagoric. Gaudí here, as elsewhere, reveals himself as a man obsessed with two strangely interacting visions; a mystical, almost primitive Christianity linked to the mythical, site of Montserrat (alluded to here in the body of the building and in the profile of the roof) and a pantheistic, almost Greek involvement with the marine based civilization of the Mediterranean. This last is perhaps most evident here in the tortured kelplike forms adopted by the wrought-iron balconies or in the aqueous part-painted, part-mosaic, part-ceramic, wall and ceiling finishes that occur in the entrance to the large light courts and rise with the open access stairs to the *piano nobili*. Again, as in the Casa Batlló, there is an implication of rising from the ocean bed towards the light. This without doubt is the secular masterpiece of Gaudí's career, where the bonelike theme evident in the facade of the Casa Batlló has been absorbed into the whole building as a series of horizontal volcanic waves. As the poet Francisco Pujols put it: "The wind, the sun and the rain drawn out of heaven in answer to pleadings and prayers, working the stone at the command of time, are the only ones who can compare with the stone masons who roughen the stone at the command of Gaudí." At a more pragmatic level, the Casa Milà is an ingenious eight-storey residential speculative development, occupying one of the typical diagonal "clipped" corners generated by Cerda's plan for Barcelona of 1859. As in the Palau Güell, an elaborate ramp leads down from the entry courts to the stables and the storage space in the basement. While located on the fashionable Paseo de Gracia it is still difficult to comprehend the economic context of Gaudí's residential work. The room planning is organic and configured throughout without a single orthogonal wall, and one wonders what sort of market it was that could support the building of residential complexes in which every unit was absolutely unique.

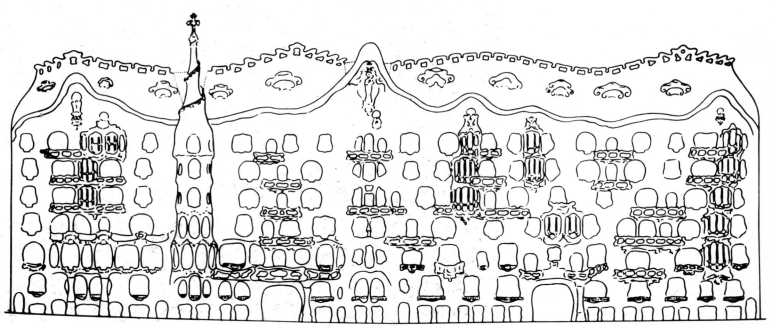

140 *Entry facade*
141 *Above: view of roof across light well*
    Below: unfolded street elevation

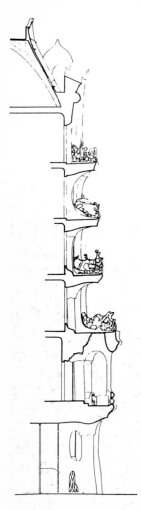

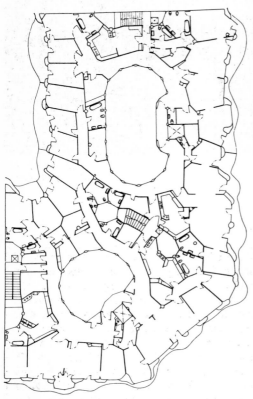

Above left: section
Below left: plan
Above right: view from the roof
Below right: entry hall

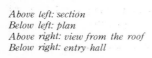

142

Left: overall view
Right: south facade

Formally opened on mid-summer night 1923, the Stockholm Town Hall is the last heroic monument of the Scandinavian National Romantic movement, which in Sweden had begun with Ferdinard Boberg's Gävle Fire Station built in 1902. First regarded as the apotheosis of Swedish architectural culture and then seen as a historicist anomaly during the functionalist (*funkis*) period of the thirties, this building now begins to take its proper place as a seminal work in Scandinavian architecture, without which the whole of Asplund's and Aalto's achievement would have been very different. Deriving in part as a plan type from the typical 17th-century Swedish castle and filtered through the skewed plan form adopted by Östberg for the design of his Bonnier Villa in 1902, this building was surely the inspiration behind Asplund's extension to the Gothenburg Law Courts (1934-37) and may even be detected in the form of Aalto's much more modest Säynätsalo City Hall of 1950.

Other than the council chamber and the usual ancilliary offices, this building consists of three major representative spaces: the Great Court, open to the sky, the so-called Golden Chamber which is a large formal reception space, and the Blue Hall which was curiously conceived in the form of an outer court which had been at some time roofed over. Each of these spaces has a distinct feeling of its own, largely deriving from its material finish and the quality of the light which it receives. Thus, the Great Court itself has an archaic, harsh, yet rooted quality as its dished surface falls down under the peristyle towards the water. On the other hand, the 150-foot-wide Golden Chamber (capable of housing a banquet of 750 people) is underlit and oriental, not to say Byzantine in tone with its marble floor, low furniture, and walls covered in gold mosaic. The Blue Hall, with its false "baldachino" roof, dressed brickwork, and Kolmard marble floor and mezzanine, changes the tone again, curiously evoking the sense of a roofed-over piazza, buried by the forces of time. The extent of the rich iconography incorporated into this building is to be best appreciated in the permanent collection of casts and maquettes which is accommodated above the vaulted entrance to the Three Crowns Tower. The wide variety of images used, varying from an Islamic crescent to a colossal statue of St. George and the Dragon, imparts to this building the feeling that it has been assembled over a long period. This impression is supported by the somewhat *recherché* materials out of which it is made: the hand-made red bricks, the grey and black granite, and the virulent green copper of the roof.

143

1906-09

FRANK LLOYD WRIGHT
Robie Residence
Chicago, Illinois, U.S.A.

Built for a bicycle manufacturer on a narrow subdivision in the then still growing district of Hyde Park, the Robie House was in many ways a condensation of Wright's Prairie Style, with its low horizontal profile, comprised of a series of long planes, stepping back in section away from the street front. These solid elements — separated by bands of fenestration — were faced in Roman brickwork whose raked joints served to give additional stress to the horizontal emphasis of the composition, the whole being capped by a low-hipped roof, cantilevering out beyond the supporting piers by approximately twelve feet at either end.

The basic plan form of the house was divided into two parallel rectangles of different width set side by side and by-passing each other within the narrow frontage of the site. The larger of these long rectangles was devoted to living and the smaller to service facilities, such as the kitchen, the garage, the maid's quarters and the boiler house, etc. This was more or less the *parti* of Wright's Heller and Husser houses of 1896 and 1899, only now realized in a more refined form.

The main living volume on the second floor was terminated in a prowlike form at either end as though it were a ship. This volume, directly covered by the form of the hipped roof, was divided by the central chimney/stair core into the living area on one side and the dining on the other. Below this principal volume and divided in a similar manner into billiard room and children's play area, was the ancillary living space of the house opening onto a narrow sunken garden court lining the street. Access to the bedroom accommodation on the third floor was achieved by ingeniously utilizing the stair in the service wing of the house. Of all of Wright's Prairie Style houses built prior to the Wasmuth Volumes on his work of 1910-11, this was the one house in which he achieved the most total integration of furniture and fittings. Even the smallest of utilitarian details were subtly integrated into the whole, including, amongst other elements, the built-in radiators, the eaves (which also served to ventilate the main space), the recessed ceiling lighting with its louvered grill-work and last but not least the fenestration itself complete with built-in fly screens.

144 View of ship-like exterior
145 Left: stained glass door
Above right: living room
Center right: ground floor plan
Below right: second floor plan

144

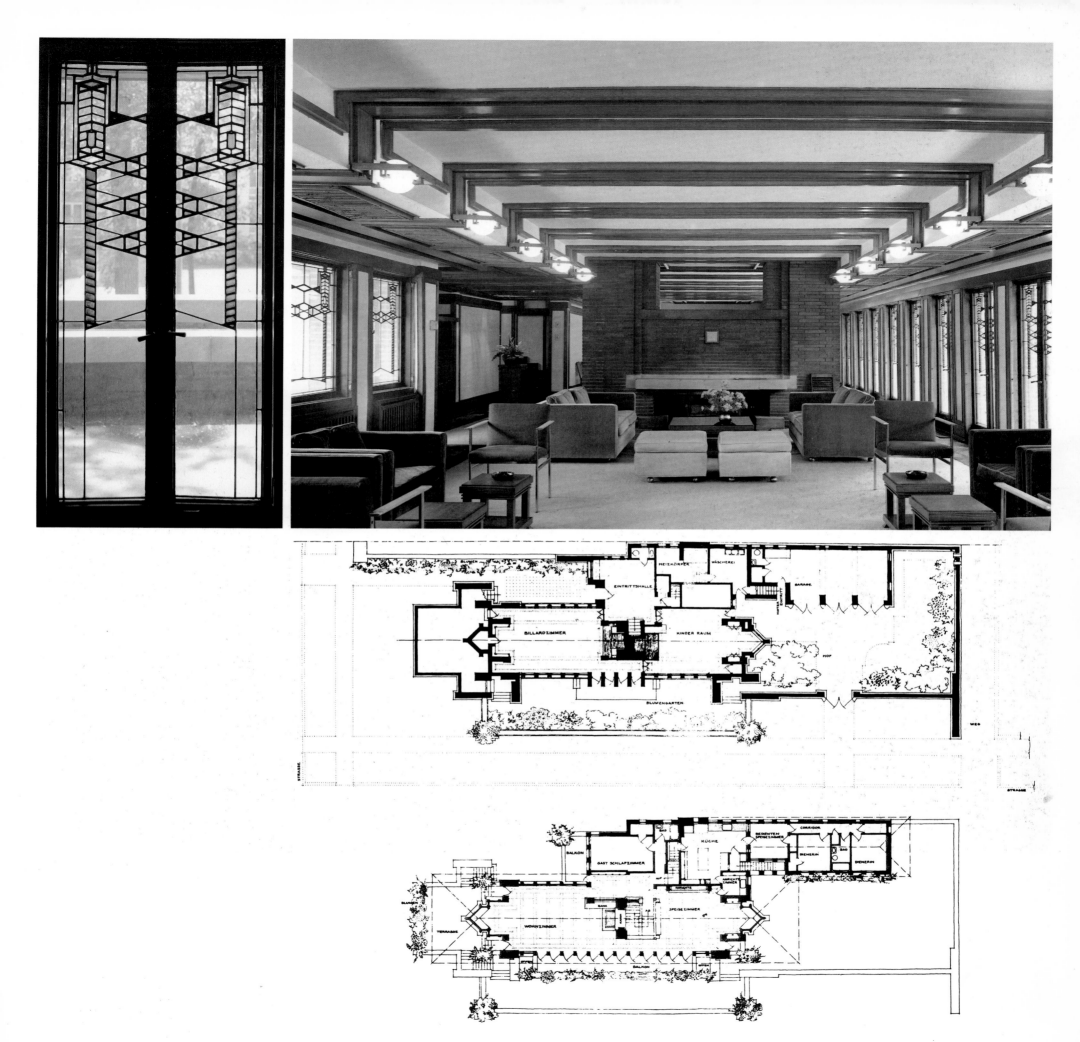

With its low-overhanging eaves, horizontal bands of fenestration, low-outriding walls and elevated basement, the Avery Coonley house epitomizes the apotheosis of Wright's so-called Prairie Style, at least in its domestic mode. And yet the plan of this "palazzo of the Prairie Houses," to quote Grant Carpenter Manson, has none of the rigour of the tartan grid imposed on the plan of Wright's Martin House, built in Buffalo in 1904. In many ways the Coonley Residence is the most "feminine" of the Prairie houses, the structure incorporating many of the more decorative themes that Wright was to return to in the 1920's; the extensive use of patterned concrete blockwork (also apparent in the Midway Gardens development of 1914) and the revealed internal timber rafters of the low-hipped roof of the living room (we may take this last as being the vestigial hall of the Gothic Revival house). As in the Unity Temple the introspective monumental quality of the blank bounding walls is foiled in a surprising way by the top-lit interior which gives the feeling of being both inside and outside at the same time. No one has captured the feeling of this interpenetration better than Manson: "In all this geometry of space and form, nature is constantly glimpsed through batteries of open casements in the distance, and is introduced into the room by jars of bitter-sweet and living plants. Across the long north wall, interrupted only by the raked brickwork of the enormous fireplace, there is a dim, painted frieze of a birch forest. These main spaces of the Coonley house combine to make what one is tempted to call "a noble apartment," for they have undeniable grandeur with their long vistas and their air of moneyed ease."

146 *Above: pool facade*
Below: aerial view
147 *Above: view from the street*
Below left: ground floor plan
Below right: interior view

146

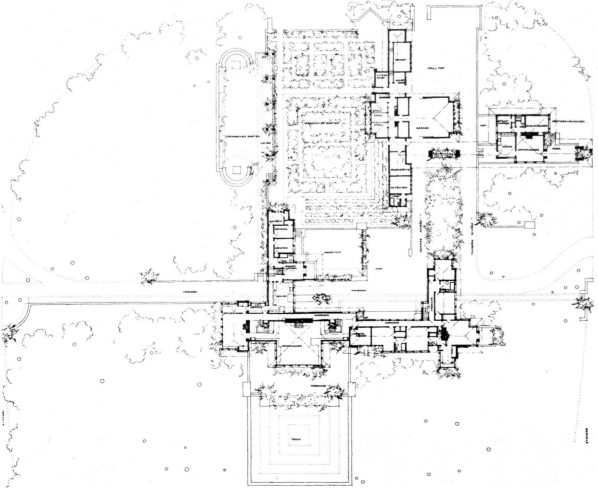

ADOLF LOOS
American Bar
Vienna, Austria

Adolf Loos's opposition to the *Jugendstil* and to the Secessionist ideal of the total work of art found its public expression in his passion for high class English tailoring and in his advocacy of American plumbing. Of all his Viennese interiors, dating from the turn of the century, this American Bar in Karnt-nerstrasse afforded him the fullest possible scope for expressing his Anglophilia. Hence the long American bar with the traditional counter mirror brilliantly reflecting the array of bottles. The same sensibility also accounts for the Thonet bent-wood bar stools and the banquet seating upholstered in black "club-room" leather. The sole break in this reinter-pretation of Anglo-Saxon culture was the elaborately coffered ceiling, whose apparent expanse was increased by its reflection in the mirrored surfaces on the upper part of the interior. The apparent volume of this narrow-fronted room was expanded almost limit-lessly by this use of opposing mirrors while the third mirrored wall facing the entrance reflected a Mackintosh-like expanse of gridded glazing above the street entrance. At the same time the dominant feature of the coffered ceiling testifies to the spirit of Neo-classicism latent in almost all of Loos's work, for while he advocated English com-fort and common sense, he never forgot for a single moment the aristocratic standards of the Prussian architect, Karl Friedrich Schinkel.

View of interior

LOUIS H. SULLIVAN
National Farmers' Bank
Owatonna, Minnesota, U.S.A.

This building, the first of Sullivan's Indian Summer, came just three years after the completion of the Carson Pirie Scott store in State Street, Chicago in 1904, and was the first of a series of five small banks built in Minnesota, Iowa and Wisconsin between 1907 and 1919. Faced in variegate red brick on a red ashlar base, this work is by far the most monumental of the five, and from an architectural standpoint it may be regarded as an effort to extend certain oriental, not to say Islamic, themes already broached in the Getty Tomb of 1891. Compositionally, however, it was not as simple, for, despite the unifying sandstone base, the structure was divided rather uncomfortably into two distinct parts: the cubic banking hall itself, situated at the corner of the intersection, and the adjunct block comprising shops, offices and a small warehouse. Sullivan's faith (or should one say delusion) that he had the capacity to create, single-handedly, a fully armed, new and totally unprecedented culture for the United States (cf. Wright's Usonian concept) was never more megalomaniacal than in this work which, like the Guaranty Building, is covered both inside and out by extensive areas of almost "delirious" terracotta decoration. For all of the precision of the furnishing and plastic authority of the ornament, there remains something disconcertingly exotic about the whole structure, particularly on the interior; an atmosphere which the unadorned brick enclosures of the offices and tellers' stalls does little to dispel. More of a railway terminus than a banking hall in the typological associations that its high volume engenders, one can never quite suppress the feeling that this space has at some time or other served the long forgotten rites of an esoteric religion. There are surely shades here of that Eldorado mythology that was soon to inform the American Art Deco expression of the late twenties. And yet as Bush-Brown has argued, this is "... Sullivan's most successful interior space, for its geometry and subdivisions and lighting all consistently reinforce the statement made by the mass. Moreover, if our attention can turn to the furnishings for a moment, the paintings, furniture and especially the clock and tellers' wickets show Sullivan's insistence upon making utilitarian things become more than mere unrelated tools; he neither exposed the machine nor hid it; rather he adorned it and made it sculptural — a mature understanding that satisfying performance does not occur if naked machines are permitted to intrude their severe lines into the human world." This somewhat romantic stance which here meets in retrospect with a contemporary critic's approval, was indubitably Sullivan's life-long conviction about the task of architecture, even if this ran counter to the pure functionalism which he is supposed to have fathered.

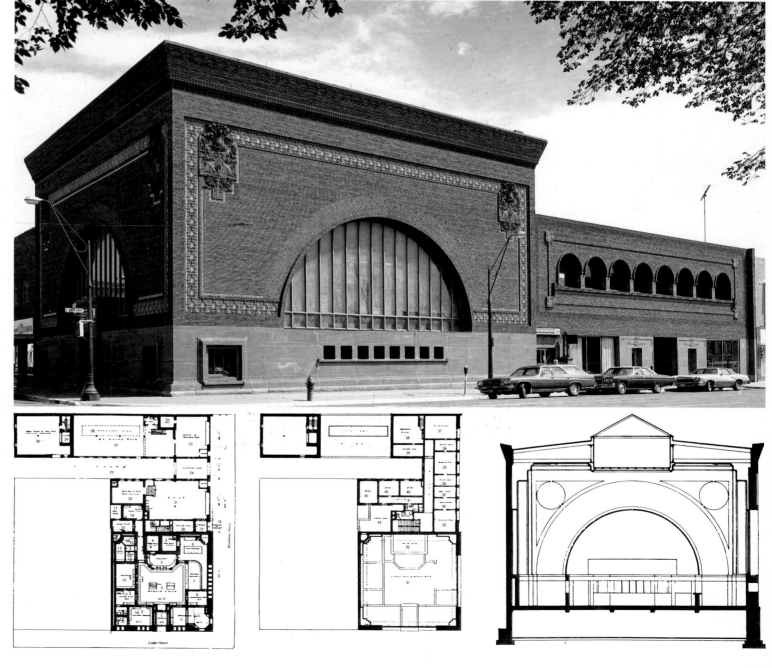

149 Above: overall view
Below, from left:
main floor plan, upper floor plan and section
150 Banking hall

JOSEF MARIA OLBRICH
Hochzeitsturm & Exhibition Bldgs.
Darmstadt, Germany

This tower, together with its adjacent pavilions, was built on the embanked earthworks of a disused reservoir, overlooking the Darmstadt Artists' Colony. As such, it may be read as Olbrich's farewell to the city which had so faithfully patronized his work over the previous decade. This complex, completed barely a year before his untimely death in 1908, represents a transitional phase in his style just before he turned to work in Düsseldorf in a manner that was unexpectedly derivative in tone — his Neo-Gothic Tietz department store and his Neo-classic Feinhals Villa, both of 1908. Against the assured air of these "historicist" pieces, the Hochzeitsturm seems exploratory and tentative. The tower itself (built in celebration of Ernst Ludwig's marriage), is patently mediaeval in its Baltic and Hanseatic references, while the pavilions are *atectonic* and crypto-classical as any building by Behrens or Hoffmann of comparable date (cf. Behrens's Oldenburg Pavilions and Hoffmann's Palais Stoclet both of 1905). No two works from the same hand and built at the same time could be more unalike than the tower and its attendant pavilions — the one of red brick and roofed in burnished copper, with asymmetrical fenestration and a blue and gold mosaic sun dial, the other a pyramidal composition of silent, rendered surfaces amounting to asymmetrical crypto-classical masses, capped by rather incongruous high-pitched Germanic roofs. This altogether disparate assembly of elements was given a certain unity by a series of stepped reinforced concrete pergolas. Olbrich obviously thought of this stepped form (which incidentally never seems to have been properly planted) as the turns of a mythic mountain/labyrinth from which, presumably, the future energy of the Artists' Colony was destined to flow.

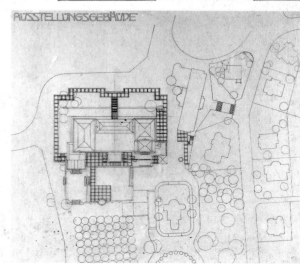

Left: view of Hochzeitsturm
Top right: view of pavilions
Center right: entrance to Hochzeitsturm
Bottom right: site plan

1908-10

PETER BEHRENS
KARL BERNHARD
AEG Turbine Factory
Huttenstrasse, Berlin, Germany

Commissioned early in 1908 and designed in close collaboration with the engineer Karl Bernhard, this vast erecting shed inaugurated Behrens's industrial work for the Allgemeine Elektricitats Gesselschaft (AEG). Contrary to Bernhard's laconic characterization of this work as " . . . nothing else but a steel framework adequate to the heavy loads of the crane, the superstructure of which is enclosed by the walls and the roof, protecting the working environment from the weather," the Turbine Factory could not have been more complex as far as its expression was concerned. In this decisive work of his mature career Behrens finally broke with the *atectonic* decorum of his geometric manner, by which his work had been more or less determined since 1903. Instead, he seems to have embraced Riegl's notion of the *kunstwollen* or "will to form" in order to impose his own creative will on the industrial format. As far as Behrens was concerned such undertakings could not be simply represented in terms of form following function. Instead it was essential that the determining forces of industrial society be reified as the sublime instruments of civilization and progress, that is, as the appropriate subject of an unprecedented monumental expression. To this end, as Stanford Anderson has remarked, Behrens sought to bring the factory under the rubric of the embassy — but not in such a way as one would mistake the former for the latter. This contradictory intention seems to account for the curious form of the Turbine Factory which juxtaposed industrial elements, such as its long curtain-wall facade, with forms drawn from both vernacular and classical sources. Seen in this light the faceted roof section appears to relate to the profile of the traditional barn while the battered concrete walls of the return facade derive with equal force from classical precedent.

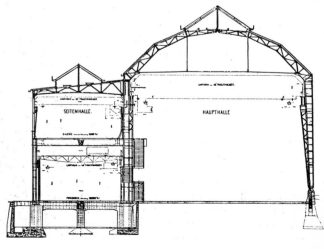

Above: exterior view
Below: section

The Gamble House, built to the designs of the brothers Charles Sumner and Henry Mather Greene may be regarded as the masterwork in a unique series of modestly scaled but nonetheless luxurious houses that the firm of Greene and Greene designed and built mostly in Pasadena in the short span of seven years, from the Theodore Irwin house of 1902 (in fact an extensive addition to a house which had been designed by the Greenes in 1900) to the Crow Residence, that Henry Greene designed in 1909. It is something of a mystery that after this last date their joint practice (lasting from 1893 to 1923) becomes increasingly without distinction. Part of this can no doubt be attributed to the cultural and economic changes that affected the region after 1911. This southern Californian oasis, initially established as a kind of sun-blessed retreat for a mid-Western and Eastern elite (the Gamble family had made their money out of soap), was rapidly becoming compromised by the expanding metropolis of Los Angeles. By 1910 wood was already becoming prohibitively expensive, and after the San Diego Exposition of 1915 the ruling taste shifted away from the Greene's homely timber construction of Japanese affinity toward the more popular, pastiche masonry style of the Spanish Colonial. In its heyday, however, the "marquetry" precision of the Greene and Greene Californian bungalow manner manifestly outclassed anything that Wright was ever to achieve in wood, and where Wright used machined scantlings to create an economic synthesis, Greene and Greene brought Western cabinet work, for a brief instant, to a level that rivaled the traditional Shinto carpentry of Japan. As C. R. Ashbee wrote in his memoirs, "I think C. Sumner Greene's work beautiful, among the best there is in this country. Like Lloyd Wright the spell of Japan is on him, he feels the beauty and makes magic out of the horizontal line, but there is in his work more tenderness, more subtlety, more self-effacement than in Wright's work.... He took us to his workshops where they were making without exception, the best and most characteristic furniture I have ever seen in this country. There were beautiful cabinets and chairs of walnut and lignum-vitae, exquisite dowelling and pegging, and all in a supreme feeling for material, quite up to the best of our English craftsmanship."

Greene and Greene created total works of art in which no detail was left to the discretion of the craftsman — the brothers designing every cantilever, bracket, joint, strap, spout, switch and air vent. The internal structure of the house, that is to say the basic framing, panelling, and staircases (usually in mahoghany) were all detailed and made in such a way as to constitute an elaborate sculpture of hand-rubbed planks, tenoned and dowelled into place with breathtaking precision. While ostentatiously overhanging eaves, exposed rafteres, and wide sleeping porches comprised the external image of this West Coast style, the main thrust of the Greene brothers resided in their Japanese influenced interiors, for which they designed everything from the furniture to the carpets, from stained glass to silverware, from light fittings to flower beds. This *Gesamtkunstwerk* possibly reached its apotheosis in the triptych glazing of the Gamble House entrance hall, where delicately assembled fragments of Tiffany glass outlined the organic silhouette of a "tree of life" against the vertical planked screen of the porch and entrance door.

153 Detail of truss and lantern, living room inglenook
154 Left: first floor and second floor plans
    Above right: front facade (Photo: T. Kitajima)
    Below right: garden facade (Photo: T. Kitajima)
155 Above: living room inglenook
    Below: dining room

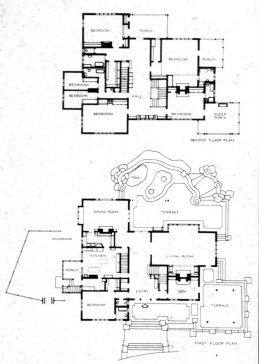

1908-28
RUDOLF STEINER
with Carl Schmid-Curtius,
Ernst Aisenpries and others
Goetheanum I & II
Dornach, near Basel, Switzerland

Both of these structures, successively erected on a hill top site near Basel, were based to varying degrees on a prescription given by the polymath Steiner to the young Anthroposophist, E.A. Karl Stockmeyer, who subsequently built a miniature prototype at Malsch, near Karlsruhe in 1908. This model was a three part, domed space, which was to be compounded out of three intersecting ellipsoids. In the built version these ellipsoids were carried at their intersection by fourteen wooden columns, whose carved profiles (vaguely reminiscent of van de Velde's columns in the Volkwang Museum) were ostensibly based on Goethe's morphological studies. After this strange and somewhat abortive attempt, Steiner modified his paradigm of the Anthroposophical cult building to a much simpler form, structurally based on the intersection of two unequal spheres; this was to be the form of the first Gotheanum, that was built in

concrete and timber, on the hill at Dornach (1913-20) to the designs of Steiner and Carl Schmid-Curtius. This decisive step in the evolution of the Anthroposophical church seems to have been based on both pragmatic and iconographic considerations. In the first place the Anthroposophical rite, now to be based on Steiner's eurhythmic mystery plays, required an auditorium and a stage; in the second place he regarded the larger and smaller spheres as standing for the "physical" auditorium and "spiritual-sensory" stage respectively. The precise degree of their intersection was such as to relate them, while still maintaining their separate identity. While the detailed structure of the first Goetheanum was predicated on a most elaborate form of number mysticism (the pentagram, etc.), the subsequent development of the site (1913-25) as an Anthroposophical colony (clustered about a "sacred" acropolis complete with its temple)

came closer than either Darmstadt or Park Meerwijk, to realizing the ultimate *Jugendstil* and Expressionist dream of building a utopian garden settlement about a central cult building or *Stadtkrone*.

The destruction by fire of the first Goetheanum on the last night of 1922, led to its subsequent replacement by a second and much larger auditorium built exclusively in reinforced concrete and completed in 1928 to the detailed designs of Ernst Aisenpries and others, three years after Steiner's death. While this building was by no means so rigorously cabalistic in its volumetric organization as the first Goetheanum it nonetheless developed the plastic lower roof profile of its predecessor into one of the most striking sculptural concrete buildings of the twentieth century, anticipating to some degree Le Corbusier's Ronchamp Chapel to be built nearby, in the Jura, some thirty years later.

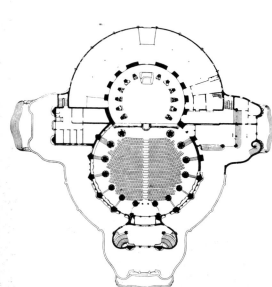

156 *Above: Goetheanum I, view through foliage*
  Below left: Goetheanum I, under construction
  Below right: plan
  Photos reproduced from Die Architektur
  des Expressionismus *by W. Pehnt*
157 *Left: Goetheanum II, entry stair hall*
  Right: Goetheanum II, main facade

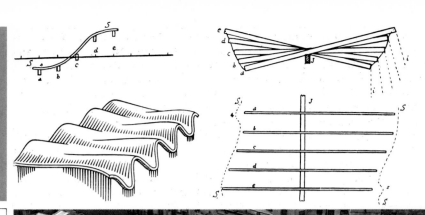

1910

BERNARD MAYBECK
First Church of Christ, Scientist
Berkeley, California, U.S.A.

Gaudí's career is of course inseparable from his highly imaginative use of the Catalonian vault, which in any event was an extremely ancient form of construction dating back to the Moorish invasion of Spain and possibly beyond. He was perhaps never to demonstrate its principle so simply as in this small scale structure, built on the grounds of the Sagrada Familia. Charged with a low budget, Gaudí chose the flat type of *solera* vault, consisting of three layers of thin, broad (**Guastavino**) tiles, bonded over each other and laid as a conoidal surface whose supporting rafters follow the trajectory of a sine curve at their extremities. These structural members span onto a central steel I-beam running down the main space of the school. The walls are made out of exactly the same material and complement the curve of the roof vault, with an undulation of their own.

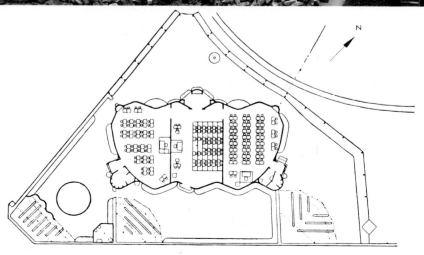

Top: detail of the vault
Center: aerial view
Bottom: plan

Despite his almost fortuitous educaiton in Paris at the École des Beaux-Arts (in the same studio that had partly trained H.H. Richardson), Maybeck (1862-1957) never seems to have aspired to the consistent practice of a style. He preferred instead to approach every building task as though it bore no relation whatsoever to what had preceded it, even within the evolution of his own work. He was perhaps the only professional of this century, who remained (in the original sense of this pejorative term) an amateur; that is to say he was a man obsessed with *ad hoc* creation as a daily activity, and there is something about his overall achievement that makes him comparable to such an eccentric figure as Bruce Goff. He seems to have practiced according to his mischievious claim that he had never been an architect but rather just a man who preferred "one line better than another." His extensive but understandably uneven output attained a remarkable level of audacity and conviction on three separate occasions in buildings which transcended the rather inconsistent folksiness of his domestic architecture. The first two "masterpieces" were built for Phoebe Apperson Hearst — Hearst Hall, erected at Berkeley, for the University of California in 1899 (Maybeck's first work of consequence in the Bay Area) and Wyntoon, a Shingle Style masonry pile built for Mrs. Hearst's own occupation in 1902. Where the former was a shingle-clad, timber-framed reception hall measuring 60 by 140 feet and roofed by Neo-Gothic, laminated timber arches, 54 feet high, the latter was a subtle composition comparable to the finest National Romantic works of Eliel Saarinen (cf. Hvittrask, built outside Helsinki in 1902). This Christian Science Church was the final golden moment in Maybeck's strange career when his exuberant and often sensitive powers of invention more or less managed to balance his almost pathological delight in the expedient use of cheap industrial materials — such as the asbestos cement sheet and factory glazing employed here. For once the brilliance of his pseudo-Japanese pagoda style was to triumph over his ever latent tendency to allow a life-long obsession with the Middle Ages to degenerate into "arty" versions of carpenter's Gothic.

Above left: south facade
Below left: detail of main beams
Right: view toward the altar
Photos: T. Kitajima

159

The Steiner House clearly represents Loos's first full scale attempt at achieving a mode of expression which would deliberately exclude fantastic and historicistic references from the form of modern building. Loos rejected the primary architectural legacies of the nineteenth century which had inspired modern architecture up to that point — namely, the Vernacular as it had been reinterpreted through the Arts and Crafts and *Jugendstil* traditions and Classical form, as this had appeared in the Romantic Classical School of von Klenze, Langans and Schinkel, and in the work of the so-called Schinkelschuler architects, of whom the Viennese architect Otto Wagner was the latest adherent. Having distinguished between art, architecture and building in his essay *Architektur* of 1910, Loos argued that most modern building programmes were inappropriate cultural vehicles for the creation of architecture. On the other hand, he saw with comparable lucidity that the newly urbanized populace of Vienna had no chance whatsoever of recovering the lost culture of their rural vernacular and that the substitute ersatz vernacular of the *Jugendstil* was by definition "uprooted" and urbanized and hence necessarily devoid of authenticity. By a similar token he regarded classicism as the style of the benighted aristocracy and hence an inappropriate means in which to re-present the status of the *nouveau riche*. As he was to write in 1910: "A house should appeal to everybody, as distinct from works of art which do not have to appeal to anyone . . . The work of art aims at shattering man's comfortable complacency. A house must serve one's comfort. The work of art is revolutionary, the house conservative. The work of art points man in the direction of new paths and thinks to the future. The house thinks of the present. Man loves everything that serves his comfort. He hates everything that wants to tear him away from his secure and safe position, and is burdensome. And so he loves the house and hates art." A sentence later Loos continues, "Only a very small part of architecture belongs to art: the tomb and the monument. Everything else, everything which serves a purpose should be excluded from the realms of art." Loos attempted to overcome this cultural impasse through combining a policy of ruthless reduction with the strategy of indulging in a *répétition différente* in which conventional elements would reappear as before but in a context which would be rendered in such a way as to make them deliberately disjunctive. While the exterior on the garden side of the Steiner Villa is obviously cast in a symmetrical if not classical format, it is patently reduced to the essentials of windows punched into bare walls. Similarly, the interior of the dining room of the house epitomizes Loos's capacity to evoke a conservative and comfortable environment which is at the same time possessed of an uncanny air of estrangement. The "fake" beams on the dining room ceiling look as though they are about to become dislodged from the surface which they are ostensibly supporting. Much to the same end the top of the wooden wainscoting passes under the sill of the adjacent clerestory so as to achieve the willful conjunction of ultimately incompatible "codes"; on the one hand the signifier of Anglo-Saxon, Yeoman tradition, on the other an oblong window, sub-divided into small rectangular panes in such a way as to resemble a traditional Japanese *Shoji*.

Left: plan and section
Right: east garden facade
Photo reproduced from Adolf Loos:
Pioneer of Modern Architecture
by L. Münz & G. Künstler

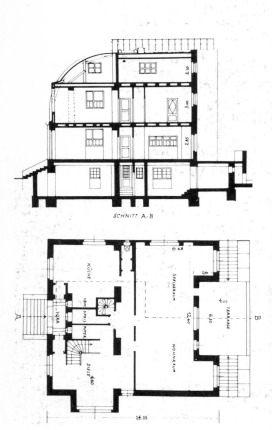

SCHNITT A-B

This large industrial complex is the first independent work of the partnership of Walter Gropius and Adolf Meyer. The style of this shoe last factory directly reflects the three years that Gropius had spent with Behrens in Berlin, prior to setting up on his own account in 1910. A number of features in the office building are reminiscent of Behrens's early work for AEG; above all the suspended glass wall which obviously derives from the glazed gable of his AEG Turbine Factory of 1908. While the industrial work of both Behrens and Gropius may appear, at first glance, to be purely functional, both men employed classical devices in the manipulation of their forms. The principle of *entasis* appears to an equal degree in the battered corners of Behrens's Turbine Factory and in the upward diminishment of the column section in Gropius's Fagus-Werk. This gradual setback of the brick-encased column toward the top of the structure, increases the effective depth of the shadow cast by the perpendicular curtain wall onto the engineering brick facade. In a similar way the Schinkelesque battered corners of the AEG Turbine Factory (executed in reinforced concrete) are reinterpreted in industrial glazing to the corner stair towers of the Fagus-Werk head building. This brilliant exercise in the aesthetic use of industrial elements served as the prototype for the Model Factory that Gropius and Meyer were to build for the Cologne Werkbund Exhibition of 1914.

End facade

161

162-3 *Overall view*
163 *Above: stair hall*
    Below: plan

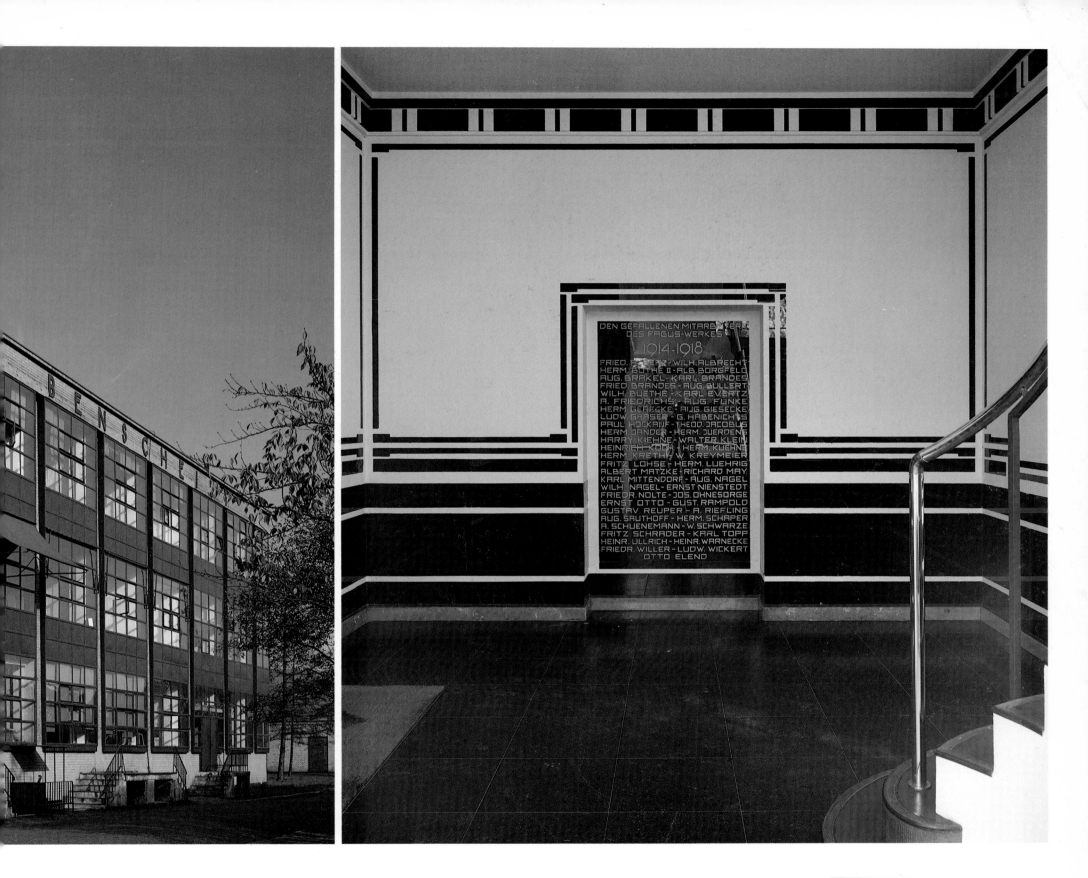

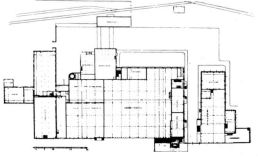

1910
ANTOINE POMPE
Clinic for Dr. van Neck
Saint Gilles, Brussels, Belgium

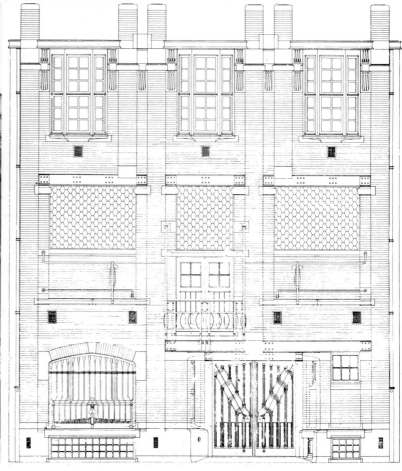

164 *Above: view of the facade* **(after alteration)**
    Below left: overall view of the altered facade
    Below right: front elevation
165 *Above left: section*
    Below left: ground floor and second floor plans
    Right: entrance

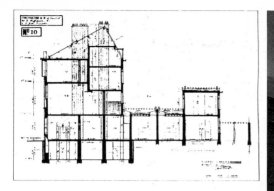

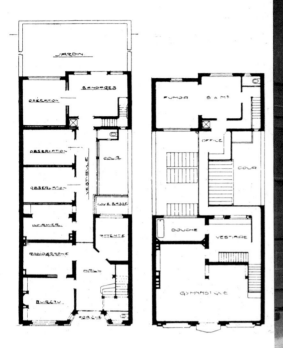

This orthopedic clinic, built for Dr. van Neck in 1910 at Saint Gilles, together with a villa, "La Sapinière," erected in the Avenue de la Sapinières, Uccle, in 1926 are the two remaining masterworks of Antoine Pompe's career. Pompe, born in 1873, practised architecture as an architect/artisan from 1904 to 1947. Like other major artists of his generation, such as Henry van de Velde, Peter Behrens and much later (and at a more comparable level) Pierre Chareau, Pompe came to architecture by way of an elaborate training as an artist/artisan. At the age of 13 he entered l'Académie Royale des Beaux-Arts in Brussels to study metal engraving under Mortelmans, and at 17 he entered an advanced drawing course at the Kunstgewerbeschule in Munich. He spent the period from 1893 to 1904 working as a designer/draughtsman for various enterprises varying from contractors in wrought-iron metalwork to furniture builders like George Hobé. In 1904 he started to work with the architect Leener on the Grand Hôtel de Bruxelles and around 1908 he miraculously acquired the commission for the van Neck Clinic.

On the face of it, this structure is simple enough: a three-storey front building with a single and two-storey extension to the rear. The ground floor is devoted exclusively to the clinic, the first floor, illuminated with three large openings in glass bricks, is a gymnasium and the second floor, announced by the three bay windows, is an apartment. The building is faced in a light gray Denain brick set on top of a dressed stone plinth. The wrought ironwork for the entry door, the window grill-work, the central balcony and the guard rails to either side are all designed by Pompe and possibly even manufactured under his direct supervision. To-

gether with the exposed sill beams and the brackets between the bay windows, all the metalwork was originally painted blue and the woodwork white. The wrought-iron facade furniture has been ingeniously designed so that the central balcony may be dismantled to admit large objects to the gymnasium while the guard rails of the flanking narrow ledges permit the cleaning of the glass bricks.

By any standards this is a remarkable work for its date, both technically and aesthetically. Technically, above all, for its use of large areas of diamond shaped glass bricks for which the sole precedent of an earlier date (at least in domestic work) would surely have been the rear stairs to Auguste Perret's 25 bis rue Franklin Apartments in Paris of 1904. Aesthetically this work represents an abrupt point of departure in Pompe's own career for only six years before he had

projected a house in a late Anglo-Saxon Arts and Crafts manner, a work that could have come easily from the hands of either Lethaby or Lutyens at a slightly earlier date. But the van Neck Clinic is clearly in advance of its time for save for the Soanesque, Mackmurdo-like modelling of the facade — particularly the upper storey — this could easily be a work from the Art Deco period of the late twenties. Taking a certain cue from Berlage rather than from the exhausted Belgium Art Nouveau or from Olbrich or Behrens, who had both turned crypto-Classic by 1910, Pompe was to arrive at his mature style almost overnight and while this work does not have the assurance of "La Sapinière" or other houses by Pompe of the mid-twenties, it was nonetheless to remain the most striking, proto-constructivist work of his entire career.

5 Industrial Production and the Crisis of Culture 1851-1910

Unremittingly, science enriches itself and life with newly discovered useful materials, with natural powers that work miracles, with new methods and techniques, with new tools and machines. It is already evident that inventions no longer are, as they had been in earlier times, means for warding off want and for helping consumption; instead want and consumption are means to market the inventions. The order of things has been reversed.

What are the necessary consequences? The modern age finds no time to adjust to the benefits that were half forced upon it and to become their master. It is like a Chinaman who is obliged to eat with knife and fork. For speculation combines with means and presents us with palatable benefits; where there are none, speculation creates a thousand useful things, large and small; when it can no longer invent something new, longforgotten and troublesome tasks are revived — the hardest prophyry and granite are cut like chalk and polished like wax, ivory is softened and pressed into shapes, caoutchouc and gutta-percha are vulcanized and used to produce imitations of carvings in wood, metal, or stone, whereby the natural aspects of the simulated materials are greatly surpassed. Metal is no longer cast or embossed, but it electrolytically deposited with hitherto unknown natural powers . . . The machine sews, knits, embroiders, carves, paints, invades far into the domain of human art, and puts every human skill to shame . . . The abundance of means is the first serious danger with which art has to struggle. This term is in fact paradox (there is no abundance of means, but rather a lack of ability to master them), yet it is justified insofar as it correctly describes the absurdities of our situation. In practice we labour in vain to master the body of materials, particularly in terms of its spiritual aspects. Science provides the tools for any further utilization in practice but no style has developed during the many hundreds of years of common use . . . What a marvellous invention is the gas lamp! How it enriches (apart from the unlimited importance to the necessities of life) our festivities! Nevertheless, in the salons one seeks to hide the gas jets so that they appear like candles or oil lamps . . .

Style is the elevation to artistic significance of the content of the basic idea and all the external and internal coefficients, which by their incorporation into a work of art are able to modify it actively. Lack of style is, by this definition, the term for what is lacking in a work, which accrues from a disregard for the basic idea and from clumsiness in the esthetic utilization of the available means for its accomplishment. The basic form, as the simplest expression of the idea is modified particularly by the materials that are used for the improvement of the form, as well as by the instruments employed. Finally, there exist many influences outside the work itself which are important factors contributing to its design, — for example, location, climate, time, custom, particular characteristics, rank, the position of the person for whom the work is intended, and so on . . .

Where will the depreciation of material that results from its treatment by machines, from the substitutes for its, and from so many new inventions, lead? And where the depreciation of labour, of paintings, of fine art, and furnishings, which originates from the same causes? Of course, I am not speaking of depreciation in price but rather of depreciation in significance, in the idea . . . How will time or science bring law and order into this until now thoroughly confused state of affairs? How will it prevent the general devaluation from expanding into the area of work which is executed by hand in the true old fashion, so that one may find more in it than affectation, antiquarianism, superficial appearance, and obstinacy?

Gottfried Semper
Science, Industry and Art, 1852

Semper's lucid account of the impact of the machine on the world of form, particularly those forms concerned with ornamentation and use in everyday

65, 65a Catholic town in 1440 contrasted to the same town in 1840, from Pugin's Contrasts, *2nd ed. 1841.*

life, highlights the cultural crisis of the mid-nineteenth century. This crisis seems to have had its origins not in the machine *per se* but in the factory system of production which, as Robin Evans has shown, had its origins as a procedure not in the earliest textile mills but in seventeenth-century corrective institutions or workhouses; that is to say in places of solitary production which attained their "behaviouristic" perfection at the end of the eighteenth century with Jeremy and Samuel Bentham's Penitentiary Panopticon of 1797.

It is a curious historical fact that a reductive but nonetheless pertinent account of the pre-history of modern architecture could be structured about two opposed social institutions, neither of which were ever actually realized in their prescribed form. First the Penitentiary Panopticon projected as a circular "workhouse" whose perimeter would have been divided into a series of wedge-shaped prison cells radiating from the governor's house and control point in the centre and second the Phalanstery, advanced by Charles Fourier in the early 1820s, as a benevolent collective, "play-palace." The one punitive and puritan (the reification of the work ethic itself) and the other productive but highly psychological and permissive. Fourier's *Phalanstère* was destined to become the radical counter-thesis to the normative principle of divided labour or "on-line" production. It should go without saying that the alienation engendered by the rationalized methods of production has yet to be sublimated by the apparent benefits of consumerism and that the socio-cultural problems induced by the division of labour are as active today as they ever were. It is significant that Fourier's baroque palace of erotic and ludic

gratification was never built and that its nearest approximation was J.P. Godin's *Familistère*, realized at Guise, France (1859-80), and that even in this instance the place of production clearly remained separate from the place of family life and nurture.

It says much for the extraordinary intelligence and insight of the Gothicist, A.W.N. Pugin, that in his book *Contrasts* of 1836-43 he should have recognised the Panopticon as the product of a reductive Humanism; that is to say, as an invention partaking of the same secular rationality that had led straight from Leonardo da Vinci to Descartes and the emergence of the centralized normative State in 17th-century France under Colbert. For Pugin the Panopticon was the reified anti-Christ of Classicism. This much is clear from the two most polemical plates of the second edition of *Contrasts* which were to compare characteristic English towns, supposedly drawn from the periods of 1440 and 1840; the one, the walled city of Christendom clearly separated from the country and inflected by the even-textured fabric of the city with the spires of numerous churches; the other projecting its disorder into the country, a city where the rising vertical features are factory chimneys, and where riverside warehouses have displaced the "sacred" boundary of the city wall. For Pugin, stalwart supporter of Cardinal Newman's Oxford Movement after its foundation in 1883, the Panopticon personified the Protestant servitude of industrialization and divided labour. For him, as for John Ruskin and William Morris, who quite patently followed in his footsteps, the evident degeneration in the quality of art objects produced more or less by industrial means stemmed directly from the exclusion of craftwork in the division of labour. As Ruskin was to put it in his text on political economy of 1860, entitled *Unto This Last*, "It is not truly speaking, the labour that is divided, but the men; . . . so that all the little piece of intelligence that is left in a man is not enough to make a pin or a nail, but exhausts itself in making the point of a pin or the head of a nail."

While Ruskin as a committed Protestant could not assuage his anguish by adopting the stance of Catholic reform, he nonetheless maintained a fundamentally religious attitude throughout his life and his socialism was nothing if not inspired by Christian virtue. Like Pugin he valued the Gothic as the bearer of Christendom, for the primary fact that unlike the learned programmatic and Pagan iconography of the Renaissance it left room for the expression of the individual Christian soul through the spontaneous contribution of his or her craft. No one could have been more removed from the hedonistic philosophy of Fourier than Ruskin, and yet when it came to the prime source of both culture and life, their views were surprisingly similar. Thus we find Ruskin writing in his *Seven Lamps of Architecture* of 1849, ". . . the question to ask, respecting all ornament, is simply this: was it done with enjoyment?"

Enjoyment for Ruskin certainly meant natural expression and the spontaneous folk celebration of God's entire creation; of Nature in all her glory with Man at the pinnacle. To this end he was against the conventionalized ornament advocated by the circle of Henry Cole. One may even see his attitude as proto-Social Realist, in as much as his opposition to Paxton's Crystal Palace and to ferro-vitreous construction in general was based on the fact that, from a physical standpoint, a diaphanous, mass-less building technique would never be able to sustain a realistic and comprehensible iconography. Ruskin opined that the micrometer precision demanded by 19th-century tool making had already destroyed the craftsmen of his time and according to his beliefs he would have restricted the use of machinery and industrial production only to the most burdensome of tasks. Like Morris in his Utopian Socialist novel, *News from Nowhere* of 1891, he envisaged a future England where the state had withered away (in his novel Morris acknowledged Marx's prophecy) and where all distinction between town and country had disappeared; a society where the city no longer existed as a slum-ridden, overcrowded centre of industrial production; a country where wind and water were once more the generic sources of power and where the waterway and the road were the sole means of transport; an economy structured about the free association of the family or the Guild (or *Werkbund*) such as the ill-fated St. George's Guild which Ruskin himself had attempted to start in 1871. Ruskin had already tried to put his anti-mechanistic cultural thesis into practice some fifteen years before, by sponsoring the building of the University Museum in Oxford, under construction to the designs of the Irish architects Deane and Woodward from 1855 to 1859; a building which took the form of a supposedly 12th-century, Gothic Revival masonry exterior, structured about a cast- and wrought-iron, top-lit, Gothic exhibition space. Ruskin's primary contribution to this work lay in the supervision of its ornamentation, in which he encouraged the by now famous O'Shea brothers to decorate the entrance arch and the capitals of

66 *Nesfield and Shaw, Leys Wood, Sussex, 1868. Perspective.*

the peripheral pillars of the central "nave," with floral elements drawn specifically from Oxford's Botanical Gardens. And yet Ruskin allowed the ornament to be both didactic (i.e. faithfully naturalistic) and free at the same time; that is creative in the sense that the O'Sheas were at liberty to introduce parrots and owls, shaped according to the fancy of their own invention.

Ruskin's influence on the English Arts and Crafts movement began around 1851, with his association with the Pre-Raphaelite school of painting, founded three years before by the painter Dante Gabriel Rossetti, after the Nazarene school of painting that had already been established in Rome by the militant Catholic Friedrich Overbeck. Yet the Pre-Raphaelite Brotherhood lacked the discipline of the Nazarenes and both it and its publication, *The Germ*, were defunct by 1853. The second, craft-oriented phase of Pre-Raphaelite activity turns upon the meeting of William Morris and Edward Burne-Jones as undergraduates at Oxford in 1853. Oxford exposed them to the lectures of Ruskin and thus to the influence of Pugin. After their graduation in 1856, they collaborated with Rossetti on the Union Society murals at Oxford, an act which was supposed to echo in its inaugural intent, the Nazarene frescoes in Rome. Although by this date Burne-Jones had already determined to become a painter, it was to be some months before Rossetti could lure Morris to London, away from his articled position in the Oxford office of the Gothic Revivalist architect, G.E. Street.

The precipitous trajectory of Morris's subsequent career — his decision to abandon architecture for painting in 1856 and then to turn from painting to craft design after achieving his ideal, Gothic Revivalist Red House at Bexley Heath, Kent in 1859 — projected him into the forefront of English progressive design in the 1860s. In the Red House (so called for its direct use of brick) Morris's architect and life-long collaborator Philip Webb developed a tile-hung "vernacular" that was soon to inform the work of Morris's more worldly contemporaries, Richard Norman Shaw and Shaw's partner, Eden Nesfield (see their seminal domestic style as it first appeared in their house Leys Wood, built in Sussex in 1868). In the Red House, Webb established the two basic principles of his architectural carrer: first his adherence to the ir-regular (L-shaped) yeoman plan form as prescribed by Pugin, along with the mandatory double-height entry hall, minstrels' gallery and staircase; second his own obsession with the integration of a building into its locale — not only with its site but also in accordance with the dictates of the local building culture. Webb became the perennially dissatisfied "vernacular" architect; forever attempting to resuscitate local craft in his pursuit of a domestic style which while momentarily dormant would one day rise out of the culture of the people.

The Arts and Crafts movement, the so-called Free School of English Architecture, the Queen Anne Revival, and the Garden City, have their common origin in this initial collaboration of Morris and Webb and Morris's foundation of "The Firm" for the production of Pre-Raphaelite applied art. After Morris's removal to London in 1864, this Pre-Raphaelite production of furniture, stained glass, embroidery, and metalwork expanded, employing such artists as Webb, Rossetti and Burne-Jones. Morris in the interim began to devote himself more and more to literature and to two-dimensional design;

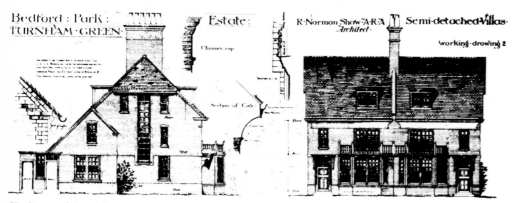

67 *Shaw, typical semi-detached house, Bedford Park, near London, 1887.*

the literature being strictly anti-Classical in its affinities (Morris produced extensive translations of Icelandic sagas and numerous volumes of poetry) and the designs being largely for wallpapers, whose conventionalized patterns were inspired by the plates of Owen Jones's *Grammar of Ornament* of 1856. Morris's career from this point forward became increasingly public, particularly after he converted the formerly loose association of Pre-Raphaelite artists into a co-ordinated team for the design and manufacture of art objects. He established this team on a commercial basis with the opening of the London showrooms of Morris and Co. in 1877. One effect of the changed scale of production was to increase the number of crafts which "The Firm" was expected to produce and to this end Morris taught himself dyeing and carpet weaving. In the same year, however, he wrote his first political pamphlet and founded the Society for the Preservation of Ancient Buildings, thereafter dividing his life equally between politics and design. In 1883, he joined Engels's Social Democratic Federation and in 1886 he founded his own Socialist League. In the ten years prior to the foundation of the League, Morris produced some 600 designs for various fabrics, but increasingly the last decade of his life was given over to writing, culminating in his famous *News from Nowhere,* published in 1891, five years before his death.

For all that they may have shared his socialist views, the Arts and Crafts architects were unable to adhere to Morris's anti-classic attitude. Not even a Puritan like Webb, whose eclectic domestic work of the 1880s (such as the house, Clouds, built at East Knoyle between 1879 and 1886) contained Classical elements drawn from Elizabethan and Georgian sources. The

progressive architects of the second half of the 1880s — men such as C.R. Ashbee, W.R. Lethaby, A.H. Mackmurdo, E.S. Prior and C.F.A. Voysey — could not bring themselves to be bound by Morris's anti-Humanism, least of all worldly figures like Richard Norman Shaw, who by the 1870s was already 'classicizing' the Queen Anne style that he and Nesfield had compounded out of the English and Dutch brick traditions. Up to his conversion to Neo-Palladianism in the early 1890s, Shaw established a formula for adopting a classic, if mannered, format in the town, such as the Old Swan House, Chelsea, of 1876, and a picturesque, vernacular one for the country, such as Leys Wood, Sussex of 1860. In 1877 Shaw designed the first garden suburb for the philanthropist Jonathan T. Carr, a development located on the outskirts of London, at Turnham Green. The brick, tile-hung, half-timbered Tudor style of this upper middle class garden village, under construction throughout the 1880s, was afterwards celebrated in the ballad of Bedford Park apocryphally attributed to Carr:

"Here trees are green and bricks are red
    And clean the face of man.
    We'll build our gardens here he said
    In the style of good Queen Anne."

This eclectic brick style extended even to the village church which, rendered without a spire in a vaguely Gothic Revival manner, audaciously displayed a Wren-like lantern on its roof. Shaw had a number of different

68 *Voysey, house in Bedford Park, near London, 1888-91. Elevations.*

69 *Voysey, project for an artist's cottage, 1889.*

architects working under his direction on Bedford Park during the next fifteen years, including Voysey who built a white-rendered, proto-modern house there for J.W. Foster in 1891. A year after taking over the commission of Bedford Park from E.W. Godwin, Shaw published, in 1878, his *Sketches for Cottages and Other Buildings.* This highly influential book illustrated numerous Shavian designs for workers' houses of various sizes. It also contained the public building typology of a small self-contained village community, featuring such structures as a school, a village hall, an almshouse and a cottage hospital. Thus in the space of two years, Shaw had not only proposed a new pattern of land settlement, but had also provided a pattern book from which to build ideal suburban communities. The idea was quick to take hold and within a decade the first paternalistic garden cities began to appear; Port Sunlight built by the soap manufacturer W.H. Lever at Liverpool in 1887, and Bourneville founded in 1895 by the confectioner George Cadbury and designed by Ralph Heaton. In 1898, in his book, *Tomorrow: A Peaceful Path to Real Reform*, Ebenezer Howard proposed his economically independent satellite garden city of limited size (30,000) surrounded by a green belt the first version of which was started at Letchworth in 1903. It is significant that this venture never really attained Howard's ideal of economic independence.

After meeting with Frank Lloyd Wright in the States around the turn of the century, the architect C.R. Ashbee was confirmed in his belief that the resolution of the dilemma posed by modern industry depended on a proper use of the machine. Like Howard and Wright, Ashbee advocated the decentralization of existing urban concentrations although unlike Morris he was opposed to the nationalization of land. While preferring liberal reform to radical socialism, Ashbee lacked a strong grasp of social reality and his Arts and Crafts country-based guild settlement foundered within two years of its foundation in 1906. A shareholder responded to Ashbee's appeal for further capital with the following words: "Cadbury's village at Birmingham is excellent as far as the cottages and all the life out of business hours goes, but modern conditions of cheap production and full use of machinery rule supreme in work hours, they have humanized leisure, you have tried to humanize work as well."

Direct social intervention was not the concern of Voysey, who in 1885 arrived at a simplicity of style that was to elude most of his contemporaries. Voysey derived his style from Webb's principles of respect for traditional methods and local materials, rather than from Shaw's formal virtuosity. In an unrealized house project of 1885, intended for his own occupation, Voysey formulated (despite the Shavian half timbering) the essential components of his style; the hipped slate roof with overhanging eaves, the wrought-iron gutter brackets, the rendered, rought cast masonry walls pierced by horizontal windows and restrained at intervals, by battered buttresses and chimneys; features which were to characterize his work over the next thirty years. Despite this simplicity, his initial apprenticeship with Mackmurdo seems to have been the source for the flowing and highly sophisticated details which became manifest in his earliest wallpaper and metalwork designs of 1890. These austere arabesques provided a necessary accent to his otherwise plain

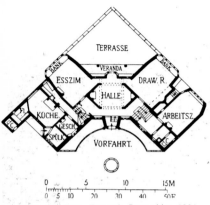

70 Prior, The Barn, Exmouth, Devonshire, 1904.
Butterfly plan.

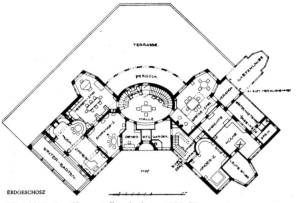

70a Muthesius, House at Freudenberg, 1907. Plan.

interiors. Unlike Morris, Voysey was possessed by a sense of restraint, almost to a fault. He stipulated that either the fabrics or the wallpaper should be patterned, but never both. His own house, The Orchard, Chorley Wood of 1899, is characteristic of his interior style; gridded balusters flooded with light, low picture rails, tiled fireplace surrounds, plain oak furniture and thick carpets. As he grew older, his two dimensional design became less figurative, and where his early furniture tended towards the organic, his later pieces were based on classical themes. Between 1889 and 1910 Voysey designed some forty houses, a number of which transcended in their white abstraction the Yeoman references of his style.

William Richard Lethaby is to be regarded as the last in a long line of English Arts and Crafts architect socialists. Following his twelve year apprenticeship with Richard Norman Shaw and his surprisingly brief career as an architect on his own account, Lethaby gave up practice to become a teacher and a public servant; initially with his principalship of the Central School of Arts and Crafts and then with his surveyorship to the fabric of Westminster Abbey. Lethaby's role in the Free Architecture movement turned on his strengths as a theoretician, evident from his first and highly influential book *Architecture, Mysticism and Myth* of 1892, in which he demonstrated how architecture had always been informed by cosmic and religious paradigms. Lethaby attempted to incorporate such symbolism into his own work, while his thesis had an immediate impact on the work of his close colleagues such as Edward Prior, whose house The Barn, built at Exmouth in 1904, was to exhibit a symbolic "brutalism" in both plan-form and fabric.

There is little doubt but that this house greatly influenced Hermann Muthesius's design for one of his earliest "English" houses, built at Freudenberg in 1907. With his entry into teaching, Lethaby shifted his attention from poetic content, to the problem of developing a correct method for the evolution of modern form. For Lethaby, the craft tradition in which he had been nurtured suddenly appeared played out. By the turn of the century he was arguing for functionalism and in 1915, while helping to organize the Design in Industry Association, he urged his fellow architects to look to Germany and the Deutsche Werkbund for the way to the future.

With the foundation of the *Deutsche Werkbund* in 1907, craft production became a matter of state policy and in this context one is hardly surprised to find that one of its founders, the Christian-socialist politician, Friedrich Naumann, had once been a disciple of Max Weber, whose concept of the *Machtstaat* or "power state" was to play such a major role in the formation of modern Germany. The other original members of the *Werkbund* were the architect Hermann Muthesius, who had become an official in the Prussian Board of Trade on his return from Japan in 1893, and Karl Schmidt, who in 1898 had founded his *Deutsche Werkstätten für Handwerkenkunst* in Hellerau, with the express intent of upgrading local craft production. Muthesius had exploited his attachment to the German Embassy in London from 1896 to 1903 as an opportunity on which to prepare the most thorough documentation ever made on the English Arts and Crafts; his three-volume study *Das Englische Haus* being published in 1904, on his return to Berlin. Where Schmidt and Naumann (like Ashbee and Wright) were convinced that

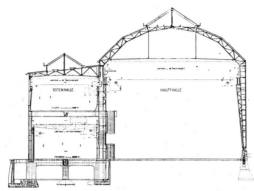

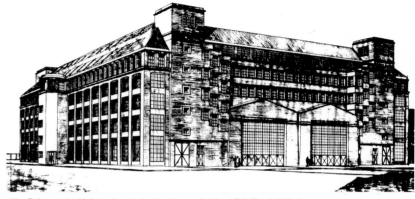

71 Behrens, cover for the AEG brochure, 1908.

72 Behrens, AEG Turbin Factory, Berlin, 1908-10. Cross section.

73 Behrens, the high-tension production factory in the AEG Humboldthain, Berlin, 1908. Early perspective drawing.

craft production could only be improved by the re-assimilation of the machine, Muthesius directly attempted to upgrade the design capacity of the society by lending his official support to Alfred Lichtwark's art school reform movement. This he did most effectively in 1903 when he secured the appointment of major artists to directorships of leading schools of applied art, Hans Poelzig going to the Breslau Academy, Peter Behrens to Dusseldorf and Bruno Paul to the School of Applied Art in Berlin. In 1907, the year that the Werkbund was founded, Muthesius was appointed to the first chair in applied art at the Berlin Commercial University. His inaugural address on the need to improve and standardize craft production on a collective basis only served to enrage further the *Fachverband für Wirtschaftlichen Interessen des Kunstgewerbes*. This national trade association of craftsmen, with its highly decentralized background, strenuously resisted the efforts of the Werkbund to evolve a state culture in applied art throughout the first decade of its existence. This conflict reflects something of the bourgeois origin of the Werkbund which sought, like Colbert in 17th-century France, to create a standard national artistic culture. On the other hand, the Werkbund's greatest supporters were removed from the government itself. They were small middle class industrialists like the typographer and printer — publisher Eugen Diederichs who, from 1912 to 1914, published the influential Werkbund year books. Since the Werkbund had been started more or less spontaneously as an association of twelve artists and twelve industrial firms, it failed to attract large industrial corporations, with the singular exception of the electrical combine *Allgemeine Elektrizitäts Gesellschaft*, which indirectly supported the

Werkbund through its appointment of Peter Behrens as its "house designer" in 1907. While the shipping lines *Norddeutsche Lloyd* and *Hamburg-Amerika* became corporate sponsors after the Werkbund moved to Berlin in 1912, the greatest success of the Werkbund lay in its influence on craft-based industrial production; that is to say on printing, ceramics and metalware, including the remarkable range of electrical equipment that Behrens re-styled for AEG between 1907 and 1910, his work for this company also ranging from graphic design to architecture.

Although the Werkbund's primary concern was product design rather than architecture, the industrial plant that Behrens also began to design for the AEG in 1908 was regarded as the architectural synthesis of its ideology. In his large AEG Humboldthain complex Behrens sought to represent the urban industrial productive unit as though it were some kind of mediaeval agrarian settlement. He seems to have envisioned it as a form of farm or rural hamlet which had undergone a strange transformation into a series of giant sheds dedicated to the manufacture of electrical equipment and grouped like glass-roofed "barns" about a "farmyard" inundated with tramways, trucks and locomotives. For Behrens the cultural mission of monumental art (i.e. architecture) was now to be extended beyond the traditional representative buildings, such as the German Embassy that he built in St. Petersburg in 1912, to embrace within its spectrum industrial production itself.

It was this drive to artistically "misrepresent" the essential status of objects (i.e. to represent as Behrens did an industrial complex as a monumental farm) that led the Viennese architect Adolf Loos to mount his

74 *A 1911 cartoonist's comment on the Goldman and Salatsch store facade.
The German text reads: "Brooding about art, the most modern man walks
through the streets. Suddenly he stops transfixed. He has found that
for which he has searched so long."*

specific attack on the Werkbund in 1908; an attack which was in effect a continuation of his opposition to the aesthetic re-design of everyday objects, already set forth in his essay, *Ornament and Crime* (1908). In an essay entitled *Cultural Degeneracy* of the same year he wrote:

The aims of the Deutscher Werkbund, as set forth by Muthesius, can be summed up in two phrases: excellence of workmanship, and the creation of a contemporary style. These aims are a single aim, for whoever works in the style of our time works well. And whoever does not work in the style of our time works carelessly and badly. And that is how it should be. For a bad form — by which I mean any form which does not conform to the style of our time — can be excused if one has the feeling that it will soon be done away with. But when rubbish is produced for posterity, its effect is doubly unaesthetic. It is the aim of the Werkbund to produce things for posterity which are not in the style of our time. That is bad. But Muthesius also says that through the cooperative work of the Deutscher Werkbund, the style of our time will be discovered. This is a waste of effort. We already have the style of our time. We have it everywhere where the designer, and therefore a member of this very movement, has not yet interfered. . . .

Can anyone try to deny that our leather goods are in the style of our time? And our cutlery and glasses? And our bathtubs and American washstands? And our tools and machines? And everything, I repeat everything, which has not fallen into the hands of the artists!

Loos's complex, subtle and often contradictory position was based upon two main insights which he seems to have acquired during his three-year sojourn in the United States from 1893 to 1896. Briefly stated, these insights may be summarised as follows. In the first place, he argued that the true greatness of our technological civilization was already an established fact and that the manifest benefits of industrial distribution (transport), electricity and plumbing were in and of themselves civilizing forces and where present in objective form, should be recognised and accepted in their unmediated state. In the second place, he felt that the process of modern urbanization (above all as he had witnessed it in Chicago in 1893), had already succeeded in the wholesale uprooting of indigenous populations. This uprooting had effectively produced an *arriviste* or proletarian class who were irredeemably alienated from their native culture. At the same time he was well aware that in many areas — such as tailoring, upholstery, saddlemaking and joinery — a traditional craft culture still persisted, and that these craft products, when randomly juxtaposed with the brute *anomie* of industrial production, would inevitably constitute the incoherent and paradoxical style of our epoch. The general thrust of Loos's criticism as it first appeared after 1896 was directed towards the *Sezession* and in particular towards Olbrich, whose aestheticization of everyday objects he regarded as an anathema. In *Ornament and Crime* he wrote: "Modern ornament has no forbears and no descendants, no past and no future. It is joyfully welcomed by uncultivated people to whom the true greatness of our time is a closed book and after a short time is rejected."

Unlike Pugin, Ruskin and the English Arts and Crafts, to which the whole of the Pre-Raphaelite reformist-historicist reaction had given rise, Loos totally rejected the strategy of the *Gesamtkunstwerk*; that is to say he refused to

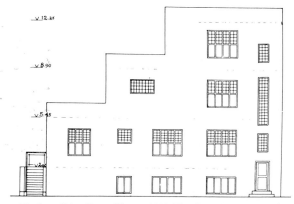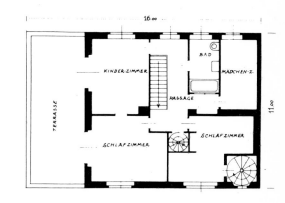

75 Loos, Scheu House, Vienna, 1912. First floor plan and elevation.

accept any approach which sought to transcend the chaotic and uncultivated consequences of industrial production through projecting an *hermetic* cultural world, be it an historicist one, as in the case of Pugin, or an arbitrarily artistic one, as in the case of Olbrich or van de Velde. It was not that he was against ornament, for on more than one occasion he used a Renaissance plastercast frieze as a decorative element. He was, however, against the *invention* of ornament. Loos regarded the "total work of art" as a sham and a tyranny and he was to satirize the oppressive impact of Jugendstil aesthetics on the lives of the *nouveau riche* in his essay *The Story of the Poor Rich Man* of 1900. At the conclusion to this parable an architect who has even designed his client's slippers upbraids the unfortunate man for wearing the elegantly profiled but brilliantly coloured footwear in the wrong room; that is to say, in a room whose basic colour they did not match. Loos's counter-thesis to this totalizing tendency was encapsulated in an aphorism that assigned a building's walls to it's architect, along with the built-in equipment and reserved for the province of the craftsman (and not the designer) all the necessary loose fittings and furnishings.

Loos's position with regard to architecture itself was most critically expressed in his essay *Architecture* of 1910, and built-out in two major works that he saw completed in Vienna in that year; the Steiner Villa and the Goldman and Salatsch store. The basic premise of *Architecture* may be roughly summarized as follows. In the first place, Loos argued that engineering forms such as a locomotive or a ship, are compatible with agrarian culture because their forms are distinctly different, whereas modern archi-

tecture, irrespective of its quality, violates the almost sacred, unconscious authority of both the vernacular and its rural context because it has been *consciously designed as though it had evolved over a long period of time*. Loos asks the rhetorical question: "Why does the architect both good or bad violate the lake?" and immediately answers himself, "Like almost every town dweller, the architect possesses no culture. He does not have the security of the peasant to whom this culture is innate. The town dweller is an upstart." In the second place Loos argued that, irrespective of cultural alienation, one still has to distinguish between *building* and *architecture* and that only commemorative or representative structures fell into the latter category. Assigning the house to the realm of building he further distinguished between the nature of domesticity and the subversive aims of art. He wrote:

. . . The work of art aims at shattering man's comfortable complacency. A house must serve one's comfort. The work of art is revolutionary, the house conservative. The work of art points man in the direction of new paths and thinks to the future. The house thinks of the present. Man loves everything that serves his comfort. He hates everything that wants to tear him away from his secure and safe position, and is burdensome. And so he loves the house and hates art.

That Loos was to adopt a proto-Dadaist stance towards relating but *not* reconciling the contradictory values inherent to the design of a contemporary bourgeois residence seems to be directly borne out by the paradoxical nature of the Steiner Villa. Loos deliberately reduced this house to a stark white

76 *Cover page for Karl Kraus's* Die Fackel *No. 1, Vienna, 1899.*

prism with nothing but stripped, pierced windows to relieve its unadorned surface. This almost cultureless form — this "architecture degree zero," nonetheless still manifested within, the apparently comfortable atmosphere of an English Arts and Crafts interior.

The subtle and subversive nature of Loos's vision, its deliberately anti-aesthetic stance, is evident in the Steiner Villa dining room, where the apparently reassuring vernacular comfort of the wooden wainscoting and the timber rafters is at the same time subtly subverted by the "anguished" and disjunctive nature of the proportions and detailing. One notes the ceiling beams whose unwieldy size and apparent weight seems to threaten their stability, the *shoji* Japanese window that impinges uncomfortably on the top of the wainscoting, and even the main window itself which is awkwardly placed in the corner of the room. Like Karl Kraus who, in outrage at the holocaust of the First World War, was to write his cacophonous dramatic collage entitled *The Last Days of Humanity* in a chaotic variety of dramatic forms and styles, Loos exploited disjunctions such as these, in order to create a disinherited "anti-architecture" which would be at one and the same time both classical and vernacular, comfortable and discordant, symmetrical and irregular. His so-called *Raumplan* or space planning, as manifest in the Scheu House, Vienna, of 1912, was a strategy for inserting within bare and symmetrical cubic forms, the irregular plan configuration and random sectional displacements of the typical Anglo-Saxon, Arts and Crafts house.

A similar subversive strategy was pursued in the Goldman and Salatsch store where a traditional, classical syntax complete with an entablature and Tuscan columns, was applied to the ground and mezzanine floors of the tailor's store (paradoxically interlaced with bay windows drawn from the vocabulary of Norman Shaw) while the upper residential floors were stripped as in the Steiner Villa and capped by a grotesquely proportioned Baroque roof.

Loos, like Kraus, confronted his epoch with an avant-gardism which was anti-avant-garde. He indulged in the brutal silence (the stripped facades, for instance) spontaneously produced by progressive technique and modern economy. At the same time he referred where necessary for the purposes of communication, to the received syntax of architecture, but always in such a way as to subtly displace the code; that is, the forms were always specific enough to be readable but at the same time distorted enough to be disturbing. His ironic but highly critical achievement, relevant even today, was perhaps best summed up by his life-long friend and mentor Karl Kraus, when he wrote:

"All that Adolf Loos and I have done, he literally and I figuratively, is to show that there is a difference between a chamber pot and an urn and in that difference there is a small margin left for culture. But the others, 'the positive ones' are to be distinguished between those who would use a chamber pot for an urn and an urn for a chamber pot."

Throughout his pre-war career in Breslau (Wrocław), from 1903 to 1914, Poelzig strove to create an *architecture parlante* in which unprecedented building programmes would assume particular forms. In this way Poelzig hoped to arrive at a repertoire of types which by virture of their specific *gestalt* would be able to communicate, presumably through their continual repetition, the purpose for which they had been designed. One may think of this as Alois Riegl's "will to form," in the service of a new typology. To this end, this steel framed water tower was given a singularly willful profile that in no way corresponded to the necessary shape of its structural frame. Invariably Poelzig wanted to create a silhouette for his structures in which the base was always wider than the top, and so the sixteen sided form was amplified with lean-to roofs that expanded the effective mass of the structure as it approached the ground. While the exterior was clad in an elegant quilt of patterned brickwork set within the discipline of a lightweight steel frame (already a German industrial vernacular form of construction), the interior was apparently much like the inside of a dirigible; that is to say, it was a cacaphony of latticework ranged about a central spiral staircase, built up out of welded and riveted plate. Strangely enough, given the enthusiasm with which he broached the theme, this was Poelzig's first and last exercise in exposed steelwork.

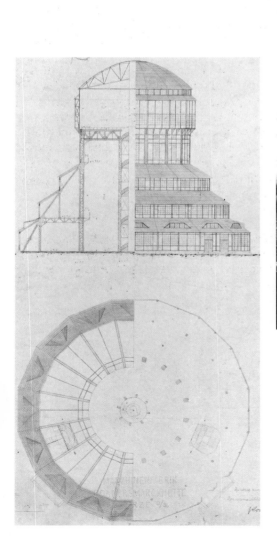

Photos: Plansammlung der Universitätsbibliothek der Technischen Universität Berlin, Berlin

Left: section/elevation and plan
Center: exterior view
Above right: interior view
Below right: steel stairs

HANS POELZIG
Chemical Factory
Luban, near Posen (Poznań), Poland

This complex is unquestionably the master-work of Poelzig's career. Its play with utilitarian building form (derived in this case from nineteenth-century warehouse architecture) is altogether more relaxed and inevitable than anything produced by Behrens for the AEG combine over the same period. The surprising thing is that the essentials of the brick and metal syntax adopted in the Luban complex had already been refined by Poelzig some five years before in his project for the Werder Mill in Breslau (Wrocław) of 1906. No one has characterized Poelzig's attitude at this time more perceptively than Wolfgang Pehnt, when he wrote: "Poelzig saw no fundamental contradiction between the demands of art and the demands of function. In his eyes the architect was — for the time being, at least — superior to the engineer in that he would take a particular set of constructional and economic demands and from them evolve new formal relationships and powerful rhythms. The Luban site, for example, owed part of its romantic strangeness of atmosphere to the varied treatment justifiable on constructional grounds of openings: round-headed windows in a load-bearing wall and rectangular where vertical and horizontal metal bands had been incorporated into the courses of brick masonry. And, of course, there was no lack of motifs, such as the mediaevalizing stepped gables with no functional basis whatsoever."

As Pehnt points out, Poelzig, like Behrens and Gropius, regarded the industrial structure as being the least constrained by any cultural preconception and therefore, as the one form which was most open to new development.

178 Gable and facade
179 Above and below: views of exterior
Photos: Plansammlung der Universitätsbibliothek der Technischen Universität Berlin, Berlin

In this unique work Perret established the Rational Classical principles which were to determine the rest of his career. Here, the internal and surface order of the structure was given by the reinforced concrete frame itself which, with brick in-fill, found direct expression on the sides and the back, while being masked by the masonry skin of the main facade and its exposed corner. Perret returned at this juncture to the use of traditional modelling or *modenature*; a technique that he would have first acquired at the École des Beaux-Arts in Paris where he had been a pupil of the "elementarist" architect Julien Guadet from 1891 to 1894. It is regrettable that this important transition for Perret should have been achieved at the expense of the Belgian architect Henry van de Velde who, on this occasion, first experienced the chauvinism which was to destroy his early career. Van de Velde had received the initial commission for the building from the theatrical director Gabriel Astruc and it was only with the commissioning of the Perret brothers as the contractors for the work, that his design encountered intense opposition; above all, of course, from *A&G Perret Constructeurs*, who argued that van de Velde's scheme was uneconomically conceived and structurally unsound. Whatever the technical refinements that may have distinguished the two rival schemes, the fact that the Perret's criticism carried the day suggests the nationalistic climate in which the whole issue was decided. Even so, Perret still adopted a *parti* identical to that projected by van de Velde and the case has since been made, first by van de Velde himself and then more recently by the Belgium champion of his cause – the architectural critic Maurice Culot – that Perret remained indebted to van de Velde for his idea of theatrical form up to the Exposition des Arts Décoratifs, Paris of 1925, when, in the temporary exhibition theatre, he achieved his own version of the ideal tri-partite stage first tentatively postulated by van de Velde for his Champs-Elysées scheme.

It is clear that Beaux-Arts ideology was influential in the cultural xenophobia that van de Velde encountered. Perret's Rational Classicism – that is, his structurally lucid but nonetheless Neo-classical expression (Louis Seize re-interpreted in terms of Viollet-le-Duc) was nevertheless an exercise in restraint, given the ruling *pompier* version of the Beaux-Arts idiom, which had more or less held sway in Paris since the Exposition Universelle of 1900 (see the Grand et Petit Palais designed for this occasion by Messrs. Louvet, Deglane, Thomas and Girault). Compared to this gratifying rhetoric in masonry and iron (Perret's theatre was close to the 1900 exhibition site) critics such as Adolf Gosset regarded Perret's theatre as cold, funereal and Teutonic. They would have no doubt found van de Velde's crypto-Byzantine manner, with its heavy "eye-browed" windows and gridded fenestration, even more unacceptable.

If the conventionalized sunflower decorative panels, filling the frame of Perret's rue Franklin apartments are to be seen, according to Robert Schmutzler, as the crystallization of the Art Nouveau, then the Théâtre des Champs-Elysées represents the moment when Classical and Symbolist culture briefly fused together to create an elegiac but geometrical expression which was anticipatory of the Art Deco. Perret would have not achieved this synthesis without the paintings of Maurice Denis and the sculpture of Antoine Bourdelle and, in fact, he was never to attain such disciplined and lyrical expression again. While this work was far from being the ultimate demonstration of his rational architecture to be derived from a subtle synthesis of classical form with structural logic (Perret's own resolution of the Graeco-Gothic ideal), it was nonetheless his first presentation of the reinforced concrete frame under a classical rubric. The Palladian A:B:A:B:A gridding of the foyer space by the frame, the daring cantilevered balconies and bow-spring arches over the main auditorium, are all strikingly architectonic structural features which testify to Perret's new found ability to render the engineer's aesthetic in classical terms.

180 Street facade
181 Left: plan
Right: interior of main auditorium

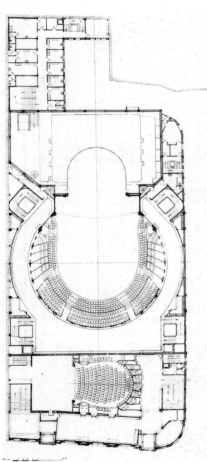

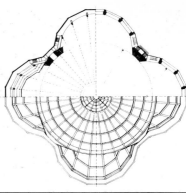

Built in Breslau to commemorate the centennial of the Pan-German victory over Napoleon at Leipzig in 1813, this colossal hall (which outstripped by 80 feet the span of the Pantheon in Rome, which had hitherto been the largest dome in the world) was certainly the most ambitious and ceremonious of the "people's monuments" or *Volksdenkmalen* erected to celebrate the birth of German national identity. The irresistible appeal of this occasion may be judged from Erich Mendelsohn, who recorded his reaction to the opening of the Jahrhunderthalle — an occasion graced with the inaugural performance of Gerhart Hauptmann's mass pageant in honour of the 1813 war — with the words: "One day we too will have to extend our technical thinking to cover sacred ends." This was surely one of the prototypes for Taut's notion of the "city-crown," first fully formulated in his book *Die Stadtkrone* of 1919. On the other hand it can also be seen as the fulfillment of the de Baudot and Viollet-le-Duc obsession with the great space as the ultimate proof of a vital civilization, even if its reinforced concrete structure was simultaneously daring and conservative; daring in its unprecedented span of 225 feet and conservative in that the extraordinary structure was largely masked on the exterior by the stepped tiers of its clerestory fenestration. Berg's invention, with the engineer Trauer, of a radial, ribbed dome, spanning onto a tension ring-beam which in turn transmitted its weight to a series of four great arches, may be taken as a step in the gradual realization of de Baudot's vision of a vast reticulated space. Eventually this structural paradigm was to receive a more integrated interpretation in Pier Luigi Nervi's Palazzetto dello Sport built in Rome in 1957, where the reticulated form of a folded concrete shell translated its configuration without any formal interruption into a series of Y-shaped buttresses carrying the perimeter thrust.

Top: beam plan
Center: interior of the dome
Bottom: section
Photo: Verlag Gerd Hatje, Stuttgart

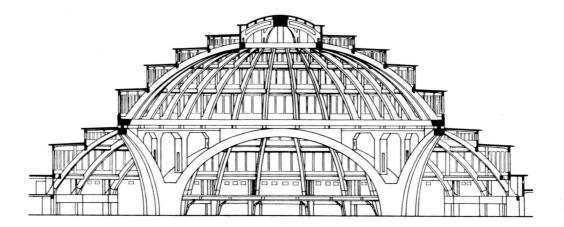

Without doubt the culmination of Wright's Prairie Style in the United States, Midway Gardens, despite its rectangular elemental Beaux-Arts plan, was a typological hybrid suspended somewhere between the continental *Kurhaus* or casino and Wright's own vision of some oriental pleasure garden, as he had first broached this theme in his somewhat Burnham-like design for the Wolf Lake Amusement Park in 1895. Deprived in this actual instance of any significant prospect onto water and having therefore nothing of consequence to relate to, Midway Gardens, like most of Wright's public structures, was highly introspective and despite the inviting articulation of its well-proportioned and heavily textured (but mostly blank) brick and concrete block facade, it kept its formal exuberance largely to itself; that is to say, the most dramatic views of its cantilvering roof planes, outriding balconies, decorative finals, statues, and illuminated sky towers were to be obtained from the terraces of the inner garden which were largely occupied by café tables. With an orchestra shell and dance floor at one end for outdoor dancing and a multi-levelled internal restaurant at the other (cf. Unity Temple), Midway Gardens may have required, as Henry-Russell Hitchcock has suggested, a certain sophistication to appreciate its possibilities. "At any rate," he continues, "it did not attract the clientele for which its cuisine and the musical and other entertainment fare – Pavlova danced here – was originally intended. So it declined to a suburban beer garden and eventually was closed by Prohibition and demolished in the early twenties" (1923).

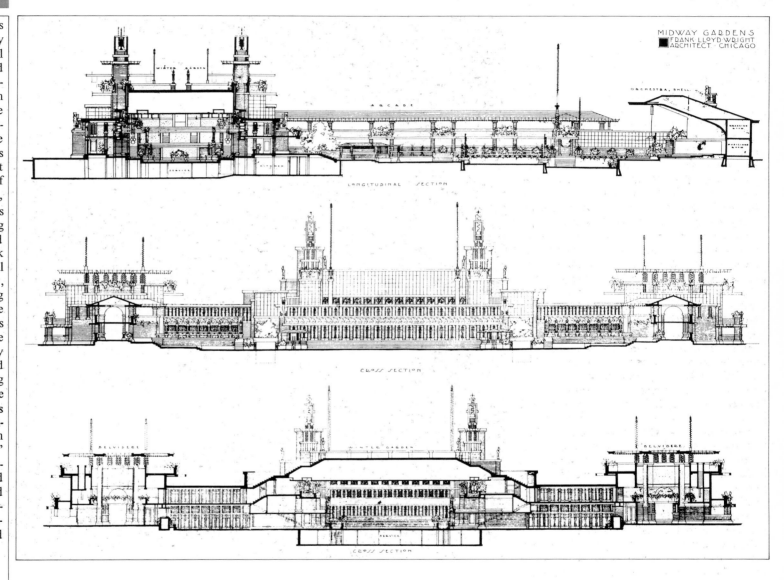

183 Top to bottom: longitudinal section, cross sections
184 Above: view from the interior court
Below left: street facade
Below right: view of the interior court
Photos: © The Frank Lloyd Wright Foundation

The Amsterdam School of Expressionism — polemically centred about Wijdeveld's magazine *Wendingen* (Turning Point) — was focused on the figure of Michel de Klerk, who was responsible for the design of the Eigen Haard (Own Hearth) estate under construction in Amsterdam from 1913 to 1919. Both architecturally and urbanistically, the Amsterdam School took its formula for new urban development (namely, brick faced horizontal residential structures forming continuous streets) from H.P. Berlage, whose famous development plan for Amsterdam South was published in 1915. Apart from adhering to the Berlagian concept of the urban block, de Klerk was to distort Berlage's brick version of Viollet-le-Duc's Structural Rationalism to his own expressive ends. Thus, unlike Poelzig whose architecture, at this time, almost always stemmed from transforming traditional elements of the industrial vernacular — his manipulation of semi-circular arches, buttress, etc. — de Klerk took liberties with both traditional building components and the requirements of the programme. This is most evident in the detailing of his window openings — above all in the fenestration of the Eigen Haard Post Office of 1917 — whose horizontal glazing bars were so compacted as to make it difficult for the occupants of the apartments to see out. Many of de Klerk's expressive distortions at Eigen Haard had no functional or institutional justification. Thus, the obelisk on the central axis of the bowed Hembrugstraat elevation served solely as a sign of the rooted nature of the community, and while it did refer to a small meeting room within the block, it was nonetheless a nostalgic symbol which depended for its general reading on the collective memory of the church spire as a form which was indicative of communality.

View from Hembrugstraat

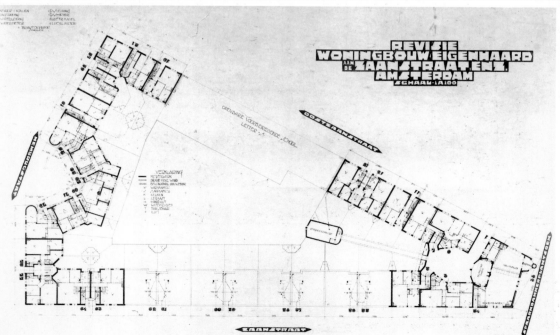

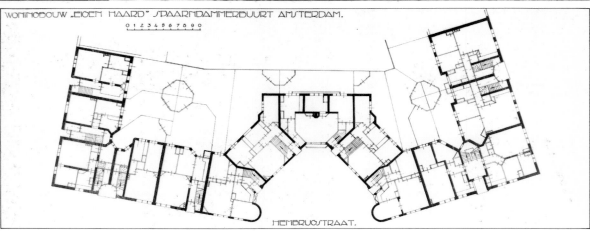

186 *Above: south corner of the block*
 Below left: ground floor plan
 Below right: window of the Post Office
187 *Above: view from Oostzaanstraat*
 Below left: view of windows facing onto Oostzaanstraat
 Below right: plan

This small pavilion, to some extent presaged by a steel monument that Taut had built at Leipzig in the previous year, inaugurated the "fantastic" phase of Taut's career as an architect; a period which lasted from 1914 to the last issue of Taut's Expressionist magazine, *Frühlicht,* or Dawn's Light which ceased publication in 1922. Openly dedicated to the anarcho-Socialist writings of the poet Paul Scheerbart, whose utopian novel *Glasarchitektur* of 1914, had inspired its form, this all-glass pavilion was in effect a prototypical cult building of the kind that Taut (after Scheerbart) was later to envisage as being built either in the centre of Kropotkinian garden cities or on suitably spectacular and remote sites situated in the midst of the Alps (see Taut's *Alpine Architektur* of 1919). In either case such an architecture would have depended for its historical rupture on the exclusive use of coloured glass, in accordance with Scheerbart's aphorism which was inscribed on the vestigial entablature of Taut's glass pavilion:

Das Glas bringt uns die neue Zeit
Backsteinkultur tut uns nur Leid
Glass brings us the new age,
    Brick culture only does us harm.

Aside from the pragmatics of exhibiting different kinds of glass (the work had been sponsored by the glass industry), Taut's pavilion embodied elements which he had taken directly from Scheerbart's text: the obscured access stairs (hidden behind screen walls in glass block) which gave access to the sacrosanct space of the faceted cupola above and the twin stairway within these stairs, which initiated the descent into the elongated "rite of passage," hidden in the body of the building and lined on the inside from floor to ceiling in coloured glass mosaics. This passage led via narrow causeways on either side of a seven-tiered cascade to the penultimate experience of a small projection room, from which the visitor was rudely expelled into the real world. An early drawing of this pavilion describes it as having been designed in the spirit of the Gothic cathedral. This partly explains the role that Taut later played in developing the Socialist-guild position that was adopted by Walter Gropius in his Bauhaus proclamation of 1919. The cover of this proclamation bore Lionel Feininger's woodcut of the cathedral of the future – shown as the cathedral of Socialism. Such structures, seen as the equivalent of the Gothic cathedrals, were posited by Taut as city crowns or *Stadtkronen*, without which, according to him, a city could not gain its proper identity.

Left: plan
Right: overall view from entrance side
Photo: Stadt Köln Nachrichtenamt, Köln

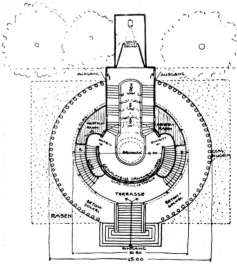

1914
WALTER GROPIUS
ADOLF MEYER
Model Factory
Werkbund Exhibition
Cologne, Germany

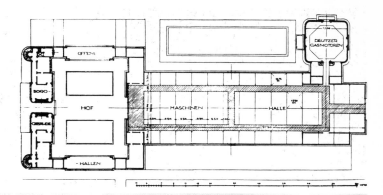

Frank Lloyd Wright's achievement prior to 1909 was first made generally available in Europe through the publication of the Wasmuth volumes in Berlin in the years 1910 and 1911. No two buildings of comparable date reflect the impact of this revelation so directly as Gropius's Fagus Factory completed in 1911 and his model factory built for the Cologne Werkbund Exhibition of 1914. It is clear that where the former was an expression deriving directly from Behrens's Turbine Factory of 1908, the latter was patently influenced by Wright, not only in the two square brick pavilions at either end with their banded cornice lines and their thin oversailing concrete slab roofs, but also in the detailing of the main facade, in which the conceit of the projecting Wrightian cornice occurs again, set on either side of the

entrance, above brick planes standing proud of the main surface. However, Wright is little more than a referent at this juncture, for the Prussian Schinkelesque tradition still pervades the basic structure of the work, particularly in the stress on the corner stair towers which here, as in the Fagus-Werk, are in glass rather than stone. The steel fenestration for this membrane was organized into a horizontal coursing pattern; a form which was no doubt made to be deliberately reminiscent of masonry; this glass membrane is returned as a continuous curtain wall throughout the full length of the rear facade of the building, organized after the hierarchical arrangement of the classical nineteenth-century Railway terminus (cf. François Duquesney's Gare de l'Est, Paris of 1852). This prototypical factory was broken

down along a symmetrical axis into two basic elements: the traditional, representative administration block or "head building" (i.e. architecture) and the utilitarian metal clad sheds housing the plant itself (i.e. building); in this case comprising two freestanding, exhibition volumes carried on three-hinged steel portals. Unlike Behrens or even Poelzig, Gropius and Meyer made no attempt here to bestow representative status on the "plant" itself. By this date they had obviously decided that such forms were best treated as pure *sachlich* engineering structures, modelled in this particular instance after Contamin's Galerie des Machines of 1889. Behrens's ponderous insistence on reifying the spirit of industrial power (as exemplified in his AEG Humboldthain complex) was reduced here to a

token idealization; evident in the small, classical exhibition pavilion built for the Deutz Motor Co., to one side of the principal axis.

189 Above: plan
Below: rear view of the administration block
190 Above: overall view
Below: The Deutz Pavilion
Photos provided by Mrs. Walter Gropius

1914

HENRY VAN DE VELDE
Model Theatre
Werkbund Exhibition
Cologne, Germany

Van de Velde's life long preoccupation with the theatre, initially manifest in the close friendships that he established with Gordon Craig and Max Reinhardt came to the fore in 1911 when Gabriel Astruc commissioned him to design the first version of the Théâtre des Champs-Elysées in Paris. However, he soon lost this commission to Gustave and Auguste Perret — that is to say to the reinforced concrete contracting firm of Perret Frères who (aside from the issue of chauvinism) were able to demonstrate that they possessed superior technical ability. The building of the Werkbund theatre three years later enabled van de Velde to realize many of the ideas that he had previously incorporated in the Paris proposal including an auditorium in the form of an amphitheatre, an open-tripartite stage with a demountable proscenium, and a circular horizon capable of optimizing the cyclorama effect. In this reinforced concrete theatre, built expressly for the Werkbund Exhibition, van de Velde succeeded in creating a theatrical space which was capable of accommodating a wide variety of dramatic performances ranging from modest pageant plays to symbolist and realist pieces which were more suited to the proscenium stage. Its mass wall and reinforced concrete frame construction, rendered over so as to form an homogeneous and plastic expression, was to serve as a point of departure for the post-war work of Eric Mendelsohn; above all for the small observatory that Mendelsohn built for Einstein in Potsdam in 1920. The brooding telluric mass of the Werkbund theatre, reminiscent in many respects of Rudolf Steiner's anthroposophical form, was to mark that point in van de Velde's career when the more animate "form-force" aesthetic of his early furniture gave way to a much more solid, not to say ponderous expression. This solemn, gray, crypto-classical auditorium was offset, on its interior at least, by the symbolist painting of the Swiss artist Ferdinand Hodler.

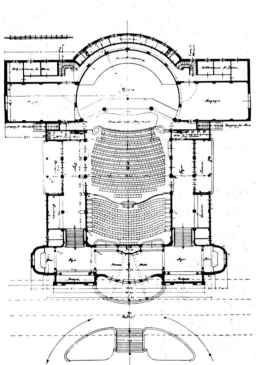

Left: Plan
Right: Overall view

Apart from Tony Garnier's *Cité Industrielle* of 1904, no other visionary project was to gain such a hold on the twentieth-century imagination as the images of Sant'Elia's *Città Nuova* or *Milano 2000*, produced sometime between 1912 and 1914 and exhibited with the group *Nuove Tendenze* in Milan in May 1914. This group show included the work of the one other Futurist architect of consequence, Mario Chiattone. The precipitous development which characterizes Sant'Elia's brilliant but short lived career (he was killed in the First World War, at Monfalcone in 1916) is as complex as it is revealing. Born in Como in 1880 and educated in Milan and Bologna, Sant'Elia, like many other architects of the *Floreale* movement, was influenced by the *Wagnerschule* and this dependency in respect of both image and drafting technique is still evident in the drawings of the *Città Nuova*. This influence was of course extensive in Italy and may have first impinged on Sant'Elia's work through the older members of the *Floreale* movement, that is to say through the work of such masters as Raimondo D'Aronco, Ernesto Basile, Giuseppe Sommaruga, Umberto Fonda, and finally Ulisse Stacchini, whose almost Piranesian Milan railway terminus still stands today. That this background in itself (despite Wagner's *Großstadt* thesis of 1911) would not have brought Sant'Elia to create the *Città Nuova* is suggested by his Sommaruga-like project for the Monza Cemetery designed with Italo Paternostro in 1912. As Reyner Banham has suggested the inspiration behind the sudden shift in his work after 1912 seems to have been the Parisien circle of Gustave Kahn with its Utopian Socialist enthusiasms — a group with which the Futurist polemicist Marinetti had been in contact a few years before. More directly perhaps the tentative prototype for Sant'Elia's *casa a gradinate* was a structure that had already been completed in Paris, in the form of Henri Sauvage's set-back apartment block, built in rue Vavin, in 1912. This unique work together with the stepped form of Sommaruga's Facanoni Mausoleum at Sarnico of 1907 (cf. Sant'Elia's power stations for the *Città Nuova*) is surely as much the architectonic precedent for Sant'Elia's vision of Milan in the year 2000 as any legacy stemming from the *Wagnerschule* itself. A further potential influence on the multiple accessways of the *Città Nuova* (for which incidentally there were never any plans) would have been Eugene Henard whose multi-levelled future street section was first exhibited at the town planning congress held in London in 1910. Of the many perspectives produced for the *Città Nuova*, the *casa a gradinate* is perhaps the most representative, since it illustrates Sant'Elia's own description of the Futurist city as it appeared in the 1914 catalogue of the show. The most relevant passage from this *Messaggio* which he wrote with the aid of Ugo Nebbia reads: "We must invent and rebuild *ex novo* our Modern city like an immense and tumultuous shipyard, active, mobile and everywhere dynamic, and the modern building like a gigantic machine. Lifts must no longer hide away like solitary worms in the stairwells, but the stairs — now useless — must be abolished, and the lifts must swarm up the facades like serpents of glass and iron. The house of cement, iron, and glass, without carved or painted ornament, rich only in the inherent beauty of its lines and modelling, extraordinarily brutish in its mechanical simplicity, as big as need dictates, and not merely as zoning rules permit, must rise from the brink of a tumultuous abyss: the street which, itself, will no longer lie like a doormat at the level of the thresholds, but plunge storeys deep into the earth, gathering up the traffic of the metropolis connected for necessary transfers to metal cat-walks and high-speed conveyor belts."

192 Centrale Elettrica
193 *Left:* Stazione Aeroplani
      Right: Casa a Gradinate

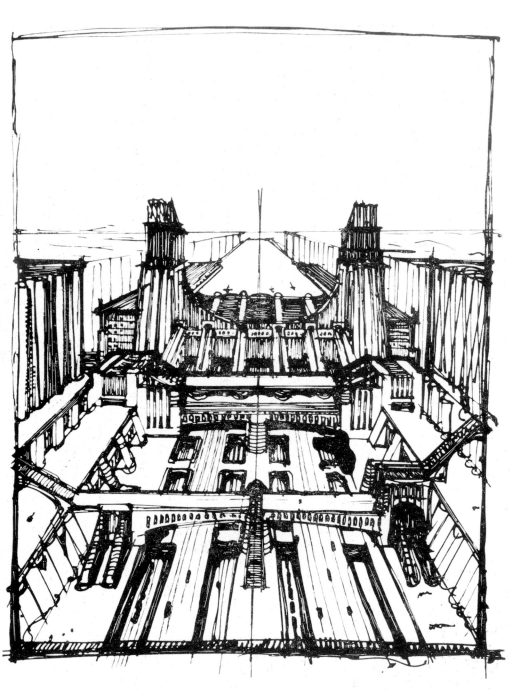

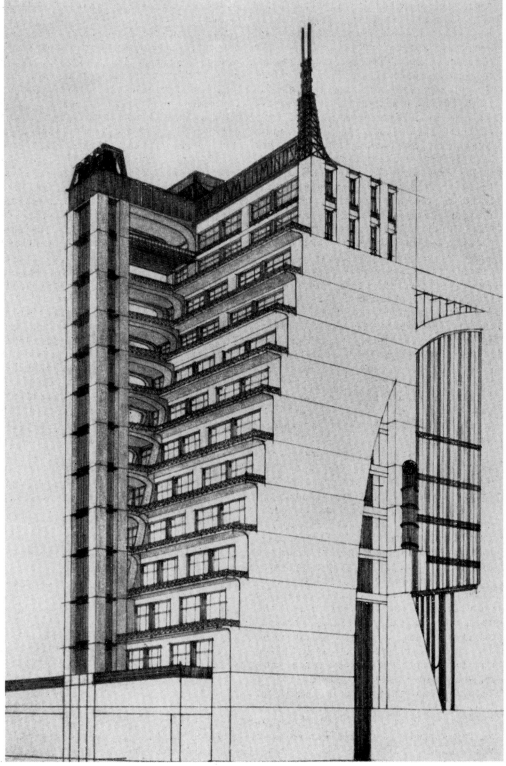

WILLIS POLK
Hallidie Building
San Francisco, California, U.S.A.

The first application of a pure curtain wall to any building in America came some six years after the completion of Peter Behrens's Turbine Factory in Berlin with its flanking glass walls. The other European precedent was the curtain wall membrane to the main administration block in the Gropius and Meyer's Fagus complex, completed at Alfeld-an-Leine between 1911 and 1913. While Polk had visited Europe soon after the completion of the Fagus-Werk it is unlikely that he was familiar with either of these precedents. One other reason for the Hallidie Building may have been Polk's decision to break with the heavyweight Richardsonian manner, that Neo-Romanesque style which

Polk once described as "Titanic inebriation in sandstone." After 1893 Polk was in any event under the influence of Burnham's highly successful Beaux-Arts Columbian Exposition staged in Chicago in that year. All the same, this in itself in no way accounts for a structure of such extraordinary precision and lightness. Such a work was hardly to be expected from Polk, given his highly eclectic practice prior to 1915. Like the Monadnock Block in the career of John Root this seven-storey structure was to be the unique triumph of Polk's career.

Natural light, budget limitations and a desire to facilitate erection, were all to influence Polk's decision to produce an all-glass facade

and this he was to achieve by exploiting the cantilevering capacity of reinforced concrete to its fullest. A regular grid of mullions held the glass membrane in place with three vertical subdivisions per floor; the top pane of each storey pivoting outwards for the purposes of ventilation. This transparent wall was suspended three feet three inches in front of the support line, which was comprised of a two-foot six-inch diameter hexagonal reinforced columns at twenty-foot centres. The weight of the glass skin alone was carried on a three-inch projecting concrete still, cantilevered out from the upstand beam. These sills simultaneously served as horizontal "firebreaks"

between one floor and the next. The upstand spandrel projected one foot six inches above the floor level, while the hollowribbed concrete slab itself was one foot six inches deep. Appropriately enough, this building, erected by the University of California, was named after a distinguished regent, A.S. Hallidie, who had been the inventor of the San Francisco cable car. Polk's ambition after 1893 to realize a refined and spirited architecture was certainly achieved in this unique crystalline facade whose pure "functionalism" was mediated only by crenellated blue and gold, cast-iron cornices at the mezzanine and roof levels.

After his visit to the Ford plant in Detroit in 1912, V.G. Agnelli began to promote the Taylorized production of the automobile in Italy. In this effort he was assisted by the highly militarized climate of the First World War which gave him the chance to impose the authority of "on-line" production under the cover of a national emergency. At first the labour force did not resist this move but the workers' subsequent occupation of this "flatted" plant, within a year of its completion, reflects the virulence with which the unions resisted the tyranny of Agnelli's rationalization. Nevertheless, the principles of ordered, sequential production for which this extraordinary building was designed, still prevail today and this no doubt goes some way towards explaining why this vast, five-storey, reinforced concrete industrial loft is still in use. The five floors are ordered sequentially to provide for (1) maintenance and motor testing, (2) engine machining and body assembly, (3) gear box and electrical work, (4) spraying, upholstering, suspension and differential steering, (5) lorry production and (6) testing. This last takes place in the open air, on the roof, where a banked reinforced concrete racetrack has been provided, on an area measuring 1680 feet by 260 feet. At the ends the banking to this track rises some 15 feet in 55 feet and this activation of the roof, together with its highly sculptural form was to inspire Le Corbusier's conception of the roofscape for his Unité apartment block built at Marseilles in 1952.

Whatever the techno-social circumstances surrounding its erection, this is a pioneering work in the application of reinforced concrete construction to an industrial plant. It was designed significantly enough by a naval engineer. Accommodating some 6,000 workers in 16,000,000 square foot of floor space, it was an undertaking of unprecedented size. From a structural point of view, however, the most remarkable innovation was the helicoidal car ramps at either end of the block which were braced by an extremely elegant system of reinforced concrete ribs, a system which in retrospect recalls the theoretical projects of de Baudot and seems to anticipate the later realizations of Pier Luigi Nervi, such as his Gatti Wool factory built at Rome in 1953.

Aerial view
Photo reproduced from LOTUS 12

CHARLES-EDOUARD JEANNERET (LE CORBUSIER)
Villa Schwob
La Chaux-de-Fonds, Switzerland

Between 1905, when he designed his first house for the Fallet family at the age of 18 and his subsequent homes carried out in a "chalet" vernacular style (his designs for the villas Stozer and Jacquement built in 1908 and 1909 respectively), Jeanneret, as he was then known, moved away from the *Jugendstil* manner that he had developed under the tutorship of his master Charles Epplattenier, toward a more explicitly cryptoclassical form of expression as exemplified in the work of both Behrens and Hoffmann after 1905. This expression first emerges in Le Corbusier's practice in La Chaux-de-Fonds, after his visit to Germany in 1911 and his brief stay in the Behrens atelier. His style changes abruptly with the Villa Jeanneret-Père built in La Chaux-de-Fonds after his return in 1912, and the new manner is consolidated in the Villa Favre (1912) and in the Scala Cinema built in the centre of the same town in 1915. This whole provincial development comes to a conclusion in the Villa Schwob designed in 1915 and built in 1916, one year before Jeanneret definitively leaves La Chaux-de-Fonds to establish himself in Paris.

The Villa Schwob is in many respects a complex synthesis of the so-called "crystallized" *Jugendstil* of Behrens and Hoffmann and the Structural Rationalism of Perret, for by the time Jeanneret came to design this house he had already spent some ten months in Auguste Perret's employ. There he would have acquired both the technical and aesthetic precepts of the reinforced concrete frame, and it is this complex architectural principle which underlies the whole of the Villa Schwob and serves to distinguish it from his previous work and the work of his predecessors. Unlike the domestic work of both Behrens and Hoffmann, the Villa Schwob is predicated on a Palladian grid and *parti*, its main body being organized in accordance with the classic A:B:A:B:A system; the A bays corresponding to the wider span volumes and the B bays to the narrower. Traditionally (but not exclusively) the B bays in this scheme are used for the purposes of service and the A bays are used for the accommodation of the principal rooms, etc. With the exception of the main stairway which occurs in the central bay near the street and the kitchen which is effectively accommodated in a single wide bay to one side, this principle of A spaces being "served" by the B spaces prevails throughout.

In the last analysis the Villa Schwob is of importance both technically and artistically. In the first case it breaks new ground, at least in Switzerland by being one of the first domestic buildings to combine a reinforced concrete frame with double glazing throughout the main volumes. The frame itself was a curious hybrid of the concrete framing systems of Hennebique and Morsch and with its flat, so-called beamless slab, it represented a significant move away from the famous French reinforced concrete patent towards Jeanneret's own DOM-INO framing method developed with his engineer friend Max Dubois. In the second case it introduced a central double height volume on the axis of the whole house as the principle device for organizing the space. The oriel windows looking down into this two-storey space seem, by virtue of their oblique references to similar features in a Turkish *saray*, to have earned the house the nickname of the Villa Turcque. Of greater import to Le Corbusier's subsequent development was the use of regulating lines (shown in *Vers une Architecture*) and the curiously grotesque cornice — a classical feature which he was soon to exclude from his vocabulary.

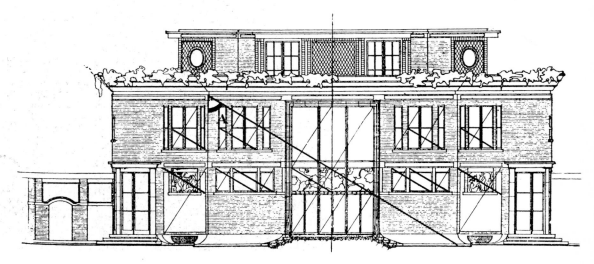

196 *Front facade*
197 *Above: view from the street*
   Below: elevation

1916-18
J.F. STAAL
MARGARET KROPHOLLER
PIET KRAMER AND OTHERS
*Housing Estate, Park Meerwijk
Bergen-Binnen, near Alkmaar, Holland*

This artists' colony-cum-garden suburb, originally comprising some seventeen houses on six acres of land was designed around 1916 by various members of the Amsterdam School, and built over the next two years on the outskirts of a small Dutch coastal town. The patron of this enterprise was an enlightened tile manufacturer named Heystee, who commissioned Jan Frederick (Fritz) Staal (1879-1940) to layout the whole site and to design five of the houses. Staal's principal collaborators, his second wife Margaret Kropholler, Cornelis Jonke Blaauw, and Piet Kramer were to divide the ten remaining freestanding houses between them while G.F. La Croix contributed the rather atypical double-fronted Wrightian villa,

which formed the centre piece of the estate. (cf. the comparable position occupied by the Ernst Ludwig House in the Darmstadt Artists' Colony of 1901). All of the other houses were executed in the Dutch Expressionist manner; that is to say, out of brick walls, creosoted siding and thatched roofs, arranged after the English Arts and Crafts tradition and clearly indebted to the work of Norman Shaw, Baillie-Scott and Edwin Landseer Lutyens. This debt however remained rather loose and the orginality of this rustic Dutch expression can hardly be overestimated. Nonetheless Kropholler's Huize Meezenest (Tom-tit's nest) was obviously indebted to the work of E.S. Prior — specifically to Prior's house, The Barn, Ex-

mouth of 1898. Huize Meezenest, with its two Prior-like, false chimneys, set on either side of the entrance and its high-pitched, thatched roof was typical of the strange Noah's Ark-like form that characterized the domestic work of the Amsterdam School at this time, not only here at Meerwijk but also in other works built along the coast; notably by such architects as Pieter Vorkink and J.P. Wormser (cf. T'Reigersnest house at Oostvoorne, 1920-21) and above all in the houses designed by the short-lived firm of Eijbink and Snellbrand. While these houses sported prow-like profiles in both plan and section, the spatial planning of their interiors was organic to the point of being literally biological.

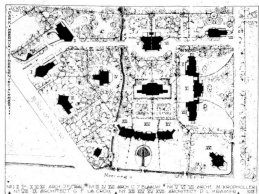

198 *Below left: Park Meerwijk, site plan*
Above right: Meezennest and Meerlhuis houses by M. Kropholler
Below right: Linked houses by J. F. Staal
199 *Above left: De Bark houses by J. F. Staal*
Below left: a house with thatched roof
Right: Meezennest and Meerlhuis houses, entrance

Within an axial composition occupying a 300 by 500 foot site and consisting of three-storey residential wings enclosing two sides of a central court and a public block four-storeys high terminating the central axis, Wright reworked the typological structure of his Midway Gardens development, realized in Chicago in 1914. In this elemental, not to say Beaux-Arts manipulation of typified elements, the multi-leveled restaurant of Midway Gardens became the public reception/banqueting hall complex of the hotel (there was also a 1,000 seat theatre in the basement), while the loggialike, open-air, semi-covered terraces flanking the Chicago beer garden were transformed into the battered form of the hotel's residential wings.

Wright's Prairie Style, which was as much influenced by Japanese culture as it was dependent on the principle of the Beaux-Arts, had here finally to confront the Japanese architectural tradition on its own terms and Wright's reaction to this challenge was not entirely consistent. Nevertheless, Wright modified the layered massing of his Prairie Style (cf. The Robie House in particular) so as to refer to the heavy-weight masonry tradition in Japanese mediaeval architecture, that is, to the battered bulwarks of sixteenth-century Japanese castle form. With evident difficulty as far as his preferential approach to ornament was concerned, Wright used local masonry throughout, a greenish-yellow, Oya lava stone which was obviously difficult to detail. Sullivan

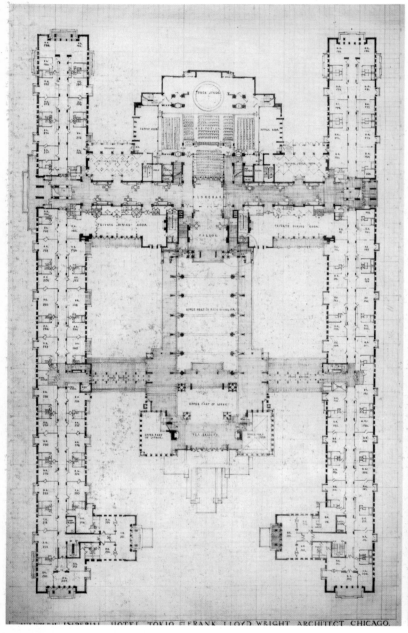

200 *Left: main floor plan*
   Right: aerial view (Photo: Y. Takase)
201 *Main entrance and the pool in front*

spoke characteristically of the ornament being cut into the surface so as to appear integral with the material. The same stone was also employed in the main public spaces of the hotel, but in a rather different context, for the dominant forms here were highly pitched rafters bearing onto massive, ornamented piers. The general effect here seems to have been Pre-Columbian rather than Shinto and yet in the timber lining (Hokkaido oak) of private rooms Wright returned to the formal order of light-weight Japanese architecture.

In many respects the Imperial Hotel completed at the end of 1920, was the "Swan Song" of Wright's seventeen-year-old Prairie culture, even though Wright had to use in its erection a group of local craftsmen rather than the Prairie Style design team that he had painstakingly assembled over the previous 15 years. The Prairie Style ethos was sustained in this foreign context by leadership of the Czech-American architect Antonin Raymond, who after supervising the building of the hotel, went on to establish his own practice in Japan.

The subsequent world renown and success of the hotel stemmed, in part, from its remarkable survival in the Tokyo earthquake disaster of 1923, a triumph that was largely due to its floating raft foundations built on short concrete piles to the designs of the engineer Paul Muller. This exemplary piece of engineering was acclaimed by Louis Sullivan in his article on the hotel written for the Dutch magazine *Wendingen* in 1924:

"So much for a system of construction altogether novel in conception and execution, carried out by a strong, persistent mind, as imaginative in its insight into fundamental principles of engineering as in its profound insight into the romance of breathing life and beauty, humanity and spirit into forms and materials otherwise helplessly inert."

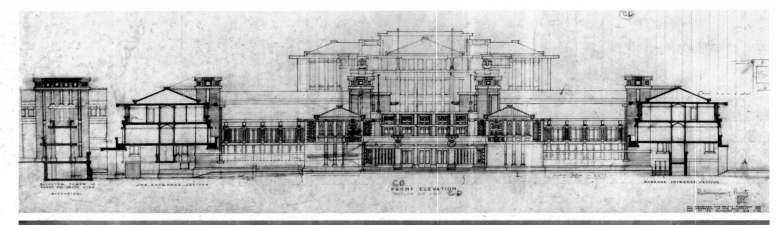

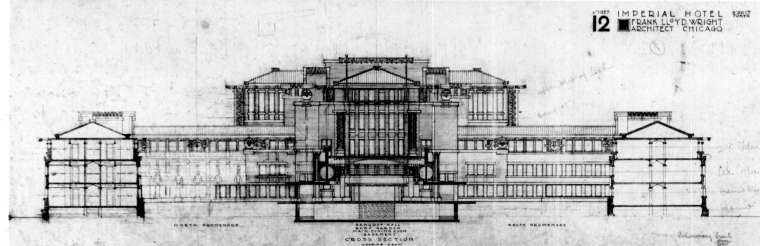

202 *Above: cross section looking west*
    Center: main lobby
    Below: cross section looking east
203 *Above left: columns of the main dining room*
    Above right: promenade of the banquet hall
    Below left: fireplace of the banquet hall foyer
    Below right: fireplace and mural painting in the parlor

Freyssinet, a pupil of the pioneer reinforced concrete engineer, Charles Rabut, was barely 28 years old when in 1907 he built the remarkable reinforced concrete bridges at Boutiron and Le Verdure. He followed this achievement with another reinforced concrete bridge realized at Villeneuve-sur-Lot between 1914 and 1919, having a clear span of some 320 feet and a crossing height above the river of 47 feet. The First World War brought Freyssinet many military commissions including a series of aircraft hangars at Istres, Bouches-du-Rhone in 1917 and these twin dirigible sheds which were built at Orly between 1916 and 1924. As with Eiffel's career, Freyssinet's genius resided as much in his constructional method as in his prowess with a given structural technique. In these paraboloid arches, he demonstrated for the first time his mastery of moving formwork for the casting of in-situ concrete. These 300-foot-wide, 200-foot-high vaults were each built in two stages. The first stage consisted of 55 feet high springing, cast in place as an integral part of the reinforced foundations on either side of the hangar. The fully "folded" and partly glazed concrete shell arch cast above this springing was built by adding one V-shaped rib at a time. These ribs were cast into movable plywood moulds which in their turn were supported by a mobile timber formwork, 7.5 meters wide. The thickness of the shell rib, varied from 3½ inches at its thinnest to 8 inches at its thickest, where the bottom chord carried the bulk of the tensile pressure in the arch. Each rib was provided with a lantern ventilator set above the top chord, while four suspended catwalks were hung from the span for the purpose of servicing the top of the dirigible. These remarkable forms, each 915 feet long, were destroyed at the end of the Second World War.

Overall view

Photo: Harlingue-Viollet, Paris

1918-47
ARNSTEIN ARNEBERG
& MAGNUS POULSSON
Town Hall
Oslo, Norway

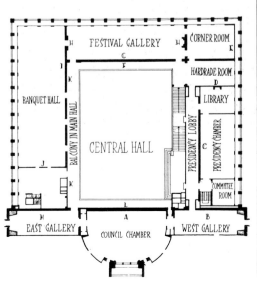

It is rare that in modern times a building will occupy the span of some thirty-five years from the date of its first siting, in this case 1915, to the year of its final opening which took place on May 15th, 1950 as part of the ninth Centenary festival for the city of Oslo. While Arneberg and Poulsson were declared the architects of the hall after a preliminary competition held in October 1919, it was to be another decade before the site had been expropriated. Even then further delays occured and the foundation stone was not officially laid until 1931. All in all, the process of construction took sixteen years with the City Council entering their chamber for the first time in 1947. A competition was held for the artistic embellishement of the hall in 1936, but these works were not all finally installed until 1950. As one might expect, the Arneberg and Poulsson's design changed radically between the 1919 design and the final scheme which was put in hand in 1931. Their 1919 project had all the classical deportment of the Neo-Renaissance Oslo Telegraph Building built to their designs between 1916 and 1924. Apart from a free-standing square tower bearing motives drawn from the Norwegian stave church tradition of the 13th century, their 1919 design was typical of the Scandinavian Romantic Classical revivalist manner. By the time of their seventh project however, in the late twenties, they had arrived at a massive brick style with a rusticated base and banded windows similar to that used somewhat later by Bryn and Ellefsen in their development of Oslo University. The basic square courtyard *parti* with two arms enclosing a fore-court facing towards the harbour was also developed by this date. In other words, except for the vestigial free-standing tower, the final designs had only one further stage to go and that was the development of the twin towers over the main mass. Somewhat like Östberg's Stockholm City Hall, the first floor in the final scheme is given over to a suite of public reception rooms: a banqueting hall, a festival gallery, a council assembly hall, and the semi-circular council chamber itself set on the axis of the courtyard composition. The twin rectilinear, 220-foot-high towers, in brick with stone and tile dressing, now served to accommodate the main bureaucratic offices of the city administration. Bastion-like and heroically profiled, Oslo City Hall still appears like an unexpected late flowering of the National Romantic spirit.

Above: overall view
Left: second floor plan

Momentarily abandoning the industrial aesthetic that had characterized his work up to his chemical factory built at Luban in 1911-12, Poelzig seems to have come under the influence of Bruno Taut's *Die Gläserne Kette* or Glass Chain. The architectural evidence suggests that he was aware of the substance of the "visionary" correspondence that took place between Taut and his friends (Gropius, Scharoun, Finsterlin, and the Luckhardt brothers) in the period between 1914 and 1918. Whatever the ultimate cause for the sudden transformation in his style, Poelzig's work acquired a strongly utopian cast at the end of the First World War; above all in his 1916 competition design for a House of Friendship to be built in Istanbul. Around this time, Poelzig began to propose a structurally rationalist, "stallactitic" architecture, compiled out of the obsessive repetition of elongated arched elements — a kind of architectonic iteration which was as homogenizing in its effect as the arch and dome had been throughout the Islamic architectural tradition. The main link between this vision and that of the Scheerbartian Glass Chain lay in the mountainous compositions that Poelzig tended to make out of these elements, for example, his Festspielhaus, projected for Salzburg in 1920-22 and his Istanbul design of four years before.

The Grosses Schauspielhaus, designed for the stage director Max Reinhardt in 1919, was the conversion of an existing market hall into a large 5,000-seat auditorium, with a 100-foot-wide stage, for the presentation of Reinhardt's mass pageant plays. Aside from the blank, boxlike, pitch-roofed exterior, which was animated by continuous low-relief full-height arch forms, the auditorium interior amounted to Poelzig's "mountain" principle in reverse: that is, it was treated as a vast cavern of stalactites — comprising a shell-like surface of suspended arches. This highly reticulated surface seems to have had the incidental advantage of reducing the reverberation time in what was an extremely large space.

Light, both natural and artificial, played a salient role in all of Poelzig's architecture, and in no work of his did it feature more strongly than in this auditorium, where the artificial illumination of the vast volume came from numerous light sources concealed within the pendentive structure of the auditorium shell. This field of light could be further animated by a starlike network of spotlights secured to the tips of the stalactites. The general principle of indirect light cascading up, over and down the convoluted surfaces of a red cavelike interior was carried over into the internal treatment of the foyer and other ancillary spaces. This was Poelzig at his most visionary; soon after, he returned to variations on his pre-war industrial aesthetic and at times even veered towards Neoclassical expression. The resurgence of his utilitarian brick aesthetic is evidenced in his Messehaus project, designed for Hamburg in 1925, yet by the time of his Capital Cinema built in Berlin in the same year, he had returned to the crypto-classical fold. The only thing left in this cinema from the glories of the Reinhardt theatre was the same concern for the expressive quality of artifical light.

206 Interior of the auditorium
207 plan
Photo reproduced from Geschichte der Mordernen Architektur *by J. Joedicke*

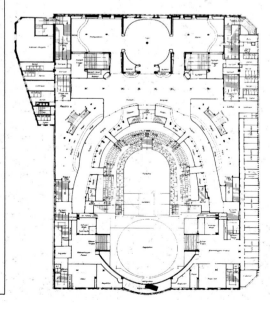

Acknowledgments

The publisher greatly appreciates the cooperation received from authorities and parties who have charge of any illustrations and photographs used in the issue.

Text illustrations

Archives de Paris, Paris: Fig. 48
Archives der Wiener Sezession, Vienna: Fig. 62
Glasgow School of Art, Glasgow: Fig. 43
Kunstbibliothek Berlin, Staatliche Museen Preußischer Kulturbeisitz, Berlin: Fig. 63
National Railway Museum, York: Fig. 8
The Crystal Palace Foundation of Patrick Beaver (Courtesy of Upper Norwood Public Library, London): Fig. 9
Victoria and Albert Museum, London: Fig. 10

Illustrations have been reproduced from the following publications by permission.

Adolf Loos: Pioneer of Modern Architecture by L. Münz & G. Künstler, Anton Schroll & Co, 1964 (Courtesy of Graphische Sammlung ALBERTINA), Vienna: Fig. 75
Art Nouveau by R. Schmutzler, Verlag Gerd Hatje, Stuttgart: Figs. 37, 40, 42, 45, 68
Chicago: Growth of a Metropolis by H. M. Mayer & R. C. Wade, The University of Chicago Press, Chicago, 1969: Figs. 19, 20, 21, 23
Geschichte der modernen Architektur by J. Joedicke, Verlag Gerd Hatje, Stuttgart, 1958: Figs. 16, 24
Le Corbusier, edited by W. Boesiger, Verlag für Architektur Artemis, Zürich, 1972: Fig. 39
Lotus 12, Lotus International, Milano, 1976: Figs. 71, 73
Otto Wagner 1841–1918 by H. Geretsegger & M. Peintner, © 1976 Residenz Verlag, Salzburg und Wien: Figs. 59, 60, 61, 64
Richard Norman Shaw by R. Blomfield, Batsford, London, 1940: Fig. 66
Space, Time and Architecture by S. Giedion, Harvard University Press, Cambridge: Fig. 17
Storia dell'architettura moderna, Vol. 1, by L. Benevolo, Giuseppe Laterza & Figli, Roma, 1960: Figs. 1, 3, 13, 15, 22, 28, 36
The Anti-Rationalists, edited by N. Pevsner & J.M. Richards, The Architectural Press, London, 1973: Fig. 41
Victor Horta by F. Borsi & P. Portoghesi, Vokaer, Brussels, 1970: Fig. 47

Illustrations have been reproduced from the following publications.

American Buildings and Their Architects by W.H. Jordy, Anchor Books, New York, 1976: Figs. 26, 27
Antonio Gaudi: l'home i l'obra by J.M. Bergos, Ariel, Barcelona, 1954: Figs. 50, 51
Architectures, Paris 1848–1914, edited by B. Marrey & P. Chemetov, Secrétaire d'Etat à la Culture, Paris, 1972: Figs. 2, 4
Bâtiments de chemins de fer 1862–66 by P. Chabat, pl. 49: Fig. 7
Builder, 15, Jan. 1848: Fig. 6
Casabella No. 329, October, 1968: Fig. 49
Contrasts by A.N.W. Pugin, 2nd, ed. 1841: Figs. 65, 65a
Corso di Disegno 5°, L'arte e la città contemporanea by L. Benevolo, Giuseppe Laterza & Figli, Roma, 1976: Fig. 35
Das Englische Haus by H. Muthesius, Berlin, 1904: Figs. 70, 70a
L'architettura del ferro: La Francia (1715–1914) by G. Roisecco, Balzoni, Roma, 1973: Fig. 14
L'architettura del ferro: l'inghilterra (1668–1916) by G. Roisecco, Balzoni, Roma, 1973: Figs. 5, 11, 38, 44
Modern Architecture by K. Frampton, Thames and Hudson, London, 1980: Figs. 25, 29
The Britannia and Conway Tubular Bridges, 1850: Fig. 12

Other illustrations

Amigos de Gaudí, Barcelona: pp. 139, 141
Archives d'Architecture Moderne, Brussels: pp. 96, 132, 164, 165
Archives de Paris, Paris: p. 70
Archives der Wiener Sezession, Vienna: p. 101
Bibliothèque Nationale, Paris: pp. 19, 21, 29, 58 above
British Railways: p. 15
Centrum v.d. Bouwkunst, Amsterdam: pp. 186, 187
Cooper-Hewitt Museum, The Smithsonian Institution's National Museum of Design, New York: p. 134
George A. Fuller Co.: pp. 42, 105
Glasgow School of Art (Drawn by Peter Porteous and Paul Spear), Glasgow: p. 92
Historisches Museum der Stadt Wien, Vienna: p. 124
Kunstbibliothek Berlin, Staatliche Museen Preußischer Kulturbesitz, Berlin: pp. 104, 151
Architectural Record, New York: p. 149
The Art Institute of Chicago, Chicago: p. 67
The British Architectural Library (RIBA), London: pp. 12 below, 94
The Cleveland Arcade Co., Cleveland: p. 56
Plansammlung der Universitätsbibliothek der Technischen Universität Berlin, Berlin: pp. 177, 207
Victoria and Albert Museum, London: p. 12 above

Illustrations have been reproduced from the following publications.

Adolf Loos: Pioneer of Modern Architecture by L. Münz & G. Künstler, Anton Schroll & Co, 1964 (Courtesy of Graphische Sammlung ALBERTINA), Vienna: p. 160
Antoni Gaudi by Sweeny/Sert, Verlag Gerd Hatje, Stuttgart, 1960: 38, 158
Art Nouveau Architecture, edited by F. Russel, Academy Editions, London, 1979 (Redrawn by John Read): p. 97
Der Moderne Zweckbau by A. Behn, Ullstein Verlag, Berlin, Frankfurt/M, Vienna, 1964: p. 163
Die Architektur des Expressionismus by W. Pehnt, Verlag Gerd Hatje, Stuttgart, 1973: pp. 156, 188, 192, 193, 198
Five California Architects by Esther McCoy. © 1960 by E. McCoy. Holt, Rinehart and Winston, New York, 1960: p. 154
H.H. Richardson and his Office: Selected Drawings by J. F. O'Gorman, David R. Godine Publisher/ Harvard College, Boston, 1974: p. 53
Kunst und Technik der Wölbung by F. Hart, Verlag Georg Callwey, Munich, 1965: p. 182
Le Corbusier, edited by W. Boesiger, Verlag für Architektur Artemis, Zürich, 1972: p. 197
Les Grands Magasins by B. Marrey, Librairie Picard, Paris, 1979: pp. 36, 37
Mackintosh Architecture, edited by J. Copper & B. Bernard, Academy Editions, London, 1978: p. 113
Otto Wagner 1841–1918 by H. Geretsegger & M. Peintner, © 1976 Residenz Verlag, Salzburg und Wien, 1976: p. 137
Passagen: ein Bautyp des 19. Jahrhunderts by J.F. Geist, Prestel-Verlag, Munich, 1978: p. 26
"Recommendations for Renovation of the Wainwright Building," St. Louis Chapter American Institute of Architects, St. Louis: p. 62
Storia dell'architettura moderna, Vol. 1, by L. Benevolo, Giuseppe Laterza & Figli, Roma, 1960: p. 69
Storia dell'architecttura moderna, Vol. 2, by L. Benevolo, Giuseppe Laterza & Figli, Roma, 1960: pp. 108, 191
The American Architect and Building News, International Edition, May 26, 1906: p. 115
The Bradbury Building, recorded by the United States National Park Service: pp. 60, 61
The Works of Sir Joseph Paxton by G.F. Chadwick, The Architectural Press, London, 1961: p. 11
Victor Horta by F. Borsi & P. Portoghesi, Vokaer, Brussels, 1970: pp. 84, 85, 86, 109
Zwischen Glaspalast und Palais des Illusion by E. Schild, Ullstein Verlag, Berlin, Frankfurt/M, Wien: p. 59

The drawings of Frank Lloyd Wright are Copyright © The Frank Lloyd Wright Foundation 1942, renewed 1970; 1963, 1965, 1980. Courtesy of The Frank Lloyd Wright Memorial Foundation.
Figs. 30, 31, 32, 33, 34
pp. 64, 127, 129, 145, 147, 183, 200, 202

Photographic Acknowledgments

Archives d'Architecture Moderne, Brussels: p. 87
Harlingue-Viollet, Paris: p. 204
Stadt Köln Nachrichtenamt, Köln: p. 188
© The Frank Lloyd Wright Foundation: pp. 126, 127, 184
Plansammlung der Universitätsbibliothek der Technischen Universität Berlin, Berlin: pp. 177, 178, 179
The Christal Palace Foundation of Patrick Beaver (Courtesy of Upper Norwood Public Library, London): pp. 10, 13
Courtesy of Mrs. Walter Gropius: p. 190
Verlag Gerd Hatje, Stuttgart: p. 182

Photographs have been reproduced from the following publications by permission.

Adolf Loos: Pioneer of Modern Architecture by L. Münz & G. Künstler, Anton Schroll & Co, 1964 (Courtesy of Graphische Sammlung ALBERTINA) Vienna: p. 160
Die Architektur des Expressionismus by W. Pehnt, Verlag Gerd Hatje, Stuttgart, 1973: pp. 156 above (Photo: Heydebrang-Osthoff), 156 below
Geschichte der modernen Architektur by J. Joedicke, Verlag Gerd Hatje, Stuttgart, 1958: pp. 58 below (Photo: Chevojon, Paris), 191, 206 (Photo: Bildarchive Foto, Marburg)
Lotus 12, Lotus International, Milano, 1976: p. 195
The Anti-Rationalists, edited by N. Pevsner & J.M. Richards, The Architectural Press Ltd., London, 1973: p. 110
Victor Horta by F. Borsi & P. Portoghesi, Vokaer, Brussels, 1970: pp. 84, 85, 109